T0379552

The Great European Stage Directors

Volume 7

The Great European Stage Directors

Series Editor: Simon Shepherd

Volume 1
Antoine, Stanislavski, Saint Denis
Edited by Peta Tait

Volume 2
Meyerhold, Piscator, Brecht
Edited by David Barnett

Volume 3
Copeau, Komisarjevsky, Guthrie
Edited by Jonathan Pitches

Volume 4
Reinhardt, Jessner, Barker
Edited by Michael Patterson

Volume 5
Grotowski, Brook, Barba
Edited by Paul Allain

Volume 6
Littlewood, Strehler, Planchon
Edited by Clare Finburgh Delijani and Peter M. Boenisch

Volume 7
Barrault, Mnouchkine, Stein
Edited by Felicia Hardison Londré

Volume 8
Bausch, Castellucci, Fabre
Edited by Luk Van den Dries and Timmy De Laet

The Great European Stage Directors

Volume 7

Barrault, Mnouchkine, Stein

Edited by Felicia Hardison Londré
Series Editor: Simon Shepherd

methuen | drama

LONDON • NEW YORK • OXFORD • NEW DELHI • SYDNEY

METHUEN DRAMA
Bloomsbury Publishing Plc
50 Bedford Square, London, WC1B 3DP, UK
1385 Broadway, New York, NY 10018, USA
29 Earlsfort Terrace, Dublin 2, Ireland

BLOOMSBURY, METHUEN DRAMA and the Methuen Drama logo are
trademarks of Bloomsbury Publishing Plc

First published in hardback in Great Britain 2019
This paperback edition 2024

ISBN: HB: 978-1-4742-5400-7
     HB Pack: 978-1-4742-5416-8
          PB: 978-1-3504-4583-3
      PB Set: 978-1-3504-4599-4
        ePDF: 978-1-4742-5995-8
       eBook: 978-1-3504-6195-6

Series: Great Stage Directors

Typeset by Integra Software Services Pvt. Ltd.
Printed and bound in Great Britain

To find out more about our authors and books visit www.bloomsbury.com
and sign up for our newsletters.

CONTENTS

List of Figures vii
Notes on Contributors x
Acknowledgements xii

Introduction to the Series *Simon Shepherd* 1

Introduction to Volume 7 *Felicia Hardison Londré* 7

Jean-Louis Barrault 21

1   Jean-Louis Barrault: His Life in His Work *Felicia Hardison Londré* 23

2   Jean-Louis Barrault's 'Total Theatre' *Suzanne Burgoyne* 55

Ariane Mnouchkine 79

3   Ariane Mnouchkine and the Théâtre du Soleil: Towards a Utopian Vision *Helen Richardson* 81

4   Ariane Mnouchkine's Théâtre du Soleil: Inside-Out *Emilie Gruat* 113

Peter Stein 127

5   Peter Stein: Life, Work, Art *William Grange* 129

6   Peter Stein: Politics in Art *K. Scott Baker* 163

Chronologies of Major Productions 189
Notes 196
Bibliography 221
Index 232

LIST OF FIGURES

1.1   Jean-Louis Barrault in costume as Hamlet at the
Marigny Theatre in 1946   36

1.2   Madeleine Renaud and Jean-Louis Barrault in
Les Fausses confidences by Marivaux   37

1.3   Jean-Louis Barrault in the title role of *Baptiste*
by Jacques Prévert at the Marigny Theatre
in 1946   46

1.4   Madeleine Renaud and Jean-Louis Barrault
show the poster for their first productions
at the Odéon-Théâtre de France   49

1.5   Jean-Louis Barrault conducts a rehearsal of *Rabelais*
on 6 November 1968 at the Elysée-Montmartre   52

2.1   Jean-Louis Barrault in the title role of *La Tentation
de Saint-Antoine* (The Temptation of St Anthony)
adapted from Flaubert and directed by Roger Blin
at the Odéon-Théâtre de France in 1967   60

2.2   Jean-Louis Barrault staged Ionesco's *Rhinoceros*
at the Odéon-Théâtre de France in 1960   71

2.3   This scene from the 1980 revival of *The Satin Slipper*,
directed by Jean-Louis Barrault, at the Théâtre d'Orsay
shows his use of masks and a catalysing object   73

3.1   *1789* at the Cartoucherie de Vincennes   85

3.2   Mnouchkine is surrounded by *Twelfth Night*
(La Nuit des rois) company members at the
Festival of Avignon, where the production opened
in 1982   87

3.3   Mnouchkine rehearses *L'Indiade, or India of Their
Dreams* by Hélène Cixous in January 1988   89

3.4   The Théâtre du Soleil got the attention of Paris
audiences in 1967 with *The Kitchen* by Arnold
Wesker   98

3.5   Théâtre du Soleil, *Iphigénie in Aulis*
by Euripides, 1990   109

4.1   Emilie Gruat and Serge Nicolai in *Le Dernier
Caravansérail* at the Théâtre du Soleil in 2003   123

5.1   Bruno Ganz in *Torquato Tasso* by Johann Wolfgang
von Goethe at the Schaubühne am Hallescgen Ufer
in 1970   138

5.2   Wolf Redl and Edith Clever in *Summerfolk* by
Maxim Gorky sit in front of the real trees that
were incorporated into Karl-Ernst Herrmann's
setting for the 1974 production   146

5.3   Otto Sander, Jutta Lampe, Werner Rehm and
Wolf Redl as nineteenth-century bourgeois characters
in Stein's 1975 production of *The Piggy Bank*
by Eugène Labiche   149

5.4   Stein's 1974 *Antikenprojekt* (Antiquity Project),
based upon the research the company

had done for Klaus-Michael Grüber's production
of *The Bacchae* by Euripides   153

6.1   Peter Stein's staging of Henrik Ibsen's *Peer Gynt* in
      1971 at the Schaubühne in West Berlin   181

6.2   Peter Stein works with his ensemble in 1974   183

NOTES ON CONTRIBUTORS

K. Scott Baker is an independent scholar based in Munich, Germany, and was previously Professor of German at the University of Missouri-Kansas City and has published on the plays of Karl Gutzkow and on Bertolt Brecht, including a 2009 article in *The Brecht Yearbook*. He co-authored *The Happy Burden of History* (de Gruyter, 2011). He recently worked in the archive of the Akademie der Künste in Berlin.

Suzanne Burgoyne, Curators' Distinguished Professor of Theatre at the University of Missouri, Columbia, is also Director of the Center for Applied Theatre and Drama Research. She teaches directing, script analysis and Theatre of the Oppressed at UM-C, has taught directing and dramaturgy at the National Institute of Belgium, and has translated and edited the plays of Paul Willems. She was a 2000–1 PEW Carnegie Scholar and has held a Kellogg National Fellowship.

William Grange, Hixson-Lied Professor of Theatre Arts at the University of Nebraska-Lincoln's Johnny Carson School of Theatre and Film, has taught at the University of Heidelberg, the University of Vienna and the University of Cologne. He has directed, held several research fellowships and published seven books on German theatre.

Emilie Gruat is an actress dramaturg and director. She holds an MA in Theatre from La Sorbonne Nouvelle in Paris. After performing with Théâtre du Soleil for six years, she chose to step out in order to conduct various research projects worldwide. In New York, she completed an MFA in Dramaturgy at Columbia University. She currently resides in Bordeaux.

Felicia Hardison Londré, Curators' Distinguished Professor Emerita of Theatre at the University of Missouri-Kansas City, taught theatre history and dramaturgy, specializing in French, Russian and American theatre. She was elected to the College of Fellows of the American Theatre in 1999 and served a term (2012–14) as Dean. Her fifteen books include the George Freedly Memorial Award-winning *The Enchanted Years of the Stage: Kansas City at the Crossroads of American Theatre, 1890–1930*. She has held a Visiting Professorship at Hosei University in Tokyo.

Helen Richardson, Professor Emerita, CUNY Brooklyn College, is former Director of the Performance and Interactive Media Arts MFA and Visiting Professor, Northampton University, UK, through a Global Talent visa. She also edits *Contemporary Performance Journal*. Her work focuses on collaborative creation and social engagement. She is author of various chapters on the collaborative practices of the Théâtre du Soleil included in *Actor Training: An Introduction, Ariane Mnouchkine* (Routledge Performance Practitioners), and 'The Impact of Jacques Lecoq on Ariane Mnouchkine and the Théâtre du Soleil' in *The Routledge Companion to Jacques Lecoq* (2016). As Artistic Director of the Stalhouderij Theatre Company, Amsterdam, an international ensemble of actors creating new works, she was recognized for best productions of the year in the Netherlands on themes exploring the encounter between the 'old' and 'new' world and issues of women's rights and economic disparity. She is a founding member of Global Theatre Ensemble and co-curator, producer and dramaturg of Global Theatre Ensemble's theatre project on Eliminating Violence against Women, commissioned by the United Nations.

ACKNOWLEDGEMENTS

It has been a particular pleasure to revisit my theatre memories of the 1960s in Paris. Jean-Louis Barrault's productions were always a strong draw for me during my Fulbright year and on subsequent trips to Paris. I am grateful to series editor Simon Shepherd for this opportunity, for his warm and witty responses to my queries, and for believing that I could handle the project even as I still had work in progress for another Methuen Drama series volume in *Decades of Modern American Drama*. With regard to both series, I thank Mark Dudgeon and Susan Furber for their invaluable guidance and prompt responses.

The five contributors to this volume were wonderfully helpful and patient. I especially want to acknowledge Helen Richardson's extraordinary generosity, as her academic and personal contributions extended far beyond her own chapter. It was Helen who put me in touch with Emilie Gruat, who brings a special inside glimpse of the workings of Mnouchkine's company.

It has also been gratifying that my long-time friends Suzanne Burgoyne and Bill Grange and my colleague Scott Baker were exactly the right scholars whose expertise coincided with the subjects of their chapters. It's a bit of a miracle to get the ideal team of contributors: my sincere appreciation to them.

Introduction to the Series

Simon Shepherd

The beginnings of directing

Directors have become some of the celebrities of contemporary theatre. Yet for most of its life, and across a range of practices, theatre has managed perfectly well without directors, celebrated or otherwise.

This is not to say that it has lacked direction, so to speak. Some form of directing, by actors, prompters, stage managers, designers, has always featured as an activity within theatre's processes. What was new was the concept that directing should be done by a role specifically dedicated to that purpose. Emerging around the 1890s after many centuries of theatre, it was both a historical novelty and geographically limited, to Europe and North America.

What these cultures had in common, at the start of the twentieth century, were the ideas and practices which we now call Modernism. In the arts it is associated with particular sorts of innovation made by short-lived movements such as Constructivism, Dada, Expressionism and Surrealism. But modernist thinking also influenced industrial innovation. This is seen in the creation of what F.W. Taylor called 'scientific' management, the systematization and hence separation of the role of a manager who bears responsibility for planning and oversight of the production process. As I have argued before,[1] the concept of director comes to be formulated at the same time as a managerial class is becoming defined. The value put upon the activity of management might be said to create the conditions for, and justify, the creation of a separable role of director.

This was apparent to Barker in 1911 when he observed that in Germany it was precisely the proliferation of management duties that made it impossible to combine the role of manager with that of actor. But German practice was perhaps in advance of the rest of Europe. Many of those now regarded as the founders of directing appeared to work in very similar ways to those who are not categorized as directors. Antoine ran his own company, selected the repertoire, took acting roles and directed plays, as did Stanislavski and Copeau. In this respect their practice differed little from, say, Henry Irving or Herbert Beerbohm Tree, both regarded as actor-managers.

Where the practice of the early directors seems consistently distinct throughout Europe is in its cultural, and sometimes political, positioning. Antoine, Copeau, Barker, Piscator, among others, positioned themselves against a dominant theatrical culture which they aimed to challenge and change. This positioning was an ideological project and hence brought with it an assumption of, or claim to, enlightened vision, artistic mission, the spirit of innovation. Adopting this rhetoric Antoine declared that directors had never existed before – that he was the first of a kind. When P.P. Howe wrote his 1910 book on that new organizational phenomenon the repertory theatre he distinguished the new director from the old stage manager on the grounds that, while the stage manager was adept at controlling the 'mechanical' aspects of the stage, the director was the guardian of the 'vision'.[2] This aesthetic formulation is, though, wholly cognate with management as industrially understood, as Alexander Dean makes clear. In 1926 he recommended that each company should have one person in the role of overall director because the director is not only responsible for each production but also, crucially, is 'the great connecting link between all parts of the organization'. Furthermore: 'Every organization needs a leader who has a vision; who sees a great achievement ahead.'[3] The non-mechanical visionary is also the Taylorist planner.

But some, it seems, were more visionary than others. You will have noted that none of the directors so far mentioned is North American. Yet while Antoine, Copeau and others were founding their theatres outside the mainstream, the same was happening in the United States. The Little Theatres of Chicago and New York started in 1912, the Neighbourhood Playhouse (New York), Portmanteau Theatre and Washington Square Players followed in 1915–16. Contemporary commentators such as Constance D'Arcy Mackay (1917) saw both the European and the American experiments as part of the same 'little theatre' movement.[4] Their practices look similar: founding theatres, against the dominant; culturally selecting audiences, possibly by a membership scheme; working with amateurs; performing explicitly naturalist dramatists, such as Ibsen. But while Antoine and Copeau have entered the canon of great directors, Winthrop Ames and Alice and Irene Lewisohn have not.

Reflecting on the contrast between North American and European practices, William Lyon Phelps suggested in 1920 that the United States lacked a public discourse that would take theatre as seriously as cars. His argument built on Moderwell (1914) and was taken up by Dean (1926).[5] Both saw little theatres as the mechanism for developing a larger theatre-going public, and hence were primarily interested in their success as organizational and economic entities, being much less interested in directors as artists. In Britain similar arguments proposed repertory theatre and the amateur movement as the mechanisms for building both democracy and a dramatic renaissance. Theatre, Barker argued in 1910, is a 'sociable' art. Thus North American and British discussions proposed that theatre could develop the cultural accomplishments of civil society. European discourses, meanwhile, were more interested in, and driven by, avant-gardist movements and experiment. For instance, Antoine positioned himself within an already existing public discourse about art, allying himself with the naturalist, and anti-racist, Zola; staging censored playwrights; distributing Strindberg's polemical preface to *Fröken Julie* (*Miss Julie*) – and making sure to invite reviewers to his theatre. For Piscator and Brecht the energizing link was to activists and ideas within both the political and the artistic avant-garde. The European director thus acquired the status of artistic activist, linked to and recognizable by existing networks of activists and makers, with their own mechanisms for dissemination and publicity. The European avant-garde, long celebrated as the supposed origins of performance art, was perhaps more clearly the originating moment of the theatre director.

The discursive position of European directors was consolidated by their own pronouncements and publications. Each of the early directors was adept in an established theatre craft, as were actor-managers. But when Barker, Meyerhold or Saint-Denis lectured on and wrote about the crafts of theatre, and even more when directors established regimes of training, they were showing themselves to be not just practitioners but theorists of a craft, not so much mechanics as visionaries. The early directors, and indeed directors since, claimed to understand how theatre works as an art form, and to have proposals for its future developments. In this sense they show themselves to be not only guardians of the vision of the play but also guardians of a vision of how theatre itself can and should work. The success of the claim to be visionary is evidence that what the director manages is not just the company or production but also the discourse about them.

Taken together new ideas about management, avant-garde practices and theories of theatre enabled the formulation of, and justified, a separated role of director. The role could then be seen as providing a specialism, missing hitherto, which is necessary to ensure the artistic seriousness and importance of theatre.

While the mechanism that formulated the role of director may have been discursive, its consequences were much more than that. Properly to carry out the guardianship of the vision meant taking responsibility for ensuring the aims and coherence of the processes of theatre-making. The artistic visionary slides into place as Dean's industrial manager. The discursive formulation results in actual power over other theatre workers. The director's control can determine not just that which is staged but also the hiring, if not firing, of those who stage it.

With the invention of directors a new power structure emerges. Yet it had been, and is, perfectly possible to make theatre without that role and its power structure. So there is a potential tension between the effectiveness and productivity of the crafts necessary for theatre and the new, but not demonstrably necessary, power structure that came to claim organizational authority over those crafts. This tension has made the role of director important and yet unstable, treated as celebrity and yet, after only a century, subject to questions as to whether it is actually necessary.

Those questions have been asked not least by directors themselves. Tangled up with the other issues summarized above they run through the volumes of this series. For the directors here have been selected not only because they are generally taken to be important, indeed 'great', but also because they reflect in interesting ways on the role of directing itself. Of course there are other important names, and interesting reflections, which have not made it into the selection list. Decisions such as these are usually difficult and almost always never satisfactory to everybody. But more stories are told than those of big names. The featured directors are not important because they possess some solitary essence of greatness but because they offer ways into, and are symptomatic of, a range of different practices and ideas. The discussion of each featured director frequently involves other directors, as well as designers, writers and actors with whom they worked and by whom they were influenced. For example, the authors of Volume 3 insist that we move our focus outwards from the featured male directors to attend to the women with whom they collaborated and on whom they depended.

The series begins with some of the earliest examples of the practice, but the only other chronological principle governing the distribution of directors is the decision to create two groups of volumes falling roughly either side of the midpoint of the twentieth century. What this arrangement highlights is the extent to which the practice of directing generates a system of self-reference as it rapidly developed an extensive discourse of its own very new art. Thus, for example, Volume 6 features directors who engage with, and perpetuate, the practices and legacy of Brecht.

Rather than suggesting a chronologically seamless evolution of practices the distribution of the directors across the series seeks to call attention to debate. Volume 1 deals with Naturalism, Volume 2 with critiques of Naturalism. The aim is to provoke thinking not so much about the director as an individual as about the art of directing in its different approaches and concerns. The vision of which the director is guardian and the assumptions as to what constitutes the art of directing are revealed as diverse and provisional. For some directors their creative work mainly involves the staging of their ideas about the world, for others creativity comes in the design of processes and the management of people, for yet others creativity has to do with the design and management of theatres. While Brook's philosophy of life may have constructed powerful and influential stagings, Guthrie's philosophy of life more or less invented the equally powerful, and perhaps more influential, concept of the role of artistic director.

If Volumes 1 and 2 display contrasted aesthetic approaches, Volume 3 has us focus on directors as founders and managers of companies and theatres. That topic of company formation and management returns again, in the context of the latter part of the twentieth century, in Volume 7. In a similar way Volume 4 brings together directors who may be seen as auteurs working within a modernist climate while Volume 5 gives us auteurs emerging from a post–Second World War Europe. In Volume 8, the directors are also auteurs, perhaps most powerfully so in that there is often no dramatist's text. But at the same time here the role of director begins to wobble, blurring into that of choreographer or visual artist.

In exploring the various directors, it becomes clear that, as noted above, some directors are major contributors to the discourses about directing, both reflecting on practices in general and foregrounding their own work in particular. This has an effect on their apparent status within the field. The existence of texts authored by directors often facilitates the study of those directors by others, which in turn generates more texts and elevates their apparent status, as a sort of greatness-construction machine. But there are other directors who are less textually established, perhaps because they actively refuse to document their work, as did Planchon, or perhaps because there are cultural or geographical boundaries that English-speaking academics tend not to cross, as is the case of Strehler. Or it may be that directors have simply fallen out of theatrical or academic fashion, as, say, for Saint-Denis. That they are no longer, or ever were, serviced by the contemporary greatness-construction machine does not make these directors any less significant. Celebrity is not in itself necessarily relevant to being important.

Introduction to Volume 7

Felicia Hardison Londré

The idea of a company

A permanent theatre company – an ensemble of artists committed to a shared vision of theatre – undergirded each of the directorial trajectories of Jean-Louis Barrault, Ariane Mnouchkine and Peter Stein. While each director attained individual name recognition for a remarkable body of work, all three also defined themselves in terms of the ensemble to which they belonged: the Compagnie Renaud-Barrault, the Théâtre du Soleil and the Schaubühne. Thus, for these three, the art of directing must be understood in terms of the practice of working with a familiar collective of actors, designers and technicians.

The juxtaposition of these three directors allows a look at directorial practice and company leadership across two generations (Barrault a generation ahead of Mnouchkine and Stein), from two nations (two French directors, one West German), and with company structures ranging from a privately-owned business (Barrault) to a 1960s-spawned workers' cooperative entity with equal wages for all members (Mnouchkine) to one with generous government subsidy (Stein). All three directors embraced both the classics and the avant-garde with significant interpretations of classical Greek and Shakespeare plays by each. Barrault, the only one of the three who acted as well as directed, was the most challenged to give his company an artistic home; over four decades they relocated to eight different theatres in Paris and adapted to many different performance venues on long international tours. Mnouchkine found her concept-accommodating permanent space early in her journey and, apart from periodic touring, remained well ensconced at the Cartoucherie de Vincennes for rehearsals as well as performances and even – to some degree – communal living. Stein's company switched performance locations when it suited a specific production but otherwise remained settled in Berlin, moving only from its original artistic home to a larger theatre. Stein described the facility constructed in 1980 according to his specifications, his second Schaubühne in West Berlin: 'It is not a theatre building in the traditional sense. It is a flexible space that can be changed. What I invented there was like three film studios, where you open the curtains and unify it to become a huge production space. ... I always try to work in spaces like that, to set up my own stage.'[1]

The directors' collaboration with other artists

Spearheading a permanent ensemble involves collaboration. Barrault's collaborative approach differed somewhat from Mnouchkine's and Stein's. This was partly because Barrault's techniques were formed a generation earlier, under the influence of Charles Dullin whose artistry had been shaped by Jacques Copeau (affectionately called 'Maître' – Master – by his company, just as Barrault and Renaud were les petits patrons, dear bosses), and partly because Barrault's actors were his employees on his privately owned company's payroll. Barrault's troupe trusted him implicitly and referred to the organization as une démocratie amoureuse (a loving democracy). Yet Barrault's greatest joys in collaboration came through his one-on-one processes with individual authors, designers and musicians. He relished working closely with contemporary writers on translations or adaptations from other literary genres, and he even regarded his private wrestling with a canonical writer's body of work as a collaboration with the spirit of that writer. His working relationship with playwright Paul Claudel will always be remembered (alongside that of director Louis Jouvet and playwright Jean Giraudoux) as one of the great page-to-stage collaborations of the twentieth century. Barrault also enjoyed his close collaborations with writers André Gide, Albert Camus, Jean Vauthier, Georges Schéhadé and André Obey. From Barrault's earliest freelance projects until the end of their lives, Félix Labisse, André Masson, Joseph Kosma and Darius Milhaud were among the designers and musicians who repeatedly collaborated with him. Barrault's 1943 production of Le Soulier de satin (The Satin Slipper) occasioned his first fruitful collaborations with both Claudel and composer Arthur Honegger. For the inaugural production of Barrault's own company in 1946, Honegger composed the music and introduced Barrault to young Pierre Boulez (1925–2016), who soon became a company member, serving a decade as music director.[2] Although Boulez left the company in 1956, Barrault continued seeking him out for certain projects, and in 1995, after the deaths of Barrault and his wife Madeleine

Renaud, Boulez was instrumental in rescuing from public auction the personal papers and company archives that now form the Fonds Renaud-Barrault in the Bibliothèque Nationale de France.[3] Barrault's work with his actors owed much to his own understanding of the actor's needs (based on his experience of playing major roles in most of the productions he directed). He told interviewer Bettina Knapp:

> An actor should be supple; naturally, he should learn the art of diction, of breath control, of using his body and face – of exteriorising his emotions – but training is not enough. It's a question of working together, as a group, of using one's imagination and heart, of being sensitive to the play one is acting in – of listening to the author and the characters he conjures up before us.[4]

For Ariane Mnouchkine and Peter Stein, collaboration usually meant the director's hands-on, shared labour alongside company members in hacking a path through the thicket of possibilities. Mnouchkine's ensemble, formed in 1964 by 'ten idealistic young students', understood 'theatre making as social practice'.[5] They bonded in their embrace of a Brechtian idea of theatre as an impetus for social change, although Mnouchkine always nudged the work away from narrow political ideology, towards a broad humanistic outlook. From the beginning, she recalled, 'We were just looking for progress, freedom, and justice. We didn't have an ideology as such, but we were idealists.'[6] The company's quest for theatrical innovation led them to explore together various popular theatre forms, later branching into elements of traditional Asian theatres. Yet, as David Williams points out, the Théâtre du Soleil company frequently reconstitutes itself with periodic 'departures and new arrivals', while company director Mnouchkine remains a 'resilient and dynamic' continuity. Williams quotes Mnouchkine's description of her troupe as one 'where change and transformation are part of the very essence of the undertaking'.[7] Although she is the last remaining member of the original troupe of ten, some long-lasting collaborations undergird her work. Among those collaborators are mask-maker/sculptor Erhard Stiefel (from 1967), scene designer Guy-Claude François (1968–80), administrative assistant Sophie Moscoso (from 1971), public relations director Liliana Andreone (from 1976), musician Jean-Jacques Lemêtre (from 1979), costumers Natalie Thomas and Marie-Hélène Bouvet (from 1976 and 1982, respectively) and playwright Hélène Cixous (from 1985).[8] In her work with the acting ensemble, Mnouchkine sees her role as giving them the tools they need 'to avoid being realistic', and that is why so many of her productions have employed Asian forms as mechanisms for staging occidental texts. The actor taps into personally experienced passions but needs metaphors or images to express them outwardly. In Asian theatrical tradition, everything can be exteriorized; there is a physical 'symptom' for 'each emotion, each sensation'.[9]

According to Sophie Moscoso, each production is rehearsed for about six months, followed by a year-long run with many productions additionally going on tour. Government subsidies help support the long rehearsal period for forty to sixty company members (comprising twenty or so different nationalities).[10] Moscoso further explained:

> The nature of our work as a company necessitates the long rehearsal period, which we find indispensable: we need time for research, discoveries, apprenticeships, blossoming of actors. This long gestation is compensated by our long run, certainly, but also by the way we organize our work, so that nobody serves a single function in the Théâtre du Soleil. There are plenty of jobs that elsewhere would be handled by this or that specialist, but here they are taken on by each and every one of us. We consider this an ethical principle, but it's also economical![11]

Mnouchkine acknowledged the need for a director's objective eye, yet the goal was always to allow individual creativity to flourish within the collective. 'A collective is not the negation of the individuals of which it's composed,' she said. 'A collective is the grouping of several creators.'[12] It was her desire to unleash each actor's own creative artistry that guided Mnouchkine's organization of the Théâtre du Soleil to make it 'as democratic as possible'.[13]

Peter Stein took the idea of a democratic collective even further – but later pulled back towards a more traditional structuring of company hierarchy. As Shomit Mitter explains it, 'the principles of democracy and egalitarianism' that Stein introduced at the Schaubühne 'flew in the face of the tradition of autocratic control which directors in Germany were accustomed to exercising, but drew on Stein's conviction that actors were more likely to give better performances if they had a say in what the company as a whole was trying to achieve'.[14] The essays by William Grange and K. Scott Baker in this volume both trace aspects of Stein's experiments with running the ensemble according to the Brechtian principles of egalitarian participation that guided his early productions at the Schaubühne am Halleschen Ufer. Ultimately it was the time wasted in obligatory company meetings with all the inefficiency of collective decision-making that took a toll on actors, designers and technicians. Interestingly, Stein's production values and techniques have reflected his evolution in rethinking the nature of the ensemble.

Influence overlapped with collaboration in Stein's artistic trajectory. Stein absorbed innovative ideas from seasoned actors Therese Giehse and Fritz Kortner about their processes in creating roles and how a director might best tap their creativity. Stein's respect for them as mentors led him to seek them as collaborators, and he served as Kortner's assistant even after he had begun directing; later he recruited Giehse to act in *The Mother*, which he directed. Stein worked closely and collaboratively on productions with his ensemble of actors – notably Jutta Lampe, Bruno Ganz, Edith Clever and Michael

König – during their fifteen years (1970–85) together at the Schaubühne. Stein also enjoyed collaboration with scenic designer Karl-Ernst Herrmann with whom he first worked in 1968 at the Munich Kammerspiele on Brecht's *In the Jungle of Cities*. Stein and Herrmann learned together over the years how the theatrical space collaborated in projecting the text's meaning. Klaus van den Berg shows how Herrmann's 'intense work with Stein' focused on putting actors into 'a meaningful environment' while 'unfolding a sequence of spaces in the course of the performance'.[15] *As You Like It* serves as an excellent example of unfolding spaces; staging the production inside a film studio offered the designer and director adaptable configurations on a large scale. They created two contrasting environments: an unadorned, enclosed Elizabethan court setting versus a sprawling forest of Arden with multiple points of interest. The audience moved from the court scenes through a small door to the open vista of a forest that encompassed various locations for a cinematic flow of encounters of different character groupings. Thus, Herrmann and Stein transformed 'linear scene progression into a spatial image of a forest with all its fragmented parts'.[16] Another of Stein's long-term collaborators, costume designer Moidele Bickel, met Stein when she was a student in Munich; she remained with the ensemble throughout the Schaubühne years. Later, she and Herrmann were part of the team when Stein worked with one of Jean-Louis Barrault's major collaborators, composer Pierre Boulez, who conducted two operas with Stein as stage director. Boulez had seen Stein's 1986 production of Verdi's *Otello* and made a concerted effort to win Stein's consent to direct Debussy's *Pelléas et Mélisande*. Boulez noted, 'What I like about Peter is that he accepts nothing without reflecting on it, and one has to overcome so many barriers in his objections and scruples before winning him over. But after all that, there is total trust and the work gets underway with total dedication.'[17] During the eight-week rehearsal period in 1992, Peter Stein attended all of Boulez's music rehearsals, and Boulez attended all of Stein's dramatic rehearsals. The collaboration worked so well that they followed it in 1995 with Arnold Schoenberg's *Moïse et Aaron*.

The directors' role and function

All three directors declined to articulate a philosophy of directing. Jean-Louis Barrault told Bettina Knapp in a 1963 interview, 'The theatre is a question of instinct. After spending many years in the theatre, an actor or director develops a sixth sense. ... There are no fixed rules, no definite theories.' Crediting Antonin Artaud for teaching him to feel his way into plays rather than to intellectualize, Barrault claimed, 'I am not a philosopher – I despise abstractions about the theatre.'[18] Similarly, according to David Bradby, 'Stein has always claimed that he has no set working method, that he shapes his methods according to the demands of the plays he tackles.'[19] Peter Stein told interviewer Jack Zipes that he would not want to be known for having 'a personal style' but that his record would show swaying 'back and forth from different positions' as he tried 'different modes of work' without imposing any specific approach. Rather his 'function' was 'to integrate these very different individual tendencies, talents, and personality structures'.[20] He told a 1994 interviewer that 'a director's approach should always depend on what is needed for the play. I find that the best stage dynamic comes if I am accepted as a brother who has very good eyes.'[21] For Ariane Mnouchkine also, the role of the director, as she fulfils it, 'varies from production to production'. At different times she might be a 'guide' or 'a wall' or a 'boxer', yet always the one whose perceptions are not tied to the physicality of one body or one store of scenic materials.[22] She acknowledges the need for a centralizing vision during the process of collective creation, yet she has seen herself primarily as a 'midwife' (*accoucheuse*) to the actors' creativity.[23] She doesn't create the baby but helps it to be born. 'A midwife is not somebody who just looks at the baby coming out easily. Sometimes she has to shout at the woman, sometimes she says "Push." ... Sometimes she says "Breathe." Sometimes she says "Don't do that."'[24]

Underpinning the production with research

Zeal to learn – to expand their knowledge across cultures and into arcane subject areas – characterizes all three directors. Ariane Mnouchkine and Peter Stein made the learning process a participatory endeavour by the entire company. In contrast, Jean-Louis Barrault would embark upon solo odysseys of intense reading and intellectual exploration, the fruits of which he would then share with his company. For example, Barrault had conceived *Rabelais* (1968) in the wake of the 1966 disturbances at his company's production of Jean Genet's *Les Paravents* (The Screens) and plunged into close study of Rabelais's five books, correspondence and other writing as well as works by Renaissance writers such as Ronsard and Malherbe and later scholars such as Jules Michelet and Léon Daudet. Barrault lugged the books with him and worked on successive drafts of his dramatization throughout the regular seasons he directed and during his company's 1967–68 international tour. But then Barrault lost his theatre and his company's assets in the events of May 1968 (to be covered in Chapter 1). Though personally devastated, he rallied the eighteen loyal company members and galvanized them with the rollicking life-affirming material of *Rabelais* that drew them into new performance techniques and ran for two seasons (1968–70).

Ariane Mnouchkine might always be best remembered for her response to the events of May 1968; she brainstormed with her company to select a topic that would resonate with all French people – beyond the habitual theatregoers; that is, in the aftermath of May 1968, directors looked for ways to reach what was then called the *non-public* (non-audience). She and the company chose the French Revolution and formed study groups to learn how ordinary people lived and what happened in 1789 to trigger the fall of the Bastille; they divided up the reading of primary sources and subsequent theories of revolution and class struggle; they attended lectures and pertinent movies. Together, under Mnouchkine's synthesizing guidance, they improvised vignettes and experimented with popular-theatre techniques whereby small stories fed into the mighty current of revolution. The result was the legendary, collectively created 1970 production of *1789*.

Peter Stein, like Mnouchkine, focused on details that would enliven and add up to a larger story. He employed 'working methods' that 'involved a strong element of research and discovery by all members of his company'.[25] A good example is that company's preparation beginning in 1971 for a production of Shakespeare's *As You Like It* (1977). Their process involved seminars, wide reading and learning Elizabethan performance skills, all of which resulted in an interim production – combining folk entertainments on pageant wagons and in processions, music and dancing, fencing and acrobatics, speeches and displays of Renaissance learning – to showcase the company's acquired knowledge and abilities: *Shakespeare's Memory* (1976).

Stein's staging of the company's research in *Shakespeare's Memory* reifies his articulation of his company's artistic aims in terms of a learning process, as noted by David Bradby: there is an 'emphasis on what is to be learned rather than what is to be shown, on process rather than on product'.[26] This is very similar to Maria Shevtsova's observation that for Mnouchkine, 'theatre is a conduit for *learning* from history rather than transforming it'.[27] Using research as a dramaturgical tool to aid the actors and designers is a time-honoured process that all three directors honed to perfection. However, turning the research itself into theatre for paying audiences is a trickier proposition. The two evenings of garnered material that constituted *Shakespeare's Memory* did not generate the favourable reviews that Stein's major productions did. According to Michael Patterson, 'throughout the programme the ensemble had difficulty in communicating the enthusiasm they had experienced in gathering the information. As Hinrichs said (1976), a lion hunt may be exciting, but all that remains is a stuffed head: "The Schaubühne cannot present its explorations to the public but merely its results; not the adventure itself, only a few trophies".'[28] Mnouchkine was generally successful at integrating historical context and other background studies into human stories that would hold an audience's interest; Emilie Gruat's essay in this volume offers an insider's perspective on how this was achieved. Barrault's all-consuming passion for whatever subject he was pursuing, coupled with his objectivity in seeing his work as the theatregoer would see it, enabled him to get away with work like *Ainsi parlait Zarathoustra* (1974), which was essentially a staging of Friedrich Nietzsche's philosophical thought.

All three directors used travel with their ensembles, whether on tour or as on special research-driven expeditions, to share the excitement of opening their minds to unfamiliar vistas of humanity. Jean-Louis Barrault especially encouraged his company members to immerse themselves in the local culture at street level, mingling with the people, visiting the shops and restaurants as well as the museums of each foreign city on their tours. Catherine Levasseur, wardrobe mistress for the Compagnie Renaud-Barrault and personal dresser of both Renaud and Barrault, recalled a serious stand-off with Barrault on their arrival in Japan, when he wanted her and the wardrobe crew to join the official welcoming tour of Osaka, which she would have loved to do but refused, knowing how much time they needed for unpacking and refreshing the limp costumes in order to be ready for the performance.[29] The Théâtre du Soleil, in contrast, absorbs various cultures from within, as the company usually comprises twenty or more nationalities. As part of the process of collective creation, Mnouchkine often sends actors out to specific locales to communicate with people whose views and histories they need to understand as a basis for certain productions. Despite the proclivity for elements of Asian theatre (gestural vocabulary, masks) in production, the tour itineraries of the Théâtre du Soleil have been mostly in Europe, often to major festivals of theatre. Peter Stein has incorporated travels by the ensemble as a component of their advance research for certain productions. When Peter Stein's fellow director in the Schaubühne collective, Klaus-Michael Grüber, was preparing his 1974 production of Euripides' *The Bacchae*, company members voyaged together at their own expense to lands around the Mediterranean, and those discoveries became the basis for Stein's *Antikenprojekt* (The Antiquity Project, 1974), a form of staged research that prefigured both *Shakespeare' Memory* and an *Antikenprojekt II* (1980), when Stein was preparing Aeschylus' *Oresteia* (1980). To prepare Gorky's *Summerfolk* (1974), the company journeyed to the USSR. Genet's *The Blacks* (1983) had some African dance steps incorporated into it, thanks to the troupe's visit to Africa.[30]

Directors defined by their repertoires

A vast world of dramatic literature opens up to the director of a company with enough actors on the payroll to cover the roles in large-cast plays that were standard before the mid-twentieth century. Given that wealth of possibilities, it is noteworthy that Barrault, Mnouchkine and Stein all chose so many of the same authors and, in a few cases, the same specific plays. Stein often refers to the Greeks, Shakespeare and Chekhov as the three pillars of European theatre; he and Barrault staged works by all three playwrights. All three directors tackled Shakespeare and then went on to explore Greek classics with Aeschylus' *Oresteia* trilogy as a key production for each of them. Both Barrault and Stein directed Chekhov's *The Cherry Orchard*, and Stein won particular acclaim with *Three Sisters*. Mnouchkine reveres Chekhov but says that since he stands alone as an era of theatre all to himself, 'there is only one way to stage his work', and she needs instead the open sky of Shakespeare.[31] Plays by Maxim Gorky appeared fairly early in the repertoires of Mnouchkine (*Petty Bourgeois*, 1964) and Stein (*Summerfolk*, 1974). Having earned early reputations for mastering serious material, both Barrault and Stein drew critical disapproval when they introduced some frivolity or lightness into their repertoires, as when Barrault staged Feydeau's bedroom farce *Keep an Eye on Amelia* in 1948, and Stein in 1973 chose *The Piggy Bank* by the earlier author of bourgeois French farce, Eugène Labiche. Both productions won popular success, although Stein told John O'Mahony in 2003, 'you know I have no sense of humour. I am German and I like tragedies very much and I do them quite well'.[32]

Peter Stein originally approached Shakespeare with some trepidation, and that is why he paved the way to *As You Like It* with the exploratory *Shakespeare's Memory*. Klaus van den Berg cites critic Peter Iden as one who recognized that 'Shakespeare was a fulcrum for the Schaubühne in building a performance approach'. Van den Berg notes further:

> In Stein's view, each play, canon or new work must be placed in a constellation with Shakespeare, and this interrelationship should be a source for action in any performance. All members of the Schaubühne were drawn into the discovery of the author as a historical subject, ... and to experiment with how cultural ideas might be presented visually. This method of quasi scientific engagement as a grounding for each production stood in stark contrast to most German production approaches in the 1970s and challenged the designers to conceive visuality as a repository of historical spaces drawn from a complex context.[33]

Stein's Shakespeare productions, in addition to his renowned 1977 *As You Like It*, are *Titus Andronicus* (1989, Teatro Ateneo, Rome), *Julius Caesar* (1992, Salzburg Festival), *Antony and Cleopatra* (1994, Salzburg Festival), and *Troilus and Cressida* (2006, Edinburgh Festival).

Jean-Louis Barrault's affinity for Shakespeare began early in his career when he acted walk-on roles and contributed fight choreography in *Richard III* under Charles Dullin's direction in 1933. He played Hamlet at the Comédie-Française in 1942 but commissioned a new translation of it for his first directorial venture into Shakespeare, again playing the title role in 1946. Other Shakespeare plays directed by Barrault are *Antony and Cleopatra* (1945, Comédie-Française), *Julius Caesar* (1960, Odéon) and *Henry VI* (1966, Odéon). Moreover, one of Barrault's early books was *Shakespeare et les français* (1949), in which he declared the necessity of Shakespeare for the French – even though the Bard's expansive poetic genius was 'cruelly' restrained by the 'clarity and precision' of the 'intransigent' French language.[34]

Having staged *A Midsummer Night's Dream* early in her career (1968), Mnouchkine turned to Shakespeare again twelve years later – as if to rediscover the value of the spoken word on stage. After the student uprisings of May 1968, a coalition of artistic directors led by Roger Planchon in Villeurbanne had cancelled the classic plays in their seasons and substituted hastily devised work on populist and topical subjects.[35] However, a decade of company-created theatre (few groups doing it as skilfully as the Théâtre du Soleil) resulted in a dearth of French playwrights, as other genres proved more welcoming to contemporary writers. By the mid-1970s, many were nostalgic for good speech and literary texts, which had always been the mainstay of French theatre. Mnouchkine's process for rediscovering the place of language in the theatre was to translate three Shakespeare plays that she directed at the Théâtre du Soleil from 1981 to 1984: *Richard II*, *Twelfth Night* and *Henry IV, Part I*. While each production synthesized elements of Asian and Elizabethan form, the Shakespearean essence of each play emerged fully.

Barrault and Mnouchkine both acknowledged Molière alongside Shakespeare, because – as Mnouchkine noted – Molière is like 'the boss of all theatre companies. You can't live in France and do theatre and have a company, without thinking at least once a week of Molière.'[36] Although Mnouchkine did not stage a play by Molière until 1995, when she did *Le Tartuffe*, she had in 1978 scripted the celebrated four-hour film biography *Molière* in which she directed actors from the Théâtre du Soleil. Interviewed about *Tartuffe* in 1995, Mnouchkine commented:

> For me both Aeschylus and Shakespeare are gods. They're not human. When you work on their works it's so magical. Everything is there. They invented it. ... But Molière's just a man – a wonderful man, a wonderful actor, a dear director of a company, but just a man. He's a genius but he's not superman. ... and he's so near us that he's modern.[37]

Barrault expressed a somewhat different perspective: 'Molière is us. From the time we are born, his phrases resonate in us, but I must say that right now I am more nourished by Shakespeare than by Molière.'[38] For Barrault, Shakespeare – writing in a time of murders, revolutions, crisis of faith (as opposed to Molière's era of order, authority, stability, prosperity) – speaks more directly to our post-war world. Barrault's preference would be to carry both Shakespeare and Molière in his pocket, but if he were forced to choose it would have to be Shakespeare as the 'more modern'.[39] Barrault directed Molière's *Amphitryon* in 1947, and he had the pleasure of being directed by Louis Jouvet in *Les Fourberies de Scapin* in 1949. What Molière is to a French director, Goethe must be to a German, and Peter Stein paid his homage to Goethe both early and late in his career with *Torquato Tasso* in 1969 and *Faust I* and *II* in 2000. Much of his meticulous work on text had been building towards the latter, uncut, twenty-one-hour 'production that (despite $265 tickets) played to sold-out houses for a year and a half in Hanover, Berlin and Vienna'.[40]

Jean-Louis Barrault, Ariane Mnouchkine and Peter Stein all attained new heights with their productions of *The Oresteia*, Aeschylus' classical Greek trilogy about the House of Atreus. Barrault spoke of his 1955 *Oresteia* as one of the milestones of his career, along with *Phaedra* and *Numancia*. Mnouchkine embedded her *Oresteia* in a four-play cycle that she called *Les Atrides* (1990–2); she began it with *Iphigenia in Aulis* by Euripides as a prequel. Mnouchkine had intended to do one of the less familiar Greek classics, but after reading and rereading them all, it was the 'top hit' of the Greeks that she found compelling. She was particularly intrigued by the character of Clytemnestra, even to the point of contemplating playing the role herself – but luckily 'the gods of the theatre sent Juliana Carneiro da Cunha' for the role.[41] It was Mnouchkine's interest in Clytemnestra that led her to begin the cycle with Euripides' play about Agamemnon's sacrifice of his daughter Iphigenia; this served as a context for her mother Clytemnestra's revenge on Agamemnon in the first play of the *Oresteia*. Tackling the plays of Aeschylus – who 'invented theatre, our western theatre' – was daunting to Mnouchkine, and she found herself, 'like the chorus, frightened and fascinated. Sick and healed. … breathless!'[42] Indeed, figuring out how to employ the chorus involved endless trial and error. She and Jean-Jacques Lemêtre knew that the chorus had to be music based, but the company comprised few good singers, so it was decided to have the chorus dance instead of singing. Mnouchkine tried having the chorus speak in unison and tried distributing lines among them, but always it sounded false. Her solution was to give all the chorus lines to the chorus leader. Even the stage setting was conceived for the chorus: a kind of bullring with enclosing stucco-coloured walls. With the intrusion of the savage protagonists, the chorus could climb a wall or hide behind a sheltering barricade.[43] Similarly, when Jean-Louis Barrault staged the *Oresteia* in 1955, Félix Labisse's scene design, all in pale wood, featured an encircling wall of wooden panels extending to the orchestra as a space for the chorus beneath the imposing central palace doorway. Barrault's concept for the *Oresteia* arose from the occult ceremonies he witnessed during the Compagnie Renaud-Barrault's tour to South America, notably in Brazil.[44] To evoke the majesty and magic of the ancient Greeks, he focused minutely on music, dance and a translation (by playwright André Obey in close collaboration with Barrault) tied to the metrics of the original Greek poetry. The method, which Barrault describes in *Memories for Tomorrow*, made the complete trilogy 'actable in three and a half hours'.[45] Composer Pierre Boulez wrote about his music's 'primordial role' in the production; he and Barrault agreed upon 'simplified rhythms and more or less repetitive melodic arcs' that would be within the actors' ranges. Moreover, Boulez cites Barrault's interest in Japanese Noh and Gagaku as traditions that informed his work with the chorus.[46] Like Mnouchkine,

Barrault used masks, which he found liberating for corporeal expression. Peter Stein's *Oresteia* shared Mnouchkine's and Barrault's respect for the original text manifested in a painstaking translation process, as described by Sue-Ellen Case.[47] Like Mnouchkine, Stein chose to have the chorus lines spoken by a single actor, but then the rest of the chorus would expand upon the commentary, almost as if adding footnotes. Thus, the playing time of the trilogy in Stein's original 1980 version was almost twice as long as Barrault's and even longer when he directed it in Russian in 1994. The significant difference in his approach was the use of modern costumes and the individuality of chorus members without masks. The review of Stein's 2007 production of Sophocles's *Electra* for the National Theater of Greece evokes his approach:

> All too often, the chorus in productions of Greek tragedy, 'makes us feel every year of the distance between the drama as it was conceived more than 2,000 years ago and the drama as we know it today.' Stein brings 'graceful attention ... to bear on this often troublesome convention. He understands and underscores the primal importance of the chorus in this chilly drama of revenge exacted with an almost monstrous glee'. He scales 'it down to human dimensions'. ' ... they move and sing together with remarkable fluidity.' 'Each face responds with a different measure of terror, sympathy, despair, or joy to the ghastly family drama playing itself out before it.'[48]

The stage director and other media

One major difference among the three directors is their relationship to other media. Before he formed his company, Jean-Louis Barrault gained considerable renown as a film actor, and this enabled him to build his financial resources and the name recognition that served him well in his subsequent stage career. As the demands of running a company necessitated his withdrawal from motion pictures, he turned to publishing his many books, his long-running *Cahiers* (Notebooks), some of his dramatic adaptations, and even numerous prefaces and forewords for theatre books by other authors. Mnouchkine, the daughter of a film producer, grew up with a cinematic sensibility that was theatricalized during her formative travels in Asia. Her widely distributed film *Molière* (1977) established her credentials in the medium, through her powerful use of images in visual storytelling. She went on to adapt some of her major stage productions to feature film realizations that she directed. Stein expanded his range with more elaborately staged and lengthier productions, beginning with his nine-hour *Faust*, after which his freelance directing took him frequently into the realm of opera and scenic spectacle.

Director and audience

Both Barrault and Mnouchkine kept the audience in mind as they crystalized ideas for a production, yet neither ever pandered to perceived audience tastes. In accepting government subsidies, they felt a sense of responsibility to offer intellectual challenges, to be provocative without vulgarity, and to transcend any narrow political agenda. Peter Stein, while far more generously subsidized at the Schaubühne than either Barrault at the Odéon or Mnouchkine at the Théâtre du Soleil, did not hold back from presenting texts or stage imagery with the potential to outrage. He professed a desire to engage with his audience and experimented with ways to make that happen: post-performance question and answer sessions, printed materials calculated to stimulate discussion. But his real challenge was to attract the working-class audience he wanted to reach. Ironically, for Stein – as with the plays of Bertolt Brecht – it was the capitalists targeted in left-leaning productions who most reliably supported his work.

One additional feature of both Barrault's and Mnouchkine's impulses to connect with their audiences was their creation of spaces for interaction between theatre artists and theatregoers. Attending a performance by the Théâtre du Soleil at the Cartoucherie de Vincennes is like being welcomed into a huge family gathering. The theatregoer gets to look into the make-up room where the actors are preparing. Some productions involve communal meals prepared by ensemble members who also break bread with the audience. Barrault, hampered by frequent changes of theatrical homes, finally achieved at the Gare d'Orsay his dream of a *foyer de rencontre*, a dedicated space with a bar for receptions or informal mingling of actors and audience after the show. Thus, when he planned his final theatre at the Rond-Point, it too had a reception room up the stairs off the main lobby. When I crashed a reception there on 7 November 1983, after a benefit performance of Virginia Woolf's *Freshwater*, Jean-Louis Barrault and Madeleine Renaud could not have been more gracious.

Jean-Louis Barrault

1

Jean-Louis Barrault: His Life in His Work

Felicia Hardison Londré

Epigraph: *Se passionner pour tout et ne tenir à rien*
(*Souvenirs pour demain*, 106).

Feel passion for everything, but cling to nothing.

JEAN-LOUIS BARRAULT, CREDITING ANTONIN ARTAUD

In performing arts circles outside of France, awareness of Jean-Louis Barrault's artistry usually begins with his famous mime sequence in the 1945 movie *Les Enfants du paradis* (Children of Paradise). Barrault portrayed the legendary whiteface mime Deburau in a cinematic paean to the popular entertainment that flourished on the Boulevard of Crime in 1830s Paris. One reviewer praised Barrault's 'astonishingly expressive silent language ... in the tiniest gestures, the movement of his fingers, the intensity of his eyes'.[1] Indeed, mime was also at the core of the production that had launched Barrault's dual careers as actor and director a decade earlier: *Autour d'une mère* (1935), described as 'thirty minutes of text to two hours of performance'.[2] That stage adaptation of William Faulkner's novel *As I Lay Dying* was the public's initial exposure to Barrault's lifelong obsession with *le langage du*

Translations from French-language works cited are those of the author of this essay unless otherwise credited.

corps (the language of the body), and it brought him to the attention of film-marker Marc Allégret, who gave Barrault his first movie role.

Deburau in Barrault's formation

Barrault's twenty-third film role, Deburau in *Children of Paradise*, resulted from a chance encounter with director Marcel Carné and poet-scenarist Jacques Prévert in Nice. The two were crestfallen that a producer had just turned down their proposal for a film and asked Barrault if he had any ideas they could use. Barrault had been collecting material on Deburau with the notion of creating a solo mime piece about the historical figure, but he became intrigued by the thought of a talking picture that would feature a mime surrounded by speaking actors. Prévert liked the concept and wrote a screenplay. In his memoir, Barrault listed friends from his youth who became involved in the film and added: 'To my joy, mime, theatre and cinema were brought together. This happened in the same year as *Le Soulier de satin*: 1943. *Annus mirabilis:* a real synthesis of one's life. And all this under the German Occupation!' He noted further that of all the characters he had played during his long career, the dreamy Baptiste Deburau was perhaps the most harmoniously close to himself.[3] The historical Deburau, popularly identified with the love-struck Pierrot character that seeped into his own persona, found the humanity of his portrayals through his real-life interactions at street level with ordinary and marginalized people. Similarly, Barrault admitted to being driven by all-embracing love of humanity. The opening lines of his 1955 book *Je suis homme de théâtre* (I Am a Man of the Theatre) describe his vocation:

> One who, for the love of a few square meters of stage boards, and who, out of love for all humanity, for the life that can be recreated on those boards, accepts WITH THE SAME LOVE, to serve all professions, all walks of life, even all the encircling vultures. ... The person who embraces all that is a theatre artist.[4]

What does his early career Deburau tell us about the internationally renowned director that Jean-Louis Barrault would become? Beyond his delight in the synthesis of art forms, there is his evident pleasure in the ensemble. Barrault named many artistic colleagues when he recalled the film's origins and again in a later interview with Guy Dumur: 'Everything I was passionate about in life came together, with my good friends, in a marvelous subject.'[5] Throughout his career, Barrault readily credited others for their contributions and for the success of the work as a whole. He would mention specific techniques learned from his teachers, stimuli from friends, ideas picked up from thinkers outside his realm of expertise. Then too, a director is always brimming with ideas for his next project and imagining how the material might work for individual talents in the ensemble. While the repertoire of Barrault's company remained strongly grounded in classic plays like those of the Greeks, Shakespeare, Molière, Racine and Marivaux, he was ever open to bold experimentation: staging plays by avant-garde writers, adapting performance texts from other genres, steadfastly paying homage to his increasingly erratic friend Antonin Artaud, exploring new territories in music, sound effects, lighting, visual stylization. His long close collaborations with poet-dramatist Paul Claudel and composer Pierre Boulez became intrinsic to his directorial identity. The friendship that grew from Barrault's staging of Claudel's plays is well known; in the preface to their published correspondence, Barrault wrote of how their mutual life passions transcended the forty-four-year age difference and that 'this profound understanding of each other, with a whiff of Eternity, and the twenty years I shared with him will always be among the most precious and enriching rewards of my life'.[6] Barrault wrote of Boulez in 1954, 'He won the respect of our company. Between him and us, there was good chemistry. We understood each other. We were like blood brothers. He became ensconced "in the family," in this family of choice that comprises a company.'[7]

Barrault and his influences

It takes nothing away from Barrault's stature as a director who was able to keep his privately owned, nomadic theatre company afloat for forty years to acknowledge how much he absorbed from his ongoing collaborative relationships with a wide range of artists and others both inside and outside his company. He told an interviewer in the early 1980s:

> I am a fanatic for influences. I've always known how to accept influences. … When one is open to influence, it's as if one receives something close to a degree of perfection that existed only as an embryo within oneself. Influence can happen only when it's a better version of something you intuited. If I suddenly want to be influenced by someone, it's like a spiritual relationship, in which I have the seed and that person is the perfection. I welcome influences.[8]

Corollary to his receptiveness to learning from others was the desire to be responsible for others. Barrault understood this as a need to become a father figure in place of the father missing from his childhood. He told Guy Dumur in 1981: 'I always wanted to be responsible for a human community. … To assume responsibility for a human collective was for me a passion equal to my passion for theatre – and the theatre made it possible for me to fulfil both passions.'[9] It was inevitable that he would form his own theatre company and run it as an ensemble.

In keeping with Barrault's embrace of the ensemble, this overview of his life and works will include some of those people who were important to him.

Above all must be acknowledged the woman who shared his love, passion for theatre, personal sacrifices for the art and leadership of the company that bore her name alongside his: Madeleine Renaud, Barrault's wife and co-director of the Compagnie Madeleine Renaud–Jean-Louis Barrault. As Denis Podalydès observed in writing about the company's forty-year odyssey that took them to ten different Paris theatre facilities,

> But the heart of it all remained, the jewel, the ever-pure diamond, the touchstone of the entire edifice, of everything that Barrault was: Madeleine Renaud. Without Madeleine Renaud, Barrault's theatre would probably have gone under rather quickly. He would have stopped making theatre, managing and animating a theatre. The theatre lived for her and when she was not there, the company was not complete.[10]

A similar picture emerges from the memoir by Catherine Levasseur, hired in 1952 for the wardrobe crew of the Compagnie Renaud-Barrault; she rose to become the personal dresser of both Renaud and Barrault as well as overseeing the company's costumes on their international tours. She shows how Barrault was infallibly courteous with everyone but could become harried when financial exigencies impinged on his multiple artistic roles. Madeleine Renaud was the steadying, calm, graceful presence, who would hide her fatigue to play the expected off-stage role as hostess-representative of French culture at endless receptions and cultural events when they toured abroad. Together Renaud and Barrault were affectionately referred to by company members as *les petits patrons*, which might translate as something like 'our adorable bosses'.[11]

Family background

The childhood formations of Jean-Louis Barrault and Madeleine Renaud could scarcely have been more different. Whereas she came from a genteel, upper middle-class Parisian family, Barrault's lineage was Burgundian peasant stock. 'I have three hundred years of wine in my veins,' he claimed.[12] As a teen Barrault loved wine-growing, especially the September grape harvest, which initiated him 'into the sensuality of life'.[13] Barrault's brother Max-Henry was four years older. Their father Jules served in the Great War was absent during most of their childhoods and died of Spanish flu or perhaps typhus less than a month before the 11 November 1918 armistice. Their mother Marcelle raised the boys mostly in Paris, under the influences of their crusty grandfather Louis Valette and her brother, 'Uncle Bob' Valette. The latter awakened Barrault's interests in painting and poetry. His mother exposed him to theatregoing, but his first love was geometry. As a student at the Collège de Chaptal for eight years, Barrault excelled at his studies and won prizes for mathematics.

At twenty, Barrault suddenly changed course. He had seen the renowned Cartel actor-director Charles Dullin perform in *Volpone* and wrote to request an audition. In Dullin's studio at the Théâtre de l'Atelier, Barrault – knowing nothing of audition protocol – performed two scenes in which he played all the roles, using different voices and postures. Dullin immediately offered to take him as a student and – swearing him to secrecy – made it tuition free.

Charles Dullin's school of theatre

The years at Dullin's school, 1931–5, grounded Barrault in *commedia dell'arte*, improvisation, gymnastics, scene study, discipline, collaboration and reverence for the art. He regarded Dullin as his long-sought father figure. On his twenty-first birthday, 8 September 1931, Barrault performed for the first time on a professional stage – in a walk-on servant role. His memoir refers to that as his 'second birth'.[14] He also befriended an Atelier company member, Etienne Decroux (who would later play Deburau's father in *Children of Paradise*). They became 'like two accomplices who had set out in the search for a new art of mime'.[15] Together they 'established the difference between wordless pantomime and silent mime'.[16] They spent three weeks figuring out and perfecting how to mime walking without moving forward in space. The two years that Barrault and Decroux devoted to codifying gestures and expressing themselves through all the muscles of the body may be considered the wellspring of Barrault's continuing interest in *le langage du corps*. In 1932, Barrault's studies at the Atelier school were interrupted by obligatory military service (which marked him physically in that the discovery of poetry books in his knapsack was punished by the shaving of his head, after which his hair grew back curly). Upon his release, he returned to Dullin and was cast in small roles in several plays.

It was in June 1935, at the end of the Atelier's season, that Barrault staged *Autour d'une mère*, his own adaptation of Faulkner's *As I Lay Dying*. Having come into an inheritance from his father, Barrault rented the theatre for six days (two rehearsal days and four public performances). Months of intense work had gone into the production, yet Dullin disapproved. Barrault recalled: 'Curtain up. It revealed us all stripped, our private parts only just concealed.'[17] The ensuing cries of derision quieted down as the audience became absorbed in the physicality of the storytelling, notably Barrault's portrayal of both horse and rider. Barrault's overnight renown led to an added matinee performance for theatre professionals, after which the eminent Cartel actor-director Louis Jouvet told Barrault, 'Everything we were formulating in our heads at the time of the Vieux Colombier, you now have in your blood.'[18] The risky production led to the movie contracts that enabled Barrault to pay his debts and begin saving up to start his own company: 'Theatre got me into the movies, and money from the movies let me do more theatre.'[19]

Barrault's Bohemian period

Reluctantly, intuiting that it was time to throw himself into a larger current of being, Barrault decided not to return to Dullin's school in the autumn of 1935. He rented the spacious top floor (*le grenier*) of an ancient building, 7 rue des Grands-Augustins, in the Saint-Germain-des-Prés area of the Paris Left Bank. There Barrault, calling himself an 'inoffensive anarchist', welcomed all who revelled in their personal freedoms. Some who frequented the space were second-wave surrealists: Robert Desnos, André Masson, Jacques Prévert, Joseph Kosma, Sylvain Itkine. Other artists appeared occasionally: André Gide, Georges Bataille, Tristan Tzara, Roger Blin, Félix Labisse, Maurice Baquet. Barrault even took in a homeless eight-year-old boy – who grew up to be the celebrated singer Mouloudji. Sometimes as many as fifty people would gather in the large studio workroom and improvise shows or share meals. Barrault developed a particularly close friendship with Antonin Artaud, who was already professing ideas that would coalesce into his theory of a 'theatre of cruelty' and that would become known to the world through his book, *The Theatre and Its Double*.

In January 1936, Barrault put together a production of Jacques Prévert's adaptation of Cervantes's *Retablo de maravillas*, under the title *Le Tréteau de merveilles*, with music by Joseph Kosma. One of various projects springing from the Grenier des Grands-Augustins, the piece was presented by the Groupe Octobre and performed at a neighbourhood cultural centre on a bill with other small offerings. This effort laid the groundwork for Barrault's later, more ambitious staging of another Spanish Golden Age play, Cervantes's *Numancia*, in 1937. Besides an acting engagement at the Théâtre de l'Oeuvre, Barrault acted in six films in 1936 and five in 1937. He always carried fond memories of those free-spirited two years of bohemian lifestyle at the Grenier, but again it was time to expand his horizons.

Madeleine Renaud

Ten years older than Jean-Louis Barrault, Madeleine Renaud (1900–94) was an established star of stage and screen, having since 1921 played ingénue roles at the Comédie-Française, where in 1928 she had advanced to the rank of *sociétaire*. In 1936, she was set to play the title role in the film *Hélène* and proposed Claude Dauphin for her leading man. Director Jean-Benoît Lévy asked her to meet Barrault, whom he described as 'not handsome and doesn't wear a tie, but he has an intense gaze and smile'.[20] Barrault took the trouble to shave and wear a tie for the appointment at Renaud's upscale apartment, where he also met Charles Granval. The distinguished actor-director Granval (1882–1943) had nurtured Renaud's early career at the Comédie-Française and married her in 1922; their son Jean-Pierre was thirteen and also present for Barrault's 'audition'. Perhaps Renaud had sought a father figure by marrying a man nearly two decades older than herself, for she – like Barrault – never really knew her father; hers had died when she was four. The affectionate dissolution of Granval and Renaud's marriage was already underway when she met Barrault. From childhood she had determined to make her own way in the world, and she was drawn to Barrault's common touch, his vitality, his lack of pretension. He was a force of nature and he won the role as her leading man in the movie.

Hélène was filmed during the summer of 1936, while their own developing love story, discreetly observed by the film crew, transcended the cinematic love story. From 19 August 1936 to the end of their lives, they were a couple, personally and artistically. They married, at the urging of her son, on 14 June 1940; Renaud bought the wedding rings.[21] Her death on 23 September 1994 came almost exactly eight months after his, on 22 January 1994. They always enjoyed recounting the circumstances of their meeting. Their dresser Catherine Levasseur noted often how happy they were in each other's presence and how tenderly they treated each other, even in the most trying circumstances.[22] It was a great leap of faith for Madeleine Renaud to give up a life of comfort and artistic security to share Barrault's dream of running his own theatre ensemble with all the accompanying hardships. According to Colette Godard in a retrospective tribute (*Le Monde*, 9 May 2008), Renaud would buy paintings when the company made money and have them auctioned off when times were hard. 'She looked after everything like the lady of the house, the mother of an extended family, both authoritative and indulgent. Nothing, it seemed, was further from her nature than the instability of the player's life, constantly on the road. And yet she did what she had chosen to do.'[23]

Numance (1937)

During the intervening years between filming *Hélène* and his marriage to Renaud, Barrault was preparing himself for the responsibility of creating a company. He made it his first order of business to prove himself to Renaud by undertaking an ambitious production, which he financed with his film earnings, more than 40,000 francs.[24] He chose Cervantes's *Numancia*, a powerful *entremés* about the walled Spanish city conquered by Romans in AD 133, as a work that would bring together poetry, chanting, stylized gesture and make-up, rhythmic movement, surrealist visual elements, fantasy (a talking river, for example), history, nightmare. André Masson designed the setting with a movable wall that allowed alternation between the besieged city and the Roman encampment. When Barrault staged a revival of *Numance* in 1965, he looked back at the 1937 production as 'a ballet of humanity, with its infliction of death, its collective life, its individual reactions, the flow of time, the silence overtaking everything, and above all this coexistence of the Real and the Fantastic'.[25]

Numance was presented at the Théâtre Antoine, a boulevard theatre, which Barrault rented for two weeks. Delivery of Irène Karinska's costumes brought a near crisis, as six thousand francs was to be paid in full at once and Barrault didn't have it. His faithful friend Robert Desnos saw the situation and insisted that the costumes not be taken away before his return. Desnos left and came back with the cash, having solicited an advance on his salary as a journalist. Directing the large cast and overseeing myriad business matters taught Barrault the rigours of his chosen vocation, and he learned to work beyond fatigue,[26] as he would do throughout his career. Reviewers especially praised the ensemble work. Audience word of mouth quickly led to sold-out houses for the seventeen performances. Certainly, the Civil War in Spain enhanced the resonance of *Numance*. The production led to Barrault's first meeting with Paul Claudel, who – in a burst of enthusiasm for the work he had just seen – wished that they could have met forty years earlier.[27] Another lasting result was the design motif of the bull's head with a human skull between its horns, which would later be adopted as the logo of the Compagnie Madeleine Renaud–Jean-Louis Barrault. Perhaps most important to Barrault was that he had proved to himself that he was worthy of Madeleine Renaud.

The war years

Barrault continued acting in films and on stage. He found Charles Granval to be an important influence on his development, especially in terms of learning to appreciate the classics as foundation for an avant-garde that might offer more than the facile shock effect of crude audacity.[28] Granval directed him in an adaptation of Jules Laforgue's play titled *Hamlet*, with music by Darius Milhaud, on a bill with Barrault's adaptation of the novel *La Faim* (Hunger) by Knut Hamsun. In the latter, Barrault both acted the leading role, Tangen, and directed a cast that included Roger Blin as Tangen's double. Jandeline, the actress who played roles such as Autumn and Night, gives us a sense of Barrault's developing directorial style:

> His enthusiasm shared with the troupe, the pleasure he imparted in rehearsal through his precise directions and the warmth of his explanations, the verve he brought to the actor's work on the character, the happy discoveries that he would often reconsider the next day. He demonstrated gestures but didn't impose them, yet saw them affirmed over time. Each of us committed fully to the difficult process with the feeling that we were participating in something innovative.[29]

Hamlet (the Laforgue play of that title) on a bill with *Hunger* (Barrault's dramatization of Hamsun's novel) opened on 18 April 1939 at the Théâtre de l'Atelier and achieved a run of seventy performances.

The happiness Barrault was finding with Renaud paralleled the creative spirits and frenetic living of Europe's inter-war years in general, but the world was about to change. Barrault was at his mother's side when she died on 14 June 1939. Then he and Renaud travelled to visit Paul Claudel at Brangues, the rather isolated chateau where the eminent poet-playwright lived with his three-generation family. On that first of several visits to Claudel at Brangues over the years, Barrault asked permission to stage three of his plays (the latter two not previously produced) – *Tête d'or* (Golden Head, 1890), *Partage de midi* (Break of Noon, 1906) and *Le Soulier de satin* (The Satin Slipper, 1929) – and was categorically refused. Barrault turned to adapting Franz Kafka's *The Trial* (*Le Procès*) but had to put that aside when he was mobilized at the end of August, even before France's declaration of war against Germany on 3 September 1939.

Then followed eight months of *drôle de guerre* (phoney war), a strange period of inactivity as prelude to the serious fighting on land after the German advance into the Low Counties in May 1940. Barrault was sent to Alsace and assigned menial tasks but was later transferred to a unit in which his reputed artistic skills could be put to use painting camouflage. In the chaos of the mid-June military rout and the civilian evacuation of Paris, Barrault and Renaud fortuitously found each other on the road and got married but again had to separate. With Pétain's signing of the armistice that began on 25 June and divided France into the northern Occupied Zone (including Paris) and the 'free French' resistance in the south, the army was demobilized. Barrault received an invitation from the newly appointed head of the Comédie-Française, Jacques Copeau, to join the company at the rank of *pensionnaire* for a year. Beyond the joy of his reunion with Renaud, Barrault welcomed the opportunity to continue his artistic development where he could address the skills he lacked.

The Comédie-Française

After his bold experiments in theatrical form, Barrault was ready to embrace tradition. Having honed his corporeal expressiveness, he yearned for vocal challenges. In quick succession, Barrault performed small roles in classics by Molière, Rostand and Corneille and then – opening on 11 November 1940 – the leading role, Rodrigue, in Corneille's 1636 classic *Le Cid* (The Cid). Barrault remembered his well-conceived Rodrigue as a 'disaster' in that he was physically too lightweight for the role.[30] However, he knew himself to be the right weight for Shakespeare's Hamlet, which he performed for the first time on 3 March 1942, under Charles Granval's exacting direction, in a 1923 translation by Guy de Portalès. The role would continue to challenge Barrault for over twenty-five years, as Shakespeare's *Hamlet* (in

André Gide's 1946 translation) would be the inaugural production of the
Compagnie Madeleine Renaud–Jean-Louis Barrault in 1946 and would
remain in their repertoire until the 1960s.[31] Reflecting back on his original
thirty-year-old Hamlet, Barrault later wrote: 'Hamlet's anguish, his frenzy,
his double nature, his black humor, his libertarian spirit – all these things
enabled me to feel close to the part. All the same, I did dance it rather too
much.'[32] Many other roles, large and small, followed.

In 1942, Barrault was given the opportunity to direct at the Comédie-
Française, an unusual opportunity for a *pensionnaire*. The leading actress Marie
Bell put in a request for him to direct her in Racine's *Phèdre*. That process
reaffirmed his simmering convictions about the director's art. In 1944, he
published a book, *Mise en scène de Phèdre*, which documents his close work on
the text through line-by-line indications of their inner and outward expression
on stage. His *Memories for Tomorrow* also offer commentary on the work
with Racine's 'quintessence of stage poetry'. He wrote: 'I kept finding in *Phèdre*
striking proofs of the relevance of everything I had thought, up to then, about
dramatic art: use of breathing, waking dream, the plastic art of the mouth, art
of gesture, rhythm, etc. The study of *Phèdre* was to mark me forever.'[33]

On 22 December 1942, Barrault accepted the invitation to become on 1
January 1943 a *sociétaire* of the Comédie-Française; the rank of *sociétaire*
was a lifetime sinecure or – as Barrault saw it – 'like "taking vows"' or
confining himself 'in an aesthetic citadel'.[34] The decision to commit to the
Comédie-Française was not made lightly, for it seemed like a betrayal of his
goal of leading a company of his own. His friend Jean-Paul Sartre responded
insightfully to Barrault's request for advice: 'I think a man like you, who has
at least one new idea per day, who is made for trying out new things in all
directions, ought to be his own master and every time to commit only himself.'[35]
On the other hand, as his friend Robert Desnos advised, the Nazi occupation
of Paris made any individual initiative suspect (as opposed to the sheltered
world of the Comédie-Française), and Barrault was highly visible from his
film roles, which could also prove dangerous for his associates. Indeed, Desnos
himself was later arrested and deported; he died in captivity. What impelled
Barrault to become a *sociétaire* was a sudden realization that his recalcitrance
seemed 'so amateurish, so unprofessional, so artificial, intellectual and naïvely
pretentious (as the "amateur" spirit always is)'.[36] He rationalized it further as
a way of perpetrating from within the illustrious company the ideals about
theatre that he had absorbed from Dullin. As events played out, Barrault's
time at the Comédie-Française totalled only six years, 1940–6, and his three
years as *sociétaire* contributed significantly to his development as a director.

The Satin Slipper

Paul Claudel remained the contemporary dramatist closest to Barrault's heart.
In April 1941, Barrault, Renaud and Eve Francis had performed scenes from
Claudel's *The Satin Slipper* in four ninety-minute radio broadcasts over four

days.[37] The play haunted Barrault and he carried the text everywhere in his knapsack. He saw that it would allow him to apply his ideas of *théâtre total* (total theatre) – as he had done with *Autour d'une mère* and *Numance* – this time to a major text, a serious piece of poetic writing. Performed uncut, *The Satin Slipper* would run approximately nine hours; Barrault imagined doing an abridged version in two parts, three hours each. With the informal blessing of Jean-Louis Vaudoyer, administrative director of the Comédie-Française, Barrault crossed France's line of demarcation to visit Claudel at Brangues in June 1942. Barrault read his adaptation to 'the master', who decided to entrust his monumental work to the relatively young director. For three days, they worked together on the text and on ideas for the staging; then Barrault returned to Paris, carrying Claudel's letter of permission for production. At the border crossing, a German soldier tore the letter to bits, but Barrault salvaged every tiny scrap and ultimately reassembled it on cellophane. The Comédie-Française reading committee agreed to produce the play if it could be further adapted for performance on a single evening. During the next eighteen months until the November 1943 premiere, Barrault acted in his assigned roles, began filming *Children of Paradise* and pursued various projects on the side while remaining emotionally focused on *The Satin Slipper*. The final version, approved by Claudel, was well under five hours, with a five o'clock curtain time that allowed theatregoers to return home before the Nazi-imposed curfew.[38]

When Barrault began rehearsals of *The Satin Slipper*, he still needed to win the confidence of the company's established artists. Three tactics enabled him to take command. First, following the advice of Robert Desnos, he locked in financial commitments by spending money on set construction. Second, he asked the administrative director to call a meeting of core artists, and their professionalism was invoked. Third, he took each actor aside for a one-on-one session to discuss the character and to work through scenes on an individual basis.[39] During rehearsals, Barrault learned that the artistic cauldron is satisfyingly fired up if the technicians and actors not involved in a scene slip into the auditorium to watch the work in progress.[40] The Nazi occupation caused difficulties in obtaining materials and press coverage. Technical rehearsals (33 scene changes, over a hundred costumes) brought further setbacks, and Barrault was not above screaming foul language as he ran back and forth. Jean-Louis Vaudoyer, the company's gentlemanly administrative director, watched from the auditorium and told Barrault to be patient, as it would all work out. Barrault stopped in his tracks and glowered as he unleashed an insulting obscenity. Renaud was near Vaudoyer in the auditorium and tried to excuse Barrault's rudeness. Calmly Vaudoyer replied, 'It's okay so long as he doesn't beat me.'[41] As Barrault's directorial skills matured, he learned to control such outbursts.

Paul Claudel came to Paris in anticipation of the 27 November 1943 opening of *The Satin Slipper*.[42] On 10 November, he attended a rehearsal at which all went well – up to a pivotal scene in Part Two that had been giving Barrault trouble: 'I was not managing to "place" the scene properly, to get it going; Marie Bell and I could not even get the text by heart.'[43] Barrault had wrestled with various ways of staging the scene, and nothing seemed to work; he ventured to suggest to Claudel that it be cut. Claudel asked them to go ahead and finish the run-through, after which he agreed that the scene was not working but that it should not yet be excised. The next morning, after writing all night in a fever of inspiration – as if receiving divine dictation – Claudel arrived with a replacement scene. Having seen the play on its feet, he felt that he now truly understood what he had written in 1928–9. He saw how to reinforce its nuances by bringing into the scene a character from earlier in the play, the hero's brother, a Jesuit priest.[44] According to Barrault, 'The same afternoon sufficed for Marie Bell to learn the new lines, while the staging resolved itself as if by enchantment.' Throughout the final rehearsals, Claudel 'perfected the smallest details, both diction and interpretation. Diplomatically, he rarely spoke to the actors, but he gave me pages of detailed notes.'[45]

At the opening matinee performance, the overture – eighteen musicians playing the score composed by Arthur Honegger – was interrupted by the air raid siren. Claudel loved the effect of disorder at the beginning of the play's journey to its great unifying harmony. The production was an unmitigated triumph that re-established Claudel's long-dormant status as a great dramatic poet. For audiences who might have dreaded huddling under their blankets for five hours in the unheated theatre, with some performances interrupted by electrical outages, it was 'an overwhelming affirmation of the national genius', giving them a desperately needed dose of hope and beauty.[46] For Barrault, it was one of the greatest adventures of his life, for he 'loved The Satin Slipper as if it were a Being'.[47] Over the course of his long career, Barrault would return often to direct or produce plays by Claudel: Partage de Midi (Break of Noon) in 1948, L'Echange (The Exchange) in 1951, a programme of texts and poems by Claudel in 1952, Christophe Colomb (Christopher Columbus) in 1953, The Satin Slipper revived in 1958 and 1980, Golden Head in 1959, and in 1972, Sous le Vent des Iles Baléares (Beneath the Winds of the Balearic Islands), a play excerpted from The Satin Slipper.

La Compagnie Madeleine Renaud–Jean-Louis Barrault

After the 1943 success of The Satin Slipper at the Comédie-Française, Barrault took advantage of opportunities to direct a variety of plays, notably André Gide's translation of Antony and Cleopatra, another success for Barrault. The 1944 Liberation of Paris and the release of the movie Children of Paradise were cause for optimism. But trouble was brewing at the venerable 'House of Molière'. Vaudoyer resigned in March 1944.

The ensuing power struggle between the leadership of the company and the French government ministry (source of subsidies needed to keep the theatre from bankruptcy) was complicated. From Barrault's perspective, the artists were totally ignored by the bureaucrats.[48] Without input from the *sociétaires*, whose careers were invested in the company, the Provisional Government of the French Republic drew up revised statutes for the organization of the Comédie-Française and allowed a two-week window for resignations by any *sociétaires* who were not satisfied with the new arrangements. Admittedly, Barrault was deeply torn by his reverence for the theatrical tradition he had embraced and from which he had gained much; however, he tendered his resignation on 31 August 1946. Madeleine Renaud surely had more to lose than he did, but she too relinquished her position, as did seven others. Fugitives from the Comédie-Française who joined Renaud and Barrault on their new venture were André Brunot, Pierre Bertin, Jacques Dacqmine, Georges Le Roy, Jean Desailly and Catherine Fonteney.[49]

Barrault and Renaud negotiated a three-year renewable contract to rent the Théâtre Marigny on the Champs-Elysées. Barrault acted in a movie to earn the start-up money. Joining the risky venture, besides the defectors from the Comédie-Française, were Marie-Hélène Dasté (Copeau's daughter, whom they called Maiène), Pierre Renoir, Marthe Régnier, and some younger actors: Simone Valère and Renaud's son Jean-Pierre Granval. The inaugural production, opening 17 October 1946, was the stage premiere of André Gide's translation of Shakespeare's *Hamlet*. Gide had put aside his initial attempt at translating *Hamlet* and published only the first act in 1929. Barrault had read it and in 1942 urged Gide to take it up again; the actor's concepts gave Gide the stimulus he needed. Arthur Honegger composed the music and brought along two younger musicians who would later win renown as composers: Pierre Boulez and Maurice Jarre. André Masson designed sets and costumes. Although Louis Jouvet had warned Barrault that '*Hamlet* has never made a franc,' and that Parisian audiences did not want to see ghosts on stage,[50] critics were happily surprised by the production with Barrault in the title role (see Figure 1.1).

They noted the character's synthesis of supple grace, athleticism, poetry, political awareness and even a light comic touch as his story unfolded in the simplified scenic space, with Honegger's score evoking sea waves, heartbeats, buzzing in the ears. A week later, 24 October, the company opened Marivaux's short delicate comedy *Les Fausses confidences*, a triumph for Madeleine Renaud (see Figure 1.2), on a bill with *Baptiste*, a piece based on the Pierrot/Harlequin pantomime in the movie *Children of Paradise*. The two bills, *Hamlet* and *Les Fausses confidences/Baptiste*, were performed in rotating repertory, with a third folded in on 12 December 1946: the premiere of Armand Salacrou's *Les Nuits de colère* (Nights of Rage).

FIGURE 1.1 *Jean-Louis Barrault in costume as Hamlet at the Marigny Theatre in 1946.* Hamlet *was the inaugural production of the Compagnie Renaud-Barrault, and Barrault kept the title role in his acting repertoire until 1966. Photo by Keystone-France/Gamma-Keystone via Getty Images (Getty #104422495).*

Integral to Barrault's creation of a company was the rotating repertory format (*l'alternance*). Like so many of his decisions, the plan to keep several productions in the repertoire at the same time was regarded by many as folly. Not since Jacques Copeau disbanded the Théâtre du Vieux Colombier

FIGURE 1.2 *Madeleine Renaud and Jean-Louis Barrault in* Les Fausses confidences *by Marivaux. This was the second production of the Compagnie Renaud-Barrault's inaugural season, often revived as a showcase for Renaud's skills as a graceful comedienne. Photo by Keystone-France/Gamma-Keystone via Getty Images (Getty #104422482).*

in 1924 had a private company proved capable of maintaining a rotating repertory.[51] Economically, the practice could be both a blessing and a curse. It is expensive to pay salaries of those who might not be involved in every production, to maintain and store the various sets and costumes, and to support the manpower needed for changeovers of scenery and lighting plots, often two or three times a week. On the other hand, the practice protects the company against the occasional failure, since a show that was not drawing audiences could be phased out in favour of an earlier success. Without rotating repertory, Barrault could not have continued performing *Hamlet* for twenty years (1946–66) – maturing with the play to discover endless nuances.[52] Without rotating repertory, he could never have experimented as daringly as he did with new plays and avant-garde staging. Looking back after thirty-five years with the company, Barrault claimed that they had maintained a ratio of 75 per cent modern plays to 25 per cent classics. For Barrault, the economic risks were outweighed by the artistic gains. Tied to the concept of rotating repertory was Barrault's idea of a company as an ensemble of three generations that would learn from and stimulate one another,[53] even as their diverse talents would grow 'by rubbing up against different styles day by day'. With the challenges of the varied repertoire, 'the artistic standard of the company rises continually'.[54] Nevertheless, there were theatregoers and even company members who expressed shock at Barrault's decision to stage *Occupe-toi d'Amélie* (Keep an Eye on Amelia) by the great turn-of-the-century genius of bedroom farce, Georges Feydeau, in the company's second season (opening 4 March 1948). To rotate boulevard-theatre fare with literary masters such as Shakespeare and Marivaux seemed like foolish audacity.[55] And yet the laugh-provoking farce proved enduringly popular and gave Madeleine Renaud as Amélie one of her finest forays into comic acting.

The second season additionally brought fulfilment of Barrault's dream of staging a dramatization of Kafka's *The Trial*, opening on 11 October 1947, and widely regarded as another risky choice. This work serves as an example of Barrault's directorial finesse in maintaining a vision over a long period of gestation and intuiting when the time was right to pounce. Indeed, he was meanwhile patiently earning Claudel's confidence, a long process that would pay off in the right to premiere the poet's deeply personal *Break of Noon* in 1948. Similarly, *The Trial* was a long-simmering obsession, a project Barrault had conceived in 1939. To turn Kafka's novel into a text for the stage, he envisioned collaboration with André Gide, who initially dismissed the idea as better suited to the cinema. After Barrault commissioned Gide to translate *Hamlet* for his company's inaugural production, the actor-director and the translator 'worked closely together, looking at the English text again word by word', Barrault recalled. 'We had got on extremely well. Gide had the straightforward simplicity that true professionals have.'[56] With the success of *Hamlet*, Barrault again prodded Gide about tackling *The Trial*. Barrault drafted a scenario with the idea that Gide would write the dialogue, for Barrault had come to value 'scripts by real writers'.[57] In Gide's small bed-sitting room, Barrault read his draft to the eminent novelist. At the very moment of the death of the protagonist Joseph K, the chandelier dropped from the ceiling with only the electric wire keeping it from hitting Barrault's head. Gide took that as a sign that the project was meant to be. Barrault recalled how their inclinations complemented each other's – Barrault always trying 'to pack too much in', while Gide knew how to write economically.[58] Rehearsals were not easy with Gide present, often barely masking his disapproval of work in progress that he seemed to expect to see fully formed.[59] Barrault, however, was using the text as a springboard for all the resources of the theatre, including mime, and orchestrating the various elements was complex. Félix Labisse's scenery evoked endless labyrinthine corridors, offices and unadorned grey spaces. Music director Pierre Boulez supplemented Joseph Kosma's musical score with urban sounds: traffic, typewriters, ringing telephones. Barrault even turned the dialogue into a vocal score, sometimes overlapping lines, even allowing speech to become unintelligible. Barrault paid rigorous attention to the interlocking rhythms of the gestures, lighting cues, scene changes and every element of *le théâtre total.* The resulting production brought a storm of controversy; many were dazzled by the theatrical innovations or by the contemporary relevance of the narrative in the post-war world, while others questioned whether it was at all appropriate to adapt a novel for the stage or whether the sequence of hallucinations even added up to a play. Such spirited debate generated excellent box office.[60]

The stylistic variety of plays and productions mounted during those early years of the Compagnie Madeleine Renaud–Jean-Louis Barrault would remain a hallmark during the company's forty years under Barrault's direction. He chose both classics and bold new works to resonate with current events and to push individual performers' talents into new realms. The stimulus for his projects could emerge from his reading across vast fields of knowledge: literature, history, philosophy, painting, crafts, agriculture, anthropology, foreign cultural studies. When an idea began to obsess him, he would read in depth virtually everything by an author or about a subject. He also took inspiration from the prospect of working with certain artists he admired, as when he sought out Albert Camus to collaborate on a work of total theatre inspired by Daniel Defoe's *Journal of the Plague Year*, using the plague as a metaphor for totalitarianism. Although the process that yielded *L'État de siège* (State of Siege) in the third season, 1948–9, was personally gratifying to both Barrault and Camus, the production failed to win the critics or audiences, and it closed after only twenty-three performances.[61] As another instance of his respect for another artist impelling him to seek collaboration, Barrault had always been in awe of the great director Louis Jouvet and was completely gratified that he could bring in Jouvet as guest director of Molière's *Les Fourberies de Scapin* (Scapino's Escapades) in 1949.

Barrault's directorial process

A record of Barrault's rehearsal techniques was published by Michel Bertay, a company member for thirteen years, with nine years as Barrault's assistant.[62] In the latter capacity, Bertay assisted with staging twenty-five premieres and thirteen revivals of earlier productions from the repertoire; that is, more than four productions each season personally directed by Barrault, who also acted in many of them. This meant that he was always working under pressure, which in turn drew upon strong management skills.[63] Barrault loved the exploratory phase of a project in consultation with his composer or scene designer, who often played a strong role in shaping the production Barrault envisioned. An object – what we now call a signifier – might also strike 'the seminal spark of the play', as when he saw the throne as a sign of power in *Hamlet*.[64] As soon as he fixed upon a text for the stage, it was as if Barrault fell in love with it, reading it over and over while jotting ideas and sketches in his pocket notebook.

Bertay saw not a cold analytical process but something like a courtship and deepening relationship.[65] As Barrault conceived the staging of a work, he would imagine all of the components, a remarkable mental juggling, for he was often seeing it simultaneously as the director, as an actor in the leading role and as a reader of the work who wanted to experience it as a member of the audience. He would channel the thinking of his designers along the lines of his own vision even as he was careful not to prescribe or impose upon their creative contributions.

The first read-through of a play was always pleasurably anticipated by the ensemble. Barrault would show the model of the sets or describe the concept. Then he would take off his jacket, loosen his tie, sit behind a table with a bottle of water and read all the roles, including only as many stage directions as necessary for comprehension. His sense of the rhythms of a work guided him as both director and actor. Bertay recalled only two occasions when such readings ended with a decision not to proceed further with the play. After his reading, Barrault would announce the casting.[66] Table reading would begin the next day and might continue for a week, although Bertay recalled no more than two or three days of work at the table for productions mounted after 1957. Barrault used that process not only for the actors' deepening of their understanding of the text, but for his own verification that his casting choices conformed to the characters and functioned harmoniously as an artistic whole; the occasional changes in casting at that phase could be wrenching to an actor, but Barrault strove to handle it diplomatically.[67]

Early in the rehearsal period, Barrault would set aside a morning in the changeover process between two shows in the repertoire and, on a bare stage, walk through the measurements of the projected scenic layout for the play in rehearsal. Together with the designer, the chief technician and others, Barrault would consider how the space related to his planned blocking, to scene changes, to audience sightlines and to lighting angles – all with a view to preventing unpleasant surprises when the scenery would be delivered from the builder. Bertay recalled:

> Jean-Louis would leap from the auditorium to the stage and back, confer with his friend the designer, move a chair, sit in it, have a table brought in and placed with exactitude, practice a movement between the two pieces of furniture, verifying the distance available for a bit of business, adjust another place for the view from the front row or for hanging lights. The entire technical team in the auditorium would watch quietly as the boss made the scenic space his own.[68]

'A bare stage is so beautiful,' Barrault wrote in his book *I Am a Man of the Theatre*. Referring to the director in the third person, Barrault dwelt upon this phase of the process: And when the director jumps from the auditorium to the stage, 'in three seconds, he has passed from one world to the other. And the stage space becomes for him like a painting in depth'.[69]

During blocking rehearsals, actors remained open to getting to know their characters, and Barrault might offer analytical or psychological guidance even as he was blocking a scene. As an actor moved, script in hand, Barrault sometimes walked with the actor, holding him or her by the elbow. Corrections in stage composition and movement differed little from what Barrault had already seen in his mind's eye even before the first reading. During this mechanical placing of action in space and continuing later in the process, he trusted Madeleine Renaud's objective eye, for she was invariably correct when something needed to be cut or altered. Between one and two weeks of rehearsal sufficed for actors to know their lines and blocking.

Then the company was ready for the stimulation of the third phase of preparation: teasing out the human element in working rehearsals. Using every minute to the fullest, Barrault was always conscious of his time and that of the actors who had been called to rehearse. At this point, actors would push back, explore and get off track. Barrault preserved his vision, treating the older actors with respect and diplomacy and those of his own generation with the insistence of their common vocabulary, while the younger ones would get more prolonged attention to techniques that would help them in the long run. He could make concessions, knowing that by temporarily giving an actor his head, Barrault could restore his master plan at the proper time.[70] According to Barrault, the director

> knows he must use a different psychology with each actor. To indulge the petty infractions of certain actors is clearly unfair to the disciplined ones, yet personalities must be taken into account. No two actors are cut from the same cloth, nor do they play identical roles. Nor can the director guide the young male lead as he does the established female star. So the man of theatre must be flexible enough to work in various modes at one time.[71]

During these intense hours together, the company would bond as a family, and Barrault particularly relished the 'almost-physical intimacy' of his relationship with the actors. The man of theatre, he wrote, 'loves his actors literally. He would nurse them if they were ill. He would make them perfect, hide their flaws. He suffers when they cannot intuit what works for them. He feels connected to them by some inexplicably mysterious and diabolical umbilical cord.'[72] In Barrault's view, all directors are driven by love, whether they watch and guide from the auditorium or whether they adopt his own 'voluptuous' approach of exploring the role alongside the actor on the stage, sometimes even shadowing the actor, 'his mouth to the actor's ear, like a guardian angel – or a kind of demon!'[73] Bertay saw it as Barrault's way of transferring his own energy to the actor and communicating the rhythm of his breathing. Sometimes Barrault would stand facing the actor, 1 metre away, hypnotizing him with his gaze. Or during a long speech, Barrault would firmly grip the actor's hands, forcing elsewhere the energy that might have gone into gestures. These sessions were often exhausting for the company, even for those not subjected to the personal focus, yet all were enriched. Barrault would reserve time at the end of these working sessions to run the sequence.[74]

The company would rehearse until mid-afternoon and then retire to rest for the evening performance of whichever play was on the bill that evening. Barrault used the post-rehearsal hours to switch first to his administrative oversight of business matters in consultation with the general manager and other staff. Then, if he was performing that evening, a twenty-minute nap would suffice, even for a demanding role like Hamlet, 'to recharge his batteries' and dissipate his earlier concerns so that he could 'welcome into himself' the character he would play.[75] A sign on his dressing room door warned against interruption while Barrault stretched out on his divan in the dark and transformed himself from director into actor. In *I Am a Man of the Theatre*, he describes in detail his sequence of breathing, muscle relaxation and listening to his body while he fell into the deep sleep of renewal that would refresh him for the evening performance.[76]

Working rehearsals gave actors the time and latitude to discover their nuances of character. Then they would run sequences and entire acts. When the stage was available for this phase of rehearsals, Barrault would sit at his table in the auditorium, taking notes. Nothing escaped him, and he was rigorous about respecting the text. His sense of rhythm was similarly exacting. After making corrections, he would run the scene again to ensure that the reworked bits were understood and absorbed by the actors. The next challenge was to sustain what the actors had achieved as they dealt with successive incorporations of costumes, scenery, music and lighting. Delivery day for the costumes that had been built in a commercial studio always brought some trepidation, as the costume parade on stage revealed unexpected constraints on a character or clashes in the overall visual harmony. For example, Barrault recalled that when the costumes arrived for *Pour Lucrèce* by Jean Giraudoux in 1953, Edwige Feuillère looked resplendent in both of her gowns, whereas the one designed for Madeleine Renaud made her look like 'a white cheese'. Several lengths of fabric were brought to the stage to drape over her, one was chosen, and four days later Renaud had a perfect costume. But when Feuillère tried hers again, one of them worked beautifully while the other lost its allure alongside Renaud. So Feuillère's now-imperfect costume had to be redone. 'Such are the mysteries of the stage.'[77]

The arrival of the scenery from the commercial workshop unleashed a new round of upsets, as did the first rehearsal with the unionized musicians. How did Barrault handle the chaos and complaints? He had observed closely what the master directors did at this point in the process and, always open to influence, stood ready to adopt whatever worked in the moment. His mentor Charles Dullin would take upon himself all of the despair, anxiety, suffering, to the point that his actors would forget their own gripes as they sought to reassure him. Gaston Baty would keep his focus on the technical rehearsals and leave his cast to their own worries. Jacques Copeau would conceal his agony even if it meant going into seclusion for a private nervous breakdown. Louis Jouvet would usually rework everything.[78] As long as the company was performing in the evenings, technical rehearsals were held following the performance into the small hours of the morning. To inaugurate a new production, there would necessarily be a hiatus in the performance schedule while the new work got the company's full attention. According to Bertay, this usually meant two or three dark nights at the theatre, never more than five, before the premiere.[79]

The final dress rehearsal – called the *couturière* because it allowed the wardrobe crew one last fine-tuning of the costumes – was open only to company employees and perhaps a few invited guests.[80] Bertay recalled that a smooth final dress tended to yield overconfidence and glitches at the opening, whereas more often the cast went home discouraged, but they triumphed the next evening. Either way, Barrault himself was in the theatre with the technicians most of the night. Then he would sleep for two hours and wake up with solutions to the problems. At 5.00 am, he would rise and write out his notes for actors and running crew, telephone instructions to the staff at 7.00 am, and then sleep again until 10.00 am. He would meet with the cast in early afternoon to work through any changes, followed by a run-through with scenery, sound and lights from 4.00 to 7.30 pm. At curtain time, 9.00 pm, Barrault ritually embraced the club that the stage manager would then use to pound the floor in the traditional *trois coups* (bam bam bam) that announced the beginning of the performance.[81]

Michel Bertay's essay sums up Barrault's directing techniques with a few miscellaneous observations, beginning with Barrault's remarkable readiness to rethink and reconceive work that was already considered successful and to bring fresh passion to the effort. A notable example was his acclaimed, legendary staging of Claudel's *The Satin Slipper* at the Comédie-Française in 1943, which Barrault restaged in 1958, in 1962 and in 1966, always finding new inspiration in the play and enhancing its emotional power. His artistic trajectory tended towards a paring down of elements to get at the essence of a text and to suggest rather than explain. He avoided over-interpretation or applying any personally recognizable stamp to productions; rather he allowed the work itself to determine the style. He refused to articulate a theory of directing other than to serve the text by focusing on what would best illuminate the playwright's intention for the spectator in the audience. The great variety of plays he staged – an amazing range of historical periods and theatrical aesthetics – testifies to the range of Barrault's genius.[82]

Touring

In the course of his 1981 radio interviews with Guy Dumur, Jean-Louis Barrault acknowledged that as an artistic director, he tended to be weak in the area of audience development. He felt that if he offered high-quality productions of plays that resonated with the times, his public would find him. Certainly, he attracted many students. Yet it was difficult for his private company to compete with state-subsidized theatres, which could offer significantly lower ticket prices.[83] Having to rent the privately owned Marigny Theatre during the company's first decade further subjected Barrault to administrative setbacks – which he turned to advantage by taking the company on international tours. As early as the end of its inaugural season, the company toured a repertoire of plays to cities in Belgium, the Netherlands and Luxembourg; this 1947 venture was instructive not only for the details of planning and managing inventories of costumes, props and scenery, but also for the affirmation of how its international reputation thus enhanced would serve the company's artistic mission and even its financial survival. Performances of *Hamlet* in Edinburgh in 1948 generated wildly enthusiastic international press coverage. A tour at the close of the Paris theatre season became a fairly regular occurrence that Barrault relished. 'Why do theatre, if not to get to know people? Make contact, exchange views, share, get to know one another, and try to understand,' he wrote in *Souvenirs pour demain*.[84] Clearing customs with wigs and fake jewels or packing, unpacking and setting up their own dimmer boards, cables, lighting instruments and sound systems in unfamiliar theatres of various capacities exhilarated Barrault as if he were 'half ambassador, half general of an army'.[85] Even towards the end of his career, Barrault was 'happiest among young people from distant lands, from various cultures and languages, all of them passionate enthusiasts for the theatre'.[86]

Barrault's first transoceanic voyage came in 1950 with the company's three-month South American tour that included bookings in Rio de Janeiro, São Paulo, Montevideo and Buenos Aires. The thirty or so performers and technicians travelled with over 24 tons of scenic equipment and costumes for nine productions; in the early years of their touring, they carried their own technical apparatus. During the fourteen days at sea, Barrault conducted rehearsals and gymnastic training. The travel was sponsored by the French government's cultural affairs branch, under Louis Joxe, in the Ministry of Foreign Affairs, with a view to rebuilding France's ties to South American nations in the wake of the Second World War. Thus, the enthusiastically received performances were supplemented with festive receptions and workshop visits to schools and hospitals.[87] Barrault loved every minute and often referred to his Brazilian cultural encounters in his various memoirs. The company returned to South and Central America three times, adding Chile to the original itinerary in 1954 and visiting Mexico, Peru, Ecuador, Columbia, Venezuela and Caribbean islands in 1956. Their 1961 tour began triumphantly as ever but met with several disasters: a theatre fire in Buenos Aires that destroyed much of their equipment, Madeleine Renaud bravely giving a graceful performance despite having just broken her foot on the stairs backstage, the theft of Renaud's valuable jewellery that Barrault had given her over the years, and a white-knuckle flight to Montevideo through a cyclone that pitched their overhead baggage onto the company members in their seats. At the end of that tour, Brazil paid homage to France by having the Renaud–Barrault company inaugurate the new theatre in the new capital city of Brasilia, which was still under construction. Barrault recalled that even as they were performing there, 'enormous rats scuttled between our legs'.[88]

The company's first North American tour came about when Madame Volterra, proprietor of the Marigny Theatre, which Barrault had rented on two successive three-year contracts (1946–9 and 1949–52), decided to reserve the 1952–3 season at her theatre for other ventures. Barrault signed another three-year contract (1953–6) for his company to return there in October 1953 and used the fifteen-month hiatus without a home theatre in Paris for an extended tour. The spring months of 1952 took the company to Italy, France, Belgium and Zurich. Then they embarked on a full-season tour to Canada and the United States. After playing Montreal and Quebec, they were welcomed to New York by the legendary impresario Sol Hurok. Since the repertoire included the short piece *Baptiste*, based upon the pantomime sequence in the movie *Children of Paradise* (see Figure 1.3), Hurok had arranged for the Fifth Avenue department-store display windows to be filled with mannequins dressed in the whiteface clown outfits of Barrault's character!

In the taxis that Hurok had ordered to transport them to their hotel via Fifth Avenue, Barrault and his ensemble must have thought they were dreaming when they saw those displays. The six-week season in New York City surpassed all expectations. For Barrault and company, it was a pinnacle of achievement, and his fondness for American audiences continued unabated on company tours to the United States or solo lecture performances there in 1957, 1964, 1967, 1969, 1970, 1976 and 1980. During the 1957 tour, United Nations Secretary General Dag Hammarskjöld invited the company to perform Molière's *Le Misanthrope* (The Misanthrope) in the Assembly's great hall, and they used his offices for dressing rooms![89]

In 1960, the French government sponsored Barrault's troupe on a three-month round-the-world tour, flying from Hamburg over the North Pole to Anchorage, followed by performances in Japan, then travel via Bangkok and New Delhi to performances in Israel, Greece and Yugoslavia. Barrault summarized it: 'around the world in eighty days!'[90] Playing fourteen different theatres in scarcely three months meant fourteen times arriving exhausted in a new city and hiding fatigue to make a favourable first impression on the welcoming party; fourteen times reawakening 'a virginity, a freshness, an entirely new enthusiasm' for a new public; and fourteen times unpacking and

FIGURE 1.3 *Jean-Louis Barrault in the title role of* Baptiste *by Jacques Prévert at the Marigny Theatre in 1946. Based upon the theatrical pantomime in the 1945 movie* Children of Paradise, *this short piece was first presented on a bill with* Les Fausses confidences. *It remained in the repertoire for many years and toured to New York in 1952. Photo by Lipnitzki/Roget Viollet/Getty Images (Getty #56210963).*

reassembling the tons of production materials they transported.[91] Barrault always insisted that cast and crew take time from their work to get out in the streets, see the sights and meet the locals. Barrault's spiritual sensibility emerged most intensely during his international tours, as he discovered the humanity in all religions and the commonalities in human nature despite extreme cultural differences. He noted in the course of describing a side trip to Delphi (to which he was drawn by wide reading of mythology in his youth as well as a mystical sense of his own oneness with both living things and inanimate objects): 'It always seems to me that, at a certain altitude of the Spirit, everything becomes alike. There is nothing left but our earth, nature, and *man* – as a Whole.'[92]

The Compagnie Renaud–Barrault tours comprised many return visits to London, Zurich, several cities in Belgium, Poland and Italy. A long tour to Japan in May–June 1977 proved exceptionally successful. They played Moscow and Leningrad in 1962 and 1976. Shorter jaunts took them to theatre festivals in France, including those in Avignon and Bordeaux. Sometimes the company actually rehearsed and premiered a new production on the road. For example, they first performed Georges Schéhadé's *Histoire de Vasco* (The Story of Vasco) on 15 October 1956 in Zurich, where it proved a resounding success as it did in Lyon and Baalbek, yet it inexplicably failed when it opened the Paris season on 1 October 1957. Chekhov's *La Cerisaie* (The Cherry Orchard), one of the company's enduring favourites, had been rehearsed in Paris but premiered in Rio de Janeiro on 20 May 1954.

From the Marigny to the Odéon

Launching the 1953–4 season at the Marigny, Claudel's triumphant *Christopher Columbus*, with music by Darius Milhaud, struck awe in its opening moments with the release of a trained white dove that soared above the stage and was again swallowed in darkness. Then a gigantic hand of God appeared from the heavens to touch the land and the troubled waters. Also that season Barrault began publishing a periodical that offered a range of scholarly and creative pieces related to the company's current work; from its first issue devoted to Claudel, the *Cahiers Renaud Barrault* (The Renaud-Barrault Notebooks) achieved a run of thirty-five years (1953–88). Another initiative of that season was a studio theatre, the Théâtre du Petit-Marigny, where new plays could be presented without undue pressure on the novice playwright; the intimate space further served Pierre Boulez for Le Domaine musical, a series of concerts to expose the public to contemporary music.

For a decade (including the 1952–3 season on the road), the Marigny was the company's home. Barrault himself staged forty-five productions there, and he brought in such eminent guest directors as Jean Vilar for Gide's *Oedipe* (Oedipus) in 1951 and Louis Jouvet for Molière's *Scapino's Escapades* in 1949. Barrault later reminisced that it was 'a beautiful experience' to get to know Jouvet as a person and to watch his masterful directing. Another memory was the death of set and costume designer Christian Bérard in front of his scenery for that show. They were setting light levels, and Bérard had just expressed his pleasure when he collapsed in the aisle and died on the spot. The final preview/press night performance took place on the day of his burial, 17 February, after which Barrault made a curtain speech acknowledging Bérard's sets and costumes. The entire audience silently rose up and stood in tribute. At that very moment, Barrault recalled, Bérard's painted act curtain broke and 'dropped like a guillotine. ... It is so beautiful, the mystery of the theatre.'[93]

With the 1956 expiration of the Renaud-Barrault Company's third three-year contract to rent the Marigny Theatre, Madame Volterra declined to renew. Barrault's dresser Catherine Levasseur speculated that Volterra thought the theatre had become too closely identified with Barrault himself in Parisian eyes, and she was not happy that he was assumed to be the proprietor.[94] Without a Paris theatre for the 1956–7 season, the company went on tour. Then they played the 1957–8 season at the enormous Théâtre Sarah Bernhardt, followed by a season at the Théâtre du Palais-Royal, one of the oldest theatres in Paris, and a challenge for finances since its capacity was 400 seats fewer than the Marigny's. It was at the Palais-Royal that the company enjoyed one of its greatest triumphs, Jacques Offenbach's *La Vie parisienne* (Parisian Life), which had premiered at that very theatre in 1866. Few in the company could be considered fully trained singers or dancers, but Barrault took the view that actors 'have to be able to sing with their bodies, with precision. And they have to sing with feeling, which is the same as playing comedy.' They mastered the cancan and, for the singing, adopted a cabaret style (perhaps tapping into nostalgia for the wartime spirit). With vocal coaching, they pulled off a production that long held its popular and critical appeal.[95] After a performance of *La Vie parisienne*, audiences would leave the theatre singing and dancing in the street. The Palais-Royal also saw the successful 1958 revival of Claudel's *The Satin Slipper*.

A new chapter in the company's existence began with the 1959–60 season and lasted nine years. André Malraux, the newly appointed Minister of State for Cultural Affairs under General Charles De Gaulle, invited the Compagnie Renaud-Barrault to move into the venerable government-subsidized Théâtre de l'Odéon, which had been functioning as a satellite stage for the Comédie-Française but would hitherto be called Odéon-Théâtre de France (see Figure 1.4).

Barrault was primarily concerned about retaining his artistic freedom while operating a state-owned facility, which effectively made him a government employee. While his artistry was never compromised, the new venture ended up posing almost insurmountable financial burdens on the company, as the subsidy was insufficient for a theatre facility that was so expensive to run. Barrault entered the new venture enthusiastically as always, but nothing prepared him for the jealousies of other theatre groups along with critical hostilities. The opening production, *Golden Head* by Claudel, drew disastrous reviews, although student audiences loved it, some returning to see it repeatedly during the fifty-performance run. 'Morally it was a great success; materially it was a flop.'[96] The next two new productions – Eugène Ionesco's *Rhinocéros* and Shakespeare's *Julius Caesar* – were also badly received, but luckily there were plenty of successes in the company's existing repertory that could be used to fill out that first season at the Odéon. The company's fortunes began to turn for the better in the third season,

FIGURE 1.4 *Madeleine Renaud and Jean-Louis Barrault show the poster for their first productions at the Odéon-Théâtre de France. Photo by Keystone-France/ Gamma-Rapho via Getty Images (Getty #558654069).*

1961–2, which included a revival of Claudel's *Break of Noon* and a new production: Shakespeare's *Merchant of Venice* (Le Marchand de Venise), directed by Marguerite Jamois and featuring the Senegalese-born actor Daniel Sorano as Shylock. By the fourth season, according to Barrault, 'the new productions were as successful as the well-tried favourites which we kept in our repertory'.[97]

During the Odéon years, which Barrault remembered fondly despite the financial stress, he opened a studio theatre for small, risky productions, as he had done at the Marigny. The Petit Odéon, inaugurated in 1965, was created in a lobby space and seated 150. Also in 1965, he became president of the Société d'Histoire du Théâtre and he was named director of the Théâtre des Nations, an annual festival of important productions from various countries that were presented at the Odéon. The company's 1966 production of Jean Genet's *Les Paravents* (The Screens), directed by Roger Blin, caused uproar because it dealt with issues of colonialism and nationalism in Algeria. Barrault considered it a great play on its own terms, with no political agenda; indeed, he believed that 'the true artist doesn't seek to provoke a scandal'.[98] It opened well, but the twelfth performance brought protesters with planned disruptions of the performance: stink bombs and other projectiles thrown from the balcony, with rioting inside and outside the theatre continuing over the next thirty performances. President De Gaulle and Cultural Minister Malraux spoke up for the play and for freedom of expression on stage, and police protected the genuine theatregoers. Cast members managed to maintain their composure and to complete every performance.[99] For example, Madeline Renaud was on stage as the Queen of the Prostitutes when light bulbs thrown from the auditorium began smashing around her; she stopped her performance, crossed to the footlights and addressed the audience: 'So you have a grudge against prostitutes too?' After the burst of laughter, she resumed her performance without further incident.[100]

In retrospect, the disruptions at performances of *The Screens* might be seen as a prelude to the catastrophic events of May 1968 that led to Barrault's dismissal as director of the Odéon. In May 1968, Paris became a focal point for the youth rebellion that simmered around the world in a movement positioned 'between Marxism and anarchism, on the one hand, and between politics and culture, on the other'.[101] Students' grievances against so-called paternalistic systems that constricted educational opportunity and fostered the Vietnam conflict soon aligned with labour unrest over working conditions. When the first riots erupted in the Latin Quarter of Paris on 10 May, Barrault and company were in London while the Odéon was being used for the Théâtre des Nations. Barrault returned the next day to his office at the Odéon, and there on 15 May, he received a phone call from a government representative instructing him not to hinder protesters who might invade the building that evening but to engage them in dialogue. There was no possibility of dialogue with the 2,500 impassioned youths who took over the Odéon and began their month-long occupation of auditorium, offices, dressing rooms and storage areas. Whether or not the students knew that Barrault himself was an old anarchist and ardent champion of young people, they – or the professional agitators who infiltrated the demonstrators – branded the Odéon-Théâtre de France as an emblem of bourgeois culture that pandered to a consumer society. They trashed the facilities, including the Renaud–Barrault company's personal stock of costumes and props. Barrault sought guidance from Malraux's ministry and was ignored, except for an order to cut the electricity in the theatre, which he refused to do, out of concern for the occupants' safety. Ultimately, Barrault realized that the Odéon had been sacrificed by the government to spare other government buildings from invasion; Barrault was made the scapegoat by the very government officials who had so often in the past spoken up to defend his artistic freedom. In June, the company returned to the vermin-infested theatre to find 'twenty years of work destroyed',[102] yet Barrault and Renaud further endured the indignity of two and a half months of government silence – refusals to meet with him or to explain the situation – until Barrault received Malraux's letter of 27 August 1968 notifying him that he was fired. Barrault felt betrayed by one he had considered a friend but who now publicly rebuffed him. Knowing that there was little he could have done otherwise left him yearning for an explanation that never came. The hurt was deep and lasting. He and Renaud, now fifty-eight and sixty-eight years old, would have to start again from zero.

Odyssey to a theatrical home

The mindless manifestations against consumer culture erupted again that summer in attacks on the Avignon Festival, where director Jean Vilar had long stood for making theatre accessible to all. Like Barrault, Vilar attempted dialogue with the protesters, but again the rabble-rousers wanted to hear only their own speeches and slogans. Vilar was less successful than Barrault at recovering from the insults to his life's work; he died broken-hearted in 1971. Barrault's survival mechanism for transcending the setback was his powerful sense of responsibility for his company, along with Madeleine Renaud's unwavering commitment to his initiatives. Moreover, Barrault had been working ahead – as was his custom – on projects he anticipated years in advance. During the difficult weeks from May to August 1968, he avoided despair by focusing on his fourth revision of his adaptation of the five books of François Rabelais (1494?–1553), the rollicking, licentious satirist who created Gargantua and Pantagruel. Knowing that Rabelais had championed tolerance even as his work was condemned by Sorbonne scholars and Church dignitaries, Barrault undertook the huge project in response to the intolerance he witnessed during Genet's *The Screens*. The experience of May 1968 reconfirmed his ideas: 'Rabelais is like a joyful shout on the rim of a volcano. The volcano of his era was the same as ours. He was born between a world falling apart and a world beginning afresh.'[103] Barrault rented a sports venue, the Elysée-Montmartre, not far from the studio where he had studied under Dullin, whom he had regarded as his first surrogate father. Claudel had become his next father figure, and now Barrault felt that he had been 'adopted by Rabelais'.[104] In the large rectangular space, Barrault created a playing area in the shape of a cross with spectators on all four sides, an appropriate rejection of the social hierarchies built into the traditional proscenium theatre (see Figure 1.5). Rehearsals were difficult, and the production seriously strained Barrault's financial resources.

Madeleine Renaud's engagement at the Théâtre National Populaire to perform in Marguerite Duras's *L'Amante anglaise* (The English Lover) occasioned the couple's first professional separation but brought them

FIGURE 1.5 *Jean-Louis Barrault conducts a rehearsal of* Rabelais *on 6 November 1968 at the Elysée-Montmartre. Part of the cross-shaped stage is visible. Photo by AGIP/RDA/Getty Images (Getty #508023419).*

needed revenue. Opening in December 1968, *Rabelais* played to sell out houses of 1,100 with as many as 600 others purchasing standing room. 'Happy human communication, joy, insolence, youth and health won the audience. ... We all witnessed the rebirth of our theate.'[105] Rosette C. Lamont described the production as a 'rock-farce, a fluid all-enveloping spectacle, the dream of total theatre come true'.[106] *Rabelais* tided the company over fifteen months; it ran in Paris and on tour until May 1970.[107] For Barrault, one of the happiest memories of his career was a performance of *Rabelais* for 4,000 students at the University of California, Berkeley.[108] At the Elysée Montmartre, the company followed *Rabelais* in 1970 with *Jarry sur la butte* (Alfred Jarry on the Hilltop).

From 1970 to 1972, the company mounted a series of productions at the Théâtre Récamier, beginning with a festival of Beckett plays in honour of Samuel Beckett's Nobel Prize. Ultimately, Barrault found the Récamier too small for his ventures, and he again looked for a theatrical home. Meanwhile, the company became stabilized enough that he could fulfil his desire to celebrate the centenary of Claudel's birth, albeit four years late. He asked his stepson Jean-Pierre Granval, an original company member, to prepare a stand-alone section of Claudel's *The Satin Slipper* that was separately titled *Sous le vent des îles Baléares* (Beneath the Winds of the Balearic Islands). They borrowed a circus tent from Cirque Fanni and performed the piece on Claudel's property at Brangues on 27 July 1972. That success led to an arrangement with the French railway system (SNCF) to set up the tent inside the great hall of the Beaux Arts railway station, the Gare d'Orsay (today's Musée d'Orsay), and perform Claudel's piece there for a thirty-day run; that success in turn led to the play's extended run of four months.[109]

In spring 1973, sponsored by Les Tréteaux de France, the company embarked on a European tour, transporting the tent in which they performed, often in a different city each evening. Despite the hazards of noise and cold, the tent performances inspired Barrault afresh. After so many world tours that had involved slight adaptations in the production for the different architecture of each theatre, it was exhilarating to perform in the same configuration in each new city. He saw a 'poetry of the ephemeral' in that they could raise the tent in an open space, create an intense communion 'of love and mutual affection' with the locals, and depart without leaving a trace on the environment, yet having planted 'tiny seeds in the hearts of people'.[110] Moreover, the concept of the circle as a theatrical space was one that would inform his next two ventures.

Barrault's arrangement with the Gare d'Orsay lasted eight years, until 1980. In 1973, he was accorded space to rent in the great hall where he could design and construct the Théâtre d'Orsay. Barrault's planning drew upon his thirty years of making theatre, on theatre history and on his love of mathematics. Asserting that the magnetic halo of an actor never extends more than 24 metres, he began with the premise that the last row of audience would be no more than 18 metres from the stage. The basic tent-inspired structure would be a theatre in the round, yet allowing some flexibility just as theatre had developed throughout history from the primitive circle to the classical Greek configuration to the thrust stage to the proscenium. In addition to the main stage and the Petit-Orsay studio stage for intimate productions, Barrault insisted on a '*foyer de rencontre*', a space for informal interaction between artists and theatregoers.[111] Finally, knowing from bitter experience that nothing is permanent, he had the theatre constructed in such a way that the stage house and risers could be salvaged and rebuilt in another location, a precaution that turned out to be wisely prescient. The new Théâtre d'Orsay opened on 26 March 1974 with a revival of *Harold et Maude* (Harold and Maude), Madeleine Renaud ever scintillating as Maude, a role that remained in her active repertoire for seven years. Inaugurating the Petit-Orsay on 24 October was Slawomir Mrozek's *Emigrés*. Subsequent seasons proved wonderfully rewarding for the company with an exciting mix of premieres and revivals; it was especially gratifying to return to rotating repertory, which had necessarily been abandoned since 1968. Barrault reminisced that it had taken three years to win a loyal following at the Odéon, whereas it took only three weeks at the Théâtre d'Orsay.[112] In 1979, he created his one-man show *Le Langage du corps* (Language of the Body), which he continued to tour for many years. When he learned unexpectedly that the company would have to vacate the Gare d'Orsay by 30 April

1980 to allow its reconstruction as a museum of impressionist art, Barrault ambitiously prepared as a farewell production an uncut staging of Claudel's *The Satin Slipper* that ran on weekends, Saturday and Sunday afternoons and evenings, with dinner breaks shared by the audience and the company. 'It was truly the apotheosis,' recalled Barrault; moreover, that production might be said to have transformed Paul Claudel's dramatic canon from the status of fusty classic to popular fare.[113]

Another extended tour kept the company going while its final home was being constructed with the wooden panels and other materials from the Théâtre d'Orsay that Barrault had so foresightedly made reusable (*démontable*). The Théâtre du Rond-Point was housed in the Palais de Glace, a former skating rink. Amazingly, in 1951, when the Compagnie Renaud–Barrault was only in its fifth year, Barrault had drawn up and presented to the city of Paris a plan for converting the Palais de Glace into a theatre.[114] The idea finally came to fruition thirty years later. Since the location at the Rond Point des Champs-Elysées was virtually across the street from the Théâtre Marigny, where the company was launched in 1946, Barrault quipped that they had travelled more than 700,000 kilometres to cross that street![115] The company finally had a home that might prove permanent, but the years had taken their toll on Barrault. He continued reading new plays, staging brilliant productions, mingling with theatregoers in the lobby, receiving international awards and recognitions, but Renaud and Barrault were no longer getting the movie roles that had sustained their personal – and often the company's – finances. Debts mounted at the Rond-Point. Barrault directed his last production, *Le Théâtre de foire* (Fairground Theatre), in 1986. Francis Huster gradually assumed leadership duties, as Renaud and Barrault devoted themselves largely to each other. In 1991, the Ministry of Culture resolved the company's finances.[116] Jean-Louis Barrault died on 22 January 1994, and Madeleine Renaud followed him eight months later, on 23 September.

A prolific writer with a poetic soul provides endless possible quotations with which to conclude a summary of his life and works. In his October 1980 radio interviews with Guy Dumur, Barrault commented: 'The history of our company is the history of the ensemble who worked, who changed workplaces, who experienced hard times and successes, who lived lives of upheaval and yet dazzled. But illuminating everything is Madeleine's grace and radiance.'[117] Of himself he wrote that he hoped to be remembered as 'a human being who accomplished his life fulfillment without hypocrisy, without vanity, without conniving, without "politics," ... one for whom all that mattered was human dignity, respect for others, and love of life'.[118]

2

Jean-Louis Barrault's 'Total Theatre'

Suzanne Burgoyne

You can like or dislike Jean-Louis Barrault, but to remain indifferent is hardly possible unless you're an idiot.
MILDAH POLIA[1]

Jean-Louis Barrault attracted attention as a promising young director with his very first production, *Autour d'une mère* (As I Lay Dying)[2] in 1935, a production for which Barrault served not only as director and leading actor but also as playwright by adapting William Faulkner's novel *As I Lay Dying*. Antonin Artaud's review said, 'This spectacle is magical like those incantations of witch doctors when the clackings of their tongues against their palates bring rain to a countryside.'[3]

Barrault went on to gain a reputation as one of the most active and controversial figures in world theatre. In 1939, playwright Lucien Descaves proclaimed: 'I believe that the four directors of the Cartel have found their master.'[4] After reading Barrault's published promptbook for *Phèdre* (Phaedra) in 1949, critic Robert Kemp agreed that Paul Claudel and André Gide were justified 'in using the terrible word "genius" to give a name to the young J.-L. Barrault'.[5] In 1953, British drama critic Harold Hobson called Barrault 'the man who has had the greatest single effect on the French theatre

---

Unless otherwise noted, all translations are by the author of this essay.

since the end of the between-the-wars period'.[6] Barrault had his detractors too, but as actress-critic Béatrix Dussane observed, 'We can all dispute one or another of his obstinate opinions, disassociate ourselves from one or another of his tendencies, but we always imply, with all of the admiration that that merits: "But he lives, and his theatre lives".'[7]

A man of many talents, Barrault acted, directed and adapted works for the stage, often for the same production. He managed his own company, the Compagnie Madeleine Renaud–Jean-Louis Barrault, and served as director of the Théâtre de France and the Théâtre des Nations. He also wrote numerous books and articles reflecting on his life, his productions and his vision of the theatre. Barrault incorporated widely varied influences from early-twentieth-century theatre, including Stanislavski and Meyerhold. During his six years as an actor in the Comédie-Française, he absorbed the French classical tradition. Serving his earlier apprenticeship as an actor at Charles Dullin's Atelier, he became the inheritor of the theatrical transformation initiated by Jacques Copeau and the Cartel des Quatre (Dullin, Jouvet, Pitoëff and Baty). Jouvet commented to Barrault, after seeing *As I Lay Dying*, 'I can see the distance that separates two generations. Everything we were formulating in our heads at the time of the Vieux Colombier, you now have in your blood. Digestion is proceeding.'[8] At the Atelier, Barrault learned mime from Étienne Decroux (Marcel Marceau's teacher) and became personal friends with Antonin Artaud.

Much has been written about Barrault's work, yet he remains an enigmatic figure. Was he, as some critics complained, a coldly calculating intellectual who conceived his productions to conform with his predetermined theories? Or, as others have proposed, should he be regarded as an imaginative artist or merely a clever artisan? Eric Bentley suggested that Barrault might be 'an eclectic craftsman like Reinhardt' rather than 'a theatrical policy-maker like Meyerhold',[9] but added that although Barrault's writings may not 'come together into a coherent philosophy of theatre', he still should 'be taken seriously – even as a thinker'.[10]

Barrault as aesthetician:
The theory of total theatre

Barrault's vision included a view of theatre both as a harmonious synthesis of theatrical elements and as a proposal that theatre may help us achieve a harmonious integration of elements within the individual, in society and in life as a whole. Thus, his vision of theatre is religious in the sense that religion is 'that which links us to things. ... What matters is the bond that unites us to everything.'[11]

Barrault has sometimes been called a mystic; however, Eric Bentley gives a good description of the general type of religious tendency to be found in Barrault's writings:

In contemporary French culture there is another strain of religiousness besides orthodoxy. This is the strain of religion without faith, theology without God.

This Irrationalism – the recoil from the classic rationalism of France among unbelievers – has taken many forms, ... In the thirties it found a spokesman in the actor Antonin Artaud ... [whose envisioned theatre has] the aim of 'giving the theatre back to its primitive purpose, replacing it in its religious and metaphysical aspect, reconciling it with the universe'. ... Today the avant-garde theatre in Paris, in so far as it can be said to exist, lives under the sign of Artaud.[12]

Since Barrault and Artaud were friends, it's not surprising to find the former echoing the latter's ideas about theatre originating in ritual activities, part of a 'profound, mysterious, metaphysical, and cabbalistic reality which was at one with life'.[13] Barrault too professed a distrust of reason. He compared the theatre to a temple[14] and the artist's dedication to the priest's vocation.[15] 'Even for those who have no God,' he said, 'life becomes something religious. And this profane religion is that of the theatre.'[16]

Barrault's aesthetic includes a number of related concepts, starting with *silence*. Barrault described a kind of mystical experience in which, listening to the silence, one hears one's pulse, one's heartbeat, one's breathing; one perceives the irreversible passing of *the present*, the unceasing flow of life in its becoming, which ultimately leads to death.[17] Barrault believed that theatre can help us overcome our fear of death (which he called 'sterile anguish') by renewing our faith in life. He spoke of theatre as *the art of justice*, which depicts the universe as a set of forces in harmonious balance. When something upsets the balance, those forces move to re-establish harmony, even at great sacrifice. Barrault drew upon Artaud's metaphor of *theatre as the plague*, suggesting that theatre 'inoculates' humans with the fear of death in order to restore a healthy balance.[18] Naturalism, he argued, only spreads the disease of 'sterile anguish'; his preferred style was *poetic realism*, which metamorphoses or transposes the material world to another level. He envisioned a theatre which presents a dual vision, allowing the audience to perceive simultaneously two levels of reality: the everyday and the metaphysical,[19] thereby transforming anguish into joy.

If fear causes the alienation of the individual from life, it also alienates one from others and from one's true self. Barrault often used the Artaudian term 'the double', attaching varied meanings to the word. He talked about the 'doubling' of the self, as when an infant becomes aware that others are watching and constructs a public persona behind which he hides; but the mask can become a cage.[20] According to Barrault, the theatre arises not only from anguish caused by the awareness of death but from loneliness, the desire to be reunited with one's true self, with others and with the universe.[21] For Barrault, one of the purposes of theatre is to assuage solitude by uniting actors and spectators in a rite of *communion*.[22]

Barrault's concept of *the sense of touch* helps explain his theory of communion. Barrault believed that humans emit and receive a sort of 'living radiation'; thus, we are 'touched' physically by emanations from the outer world.[23]

> The sense of touch is the sense which pierces through things. It is this sense that makes us 'see' the other side of things, which puts us in contact with the unknown, which makes us glimpse the invisible. It is the sense which reaches 'beyond the known limits'.[24]

Thanks to the sense of touch, dramatic art is fundamentally carnal, sensual activity.[25] During the theatrical performance, the audience forms 'a kind of magnetic battery'.[26] The process of energy exchange between actors and audience merges the audience members into a collective entity. Not being watched, spectators let down their defences and recover the unity of what Barrault called the 'collective soul'.[27]

In another context, Barrault linked the term 'double' to the concept of theatre as *a waking dream*. Barrault said that 'our double also lives his life ... It is he who, at night, lives our dreams. The life of the theatre is a life dreamed, in a waking state.'[28] Barrault's ideas in this regard may have been influenced by the surrealists. Breton, for example, considered dreams not 'mere' illusion but a revelation of reality.[29] Barrault said, 'all is real, even the dream'.[30]

Techniques of total theatre

If theatre is to assist humans in experiencing life as a unified whole, then it must provide a total experience and rediscover the true and essential theatre of the Greeks, the Middle Ages, the Elizabethans, the Orient. For Barrault, total theatre referred to 'the total utilization of the means of expression of the human Being'[31] for the purpose of stimulating all the spectators' senses simultaneously and awakening their metaphysical awareness of the flow of life. Theatre, he said, is physical, extreme sensation, which 'touches' not only the five senses but 'all the nerves, all the radars, all the instincts'.[32]

Barrault broke down the flow of life into three primary elements: *movement, exchange* and *rhythm*. He saw the actor as the perfect theatrical instrument because the human body contains a centre of *movement* (the spinal column), a centre of *exchange* (the respiratory system) and a centre of *rhythm* (the human heart). In addition, the human being radiates that living energy capable of 'touching' the audience. Barrault did not exclude speech from total theatre but emphasized its rhythmic and sound values; like Artaud, he proposed that speech may have incantatory powers which induce a kind of trance in the audience.[33]

However, in order to translate the relationship between the individual's inner life and the outer world, the human body must be presented in interaction with its space.[34] Like Copeau, who rebelled against the emphasis on spectacular scenery and called for 'a bare stage',[35] Barrault proclaimed, 'if there were only one man standing alone on four raised planks and acting with the totality of his means of expression, that would already be total theatre'.[36]

For Barrault, as for Copeau and the Cartel, the actor is the central instrument of theatre and serves as artistic material for the primary artist, the author.[37] In Barrault's total theatre, however, the distinction between subject and object, actor and scenery, may be eliminated: 'Men and objects act together: men play at being objects and objects play at being men.'[38] Although Barrault didn't mention his expertise in *mime* in this context, that expertise makes his vision of the blending of human and Nature realizeable on stage.

Artaud and total theatre

Charles Lyons observes that 'Barrault has traced his concept of "Total Theatre" to the period of his friendship and his work with Antonin Artaud.'[39] Discussing his debt to Artaud, Barrault reflected, '*Le Théâtre et son double* (*The Theatre and its Double*) is undoubtedly the most important thing written about theatre in the twentieth century.'[40] When comparing Barrault's theories with Artaud's, one finds comparable concepts and a striking similarity in terminology. Both Artaud and Barrault felt that modern man's reliance on intellect had alienated him from the true source of life.[41] Artaud envisioned movement and gesture as primary in the theatre. Like Barrault, Artaud wanted all theatrical elements to play an active part in the performance.[42] And like Barrault, Artaud viewed simultaneous sensory stimulation as the magical key to unlocking the mysteries of the spirit: 'There is no transition from a gesture to a cry or a sound: all the senses interpenetrate, as if through strange channels hollowed out in the mind itself.'[43] Pointing to theatre's origin in ritual and magic, Artaud called for a return to the authentic metaphysical theatre. Barrault probably borrowed his concept of the living energy field and the 'touch' from Artaud, who viewed humans as creatures composed of energy. He and Barrault worked together to develop a system for the actor as 'affective athlete', based on the cabala, which involved training in respiration, as well as learning 'which points of the body to touch' in order to throw 'the spectator into magical trances'.[44] Comparing theatre to the plague, Artaud seemed to believe that theatre could release psychic energy from the audience, which 'frees the repressed unconscious'.[45]

One can see similarities between the ideas about total theatre proposed by Artaud and those of Barrault: a magical and metaphysical view of theatre,

FIGURE 2.1 *Jean-Louis Barrault in the title role of* La Tentation de Saint-Antoine *(The Temptation of St Anthony) adapted from Flaubert and directed by Roger Blin at the Odéon-Théâtre de France in 1967. For Barrault, age fifty-seven in this photograph, the language of the body was a lifelong exploration. Photo by Reporters Associés/Gamma-Rapho via Getty Images (Getty #599798093).*

an emphasis upon simultaneous sensory stimulation, the active participation of all the elements of the spectacle, language as incantation, theatre as plague, etc. But Barrault is not Artaud (see Figure 2.1). There are crucial differences. For one thing, Artaud cried, 'No more masterpieces!'[46] The *mise en scène* should not be subordinated to a written text;[47] furthermore, the works of the past must be discarded. Barrault, on the other hand, followed Copeau and the Cartel both in their ideal of faithfulness to the text and in seeing great value in precisely those past masterpieces. Furthermore, if one reads Artaud and then reads Barrault, one has the feeling that, by contrast, when Barrault used the same terminology – hallucination, magic, plague, the double – the words became pale wisps which evaporate in the light of reason and faint echoes of Artaud's fiery proclamations. And yet Barrault seemed to be writing with as much enthusiasm, as much sincerity, as Artaud – not merely mouthing the words of another. Gradually, one becomes aware that a word such as 'magic', for instance, did not mean the same thing to both men. When Artaud said theatre was a magical operation, he was speaking literally. He compared the theatre to alchemy, suggesting that theatre is the double and the means of magically manipulating 'an archetypal and dangerous reality … This reality is not human but inhuman, and man with his customs and his character counts for very little in it.'[48] Underlying Artaud's concept of Theatre of Cruelty is his vision of life as inherently cruel – inherently evil: 'In the manifested world, metaphysically speaking, evil is the permanent law ... Good is always upon the outer face, but the face within is evil.'[49]

Barrault did not study the occult in depth, as did Artaud. Furthermore, Barrault sought to renew the audience's faith in life through theatre, not to unleash evil. In the final analysis, Barrault seems to have been most influenced by the *form* of theatre proposed by Artaud, as Artaud was perceptive enough to note in his critique of Barrault's *As I Lay Dying*. Artaud found the production moving, particularly the miming of the horse. He applauded Barrault's use of 'new relations between sound, gesture, and voice', and 'direct physical appeal'.[50] However, he added:

> If any reproach can be made against his gestures, it is that they give us the illusion of symbol when in fact they are defining reality ....
> This performance is not the peak of theatre, I mean the deepest drama, the mystery deeper than souls, the excruciating conflict of souls where gesture is only a path – there where man is only a point and where lives drink at their source.[51]

If Barrault's theatre is mystical, it is much less extreme, much more closely related to ordinary life than Artaud's. One might prefer Artaud as a prophet – this man who was the living embodiment of his ideal artist, a victim 'burnt at the stake, signaling through the flames'[52] of physical and mental torment. However, one must recognize that, as an unsympathetic Bentley observes, 'consequently he went into the madhouse, while Barrault stayed in the theatre'.[53]

Barrault as director: Examples of total theatre in production

Was Barrault an intellectual who imposed his theories on his productions or was he an intuitive artist? Perhaps one reason some critics considered Barrault too intellectual derives from the great amount of research he did for each production.[54] Like Copeau, he wrote out his *mise en scène* before starting rehearsals.[55] At the first rehearsal, Barrault himself read the whole play to the cast, to inspire them and to serve as a model.[56] Then followed a week of table work. Marie-Helène Dasté, Copeau's daughter and a member of Barrault's company, recounted that Barrault had no 'system' for directing actors; his way of conveying instructions was 'acrobatic': Barrault demonstrated the movement the actor should perform.[57] Barrault described himself as the 'impassioned coach' rather than 'critic' type of director.[58] One of Barrault's important attributes was his love for theatre and all its artists, particularly the actor. In that regard, he followed the example set by Copeau and carried on by the Cartel.[59] Barrault credited Dullin, saying, 'I learned above all at the Atelier to love the theatre.'[60] Jouvet's proclamation that 'one is a director as one is a lover' is an apt description of Jean-Louis Barrault.[61]

Although Barrault's writings developed his theories about total theatre, he directed works ranging in period and style from the classical to the contemporary, from Aeschylus to Ionesco. Barrault brought his understanding of life and theatre to his interpretation of the plays he chose to direct, which led to 'a certain guiding line in the artistic vision', no matter how different the productions might be from each other.[62] However, of the hundred plays he directed, Barrault found his ideal of total theatre appropriate for only about a tenth of them.[63] The one concept relevant to most of his productions is his view of poetic realism as a theatrical style which reveals two levels of reality.[64] The following analysis focuses primarily on Barrault's total theatre productions and gives examples of specific techniques he used – techniques corresponding with ideas in his aesthetic – to achieve an imaginative transposition of everyday reality. Let us begin, as Barrault did, with silence.

Silence

> Through the closed curtain resonate, vibrate, the first chords of music. Just a few very short chords of music. When the curtain rises, complete silence onstage. There is nothing but the setting, the snow and an atmosphere of very cold light.[65]

Silence is a key concept in Barrault's aesthetic, and not only because of his passion for mime. During a moment of silence, one becomes aware of the present flowing towards death. Faced with silence, with the unfathomable mystery of life, man begins to invent a world, and it is this imaginative transposition of the facts of existence into a vision of life that the theatre re-creates. Barrault chose to begin his production of Kafka's *Le Château* (The Castle) with the long silence described earlier. In the silence, Joseph K. entered and gazed about, as if not knowing quite what to do or which way to go.[66] These moments of silence and hesitation created 'the atmosphere of ambiguity', which cloaked the production.[67] Barrault applied to other productions the technique of beginning with silence, as in *Phaedra, Hamlet* and *La Cerisaie* (The Cherry Orchard). Barrault saw in the silences of *The Cherry Orchard* the passing of the present, the secret flow of life which 'murmurs like a soul'.[68] His production began and ended with a silence which, contrasting with the flurries of activity of the inhabitants' arrival and departure, pointed up the ephemerality of their existence.[69] Barrault's *Cherry Orchard* was faithful to the text, the poetic transposition subtle, consisting largely of undercurrents of feeling and a sense of time passing, expressed in silences occurring throughout the play.[70] Barrault based his whole production of As I Lay Dying on the concept 'of starting from Silence and living in the Present'.[71] Two hours of playing time included only thirty minutes of spoken text. In the silence, the little sounds of life – the characters' breathing, the rhythm of their barefeet on the stage floor – took on heightened importance.[72] Barrault embodied his vision: 'Real life is Silence.'[73]

If real life is silence, so also is death. An orgiastic dance with frenzied music and strobe lights led up to the ending of Rabelais: 'As the dance reaches a mesmeric climax, the lights bang up, the strobes cut, the dancers freeze, the music stops, and Panurge lies dying, having drunk too deeply of life.'[74] Once again, Barrault confronted the audience with silence: in this case, the silence of death.

Mime

In As I Lay Dying, Barrault used mime to celebrate 'the mystery of man living and dying',[75] as well as to embody the 'very close relationship between man and the Universe'.[76] In one famous mime sequence, Barrault performed the taming of the horse by the son Jewel, simultaneously playing both horse and rider: 'the horse rears, bolts, ... , and suddenly kicks, throws Jewel who rolls, picks himself up, thrashes the horse and brings him to a standstill. Then he caresses the horse and suddenly remounts him.'[77] In the same production, Barrault employed mime to symbolize Nature's cycle of life and death: 'Dewey Dell, the daughter, while picking cotton, made love, and immediately afterwards danced a dance of fecundity. She was becoming pregnant before our eyes.'[78] Following her dance of life, her little brother Vardanian mimed catching a fish and killing it gleefully. At the same time, the figure of the mother, ill and dying, appeared.[79]

Barrault transformed the scene of Joseph K.'s death at the end of Le Procès (The Trial) into a tragi-comic ritual. Joseph K.'s guards supported him by his elbows, taking him on a journey to the place of execution, while 'Barrault mimes a fast walk with knees raised high'. Once there, Joseph K. anxiously sought 'an attitude to die in. When one side of the block doesn't seem right, he tries the other. Meanwhile the guards perform what Kafka calls the "odious ceremony of courtesy",' passing the knife back and forth until one of them stabbed K, 'with a twist and flourish. The simple mention of the ceremony in the text becomes on the stage a complete pantomimic sequence.'[80] The scene expressed the 'black humour'[81] Barrault saw in Kafka, a double vision of man's death as simultaneously comic and tragic.

Humorous mime in Barrault's production of Le Bourgeois Gentilhomme (The Bourgeois Gentleman) also projected a double vision. After each chef danced in and presented his plate (including a red-nosed wine steward who rhythmically tripped and fell), the guests mimed eating at a double-time pace to the accompaniment of a fast rhythm from wood blocks in the orchestra.

The sequence was funny, but the wood blocks chattering like hungry teeth and the actors' mime gave a disturbing impression of the voracious animal nature that underlay the characters' pose of sophistication.[82]

Mime helped transpose *The Trial* from the level of everyday reality to that of a nightmare. For example, when Joseph K. entered the room where the accused were waiting, Barrault noted that 'the accused make the movements of drowning men. Impression of immersion: they hold their heads up in the air as if in order to be able to breathe.'[83] The audience thus viewed the chorus of accused through Joseph K.'s eyes, feeling his suffocating shame.[84] Everyday reality in *The Trial* acquired the fluidity of a dream: 'Just as Dali had invented the soft watch, in *The Trial* the ground was sometimes soft, especially the steps. By means of mime, of course.'[85] However, Barrault continually juxtaposed the everyday reality with the dream. Critic Claude Roy commented on 'the incessant transition from suggestion to representation'.[86] Some objects, such as the typewriters in Joseph K.'s office, were mimed; others, including the executioners' dagger, were real.[87] Barrault projected a vision in which Joseph K.'s everyday life seemed more illusory than the ultimate and mysterious reality of his death. A similar mixture of real and mimed objects appeared in other Barrault productions, including *Hunger* and *Rabelais*.[88]

Choreographed movement

Barrault also used precisely choreographed group movement to draw the audience into another level of reality. In the second scene of *The Castle*, Joseph K. suddenly became aware of seven peasants standing at the inn counter who had turned to look at him. Barrault explained to the actors playing the peasants:

> You need to have your feet placed parallel to each other, the knees a bit flexed, ... your heads should all be tilted at the same angle, as if your skulls had all been hit by a hammer in the same place ... (Kafka says that the skulls give the impression of having been flattened) ... you will all look alike, but only on that side (left) where all the costumes have the same patch of leather ... the same bump on the skull. Thus all at once, these people who were different are all going to resemble one another. And when you move again you will again be different. This is very important. The peasants all look alike, but to Joseph K. Not to the audience.[89]

Thus, Barrault allowed the spectator to see the peasants through Joseph K.'s eyes for a brief moment, then the vision dissolved and the audience could again view these characters objectively – a shifting of levels of reality.

In designing the movement for his production of Aeschylus' *Oresteia*, Barrault took inspiration from occult ceremonies, *macumbas* and *candomblés*, that he had witnessed in Brazil. By creating choreography that corresponded to these ritual dances, Barrault felt he was drawing the audience into a level of reality in which the relationship between men and gods was intimate, approaching what he believed to be the true spirit of the *Oresteia*, not the serene and harmonious Greece of the schoolbooks, but 'an archaic, vital, human, anguished Greece in constant contact with the mystery of life: a magical Greece'.[90] Designed movement also helped to express the dark forces, the 'doubles', in Barrault's *Phaedra*. For instance, during Phaedra's declaration of love to Hippolytus, she was 'magnetically drawn towards him'.[91] Barrault wanted the audience to receive the impression that Phaedra had surrendered to the will of the gods and that it was not she who was moving but the double who was moving her.

The most everyday type of scene could be transformed into a kind of ballet by Barrault. The street scene at the end of *As I Lay Dying* became a dance directed by a traffic cop, with both pedestrians and automobiles portrayed by actors.[92] A similar sequence in *Hunger* (*La Faim*) contrasted Tangen's famished delusions with the daily activities which the well-fed people in the street took for granted.[93] Transposition through choreography in the first act of *Rhinocéros* (Rhinoceros) was only slight. Barrault used movement to emphasize the juxtaposition of the lesson in (false) logic being given to the Old Gentleman by the Logician and the 'lesson' on how to live one's life being given to Berenger by Jean. Ionesco wrote the comparison between the two discussions into the script, but Barrault reinforced it by giving the corresponding characters in each pair similar gestures and parallel, sometimes simultaneous, blocking.[94] Precisely designed, the movement was nonetheless basically realistic.

Only as the play progressed and characters began to turn into rhinoceroses did the movement transform into extreme, often enlarged and slow-motion patterns,[95] as everyday reality disintegrated into a fantastic nightmare vision. Thus, the transposition of movement in Barrault's productions varied from subtle to extreme – according to the specific requirements of each play.

Voice and diction/respiration

Barrault also sought a vocal transposition appropriate to each play. For instance, he believed that the choruses in the *Oresteia* had been 'written to obtain incantatory rather than poetic effects',[96] thereby drawing the audience into the ritual act of justice embodied in the play. In Barrault's *Oresteia*, the choruses were 'successively spoken, spoken rhythmically, psalmodized, spoken to music, chanted to drum accompaniment, chanted or sung to music, etc.'[97] Barrault's treatment of the choruses was not, of course, entirely new; Copeau among others had pointed out that choruses in Greek tragedy range from speech to song.[98]

The plays of Paul Claudel were considered unstageable until Barrault discovered a way to make the author's poetic dialogue actable. Applying one of his theoretical concepts to his analysis, he found in Claudel's dialogue the elements of the flow of life: movement, exchange (respiration), and rhythm, which allowed the actor to shift easily

> from a gesture to a word, from a word to a breath, from a cry to a step, from a look to a phrase. ... Claudel's dialogue is the buccal and respiratory part of corporal expression. ... It flows according to the rhythm of the heartbeat: short/long, whence comes the iambic rhythm that one so often finds in it.[99]

The vocal transposition required by Claudel's dialogue, combined with the transposition of movement, would, according to Barrault, give the audience a direct, physical impression of the interrelatedness of all life.[100]

In accordance with his analysis of *Phaedra* as a symphony, Barrault viewed the actors as an orchestra and noted the vocal range of each character.[101] He also used vocal placement to give the impression of the dark supernatural forces acting through a character. For instance, Barrault noted that as Oenone tells Phaedra that she cannot avoid her destiny, she 'seems to speak for the gods. ... Her voice is like a voice from beyond the grave.' He called the effect of the character's vocalization 'hallucinatory'.[102] In his production of *Hunger*, Barrault echoed spoken lines with a hummed response to give an impression of 'mystery'.[103]

Barrault also experimented, as in *As I Lay Dying* and in *The Trial*, with a kind of nonsense dialogue: 'words that have no sense but whose sound plastically reproduces conversation and situation'.[104] For instance, when the chorus of the accused commented on Joseph K.'s appearance in the waiting room, Barrault noted: 'The chorus of the accused is spoken in a shrill tone. The words are distorted, chattering. The sounds are close to the real words, but in a nonsense dialogue that is incomprehensible, although well-pronounced. Only the words in italics should be understood distinctly.'[105] The nonsense dialogue, like the mime and ensemble movement described earlier, helped the audience share Joseph K.'s experience of his world turning into a nightmare.

For *Rabelais*, Barrault satirized the evil militarists vocally as well as physically: 'The entrance of Picrochole and his henchmen was required to have the formal movement of Kabuki, and the actors to achieve a ferocious Japanese monosyllabic shrieking and grunting.' In addition, the actors chose caricatured voices of film stars to go with their 'kitchen armor' clown costumes. They thus created a double vision: 'Seen as Himmler, Goebbels and Goering, they perform as Groucho Marx, James Cagney and Tommy Cooper.'[106]

Barrault proposed that respiratory technique is useful to the actor, not only in sustaining vocal delivery but also as a means of expression.[107] In *The Trial*, for instance, during Joseph K.'s strange journey through the suffocating atmosphere of the corridors of the Palace of Justice – during which he almost fainted for lack of air – he reached the exit. Joseph K. took a deep breath, 'while the others, asphyxiated by the pure air, put their hands to their throats'.[108] Metaphorically, the suffocating atmosphere of the Palace of Justice corresponded to the stifling systematization in society; the chorus of accused had become acquiescent slaves, unable to breathe in the pure air of freedom. Barrault used a similar metaphor in his production of Camus's *L'État de siège* (State of Siege). After the city had been liberated from plague, which represented totalitarian oppression, the actors turned towards the sea, stretched out their arms and breathed in purified air.[109]

In *As I Lay Dying*, respiration played a major role in depicting life in the present. Upon waking for the new day, each member of the family took three breaths, yawning and stretching.[110] Before going off to make love in the fields, Dewey Dell took a deep breath, as Barrault noted, like a good-natured animal.[111] Darl looked out over the countryside and breathed as if trying to draw the whole of life inside him.[112] The mother's death, too, is powered by respiration:

> The mother is nearing death. Her eldest son is making the coffin. The wheezings from her chest fit in with the raspings of the saw. All the rest of the family, like an enormous jellyfish, contracts and relaxes in union with the mother and the carpenter. The whole theatre is in death throes – a pump rhythm, an octopus rhythm – and all of a sudden, at the climax of a breath: total stoppage. The mother's hand, which had been raised as when someone wants to look out into the distance, falls slowly in the silence, like a water level going down. Life is emptying out. The movement is prolonged throughout the body until the rigidity of a corpse is reached. She is dead.[113]

In this scene, Barrault juxtaposed respiration (one of the elements of the flow of life) with the rasping of the saw crafting the coffin (a sound of death), thus interweaving life and death in a striking auditory image. Furthermore, the scene visualized Barrault's concept of the relationship between the individual and the collective. The family moved in rhythm with the mother's dying agony, sharing her suffering. During the silence, they were motionless; the mother was the only one to move, as life flowed from her body. In the silence of death, she was alone. Each of us dies alone.

Thus, in the productions discussed earlier, Barrault integrated speech and respiration with silence and movement to express the vision of life he found in each play.

Music/sound

Barrault insisted that music and sound effects should be integrated into the action rather than incidental. The music composed by Darius Milhaud for his production of Paul Claudel's *Christophe Colomb* (Christopher

Colombus), he said, 'fitted into the play like one of the characters. In fact, it acted with us'.[114] In approaching the music as a character, Barrault carried out Claudel's intentions, but Milhaud explained that Barrault also told the composer precisely what he wanted:

> He read the text, explained to me the role that he wanted the music to play in it. He explained it almost choreographically. ... All the while making commentaries in which his gestures, his voice, his walk expressed the essence of the drama. Jean-Louis Barrault, precise, exact, furnished me with the length of time required for each musical intervention, which ranged from several measures to support the entrance of characters to long melodies or to elements of background music.[115]

Barrault's method of working with Milhaud resembled his method of working with actors: a reading of the play, complete with mimed action and commentary, which expressed the spirit of the work, plus very precise instructions.

For his *Oresteia*, Barrault asked Pierre Boulez to compose a score based more upon oriental than occidental music but gradually evolving towards a Western sound, a 'musical transformation which should correspond to the transformation of civilization in the play'.[116] Music also evoked primitive ritual and magic; critic Guy Verdot commented on 'the masterly barbarism of a tom-tom which reintroduces, without idle recourse to archaeological accuracy, ritual frenzy into the celebration'.[117] Barrault used music and rhythm in various productions to draw the audience into a mood conducive to trance. For *Rabelais*, Barrault used a six-track tape of recorded music and text 'to throw the sound around the auditorium within one sequence of words or music, so that the voices or instruments appear to be freely moving in the air'.[118] In this case, sound really became an actor, moving through space and interacting with the players. For example, in one scene

> Rabelais' words are frozen in one of the many winters of his creative life. But after winter comes the spring and the words unfreeze. The company begins to hear the words coming to life again, and as swarms begin to pass through the air, the voyagers leap to catch and examine them. But the words melt away and cannot be preserved.[119]

This sequence created an experience in which sound and space intermingled; the recorded words almost became concrete objects – but they dissolved like the ever-ephemeral present moment.

Barrault demonstrated a particular interest in sound effects based on physiological rhythms which, he believed, would have a direct physical impact on the spectator. In *Hunger*, he employed 'heartbeats, buzzings in the ears, "physiological" musical effects'[120] to transmit the physical sensation of hunger. In *Hamlet,* a magnified heartbeat announced the arrival of the Ghost.[121] In the *Oresteia,* the drums sometimes beat a rhythm which matched the heartbeats of the chorus.[122] In *The Trial,* Joseph K.'s anguish and dizziness was reinforced by the 'sound of a heart that beats and grows feebler'.[123]

Thus, in examples discussed earlier, Barrault used means as elaborate as an orchestrated score or as simple as the rhythm of barefeet on a floor (*As I Lay Dying*) to stimulate the spectators' sense of hearing and to involve them more profoundly in the world of each play.

The actor as scenery

Barrault suggested that the actor himself, through developing his technique, might portray not only human characters but also non-human objects and environmental elements. In practice, examples of the actor as scenery come in two categories. In some cases, Barrault assigned one or more actors to portray a specific object or element. In other cases, the actor simultaneously played a human character and his environment.

A famous example of the first category in *Christopher Colombus* was described by Paul-Louis Mignon as 'the audacity of Barrault's use of an actor with a pole to represent a door – and then to have Barrault lean upon him!'[124] Two actors played the part of Columbus's mule with 'a sad and affectionate air'.[125] In *Le Soulier de satin* (The Satin Slipper), Barrault cast an actress who 'personifies the moon in the centre of her open disk, then folds or unfolds it, making her crescent progressively slimmer until she eclipses herself'.[126] Barrault used ensemble movement as well to represent natural environments, such as the river in *As I Lay Dying* and the waves of the sea in Claudel's *The Satin Slipper* and *Christopher Colombus*, as well as in *Rabelais*.[127] In *The Satin Slipper*, a masked actor representing a piece of wreckage floated amid the waves.[128] Actors also used their voices to create environment: 'howling like the tempest, murmuring like the breeze',[129] in *Christopher Colombus*.

In the second category of examples, the actor – without abandoning his character – simultaneously depicted the environment. The sailors in *Christopher Colombus* gave the impression of wind in the tempest scene by miming the reaction of their bodies to the storm.[130] In *As I Lay Dying,* the actor playing Darl set fire to the mother's coffin; through his mimed reaction, he projected the vision of leaping flames.[131] For the scene in which Columbus rescued a dying sailor from the sea, Barrault explained that 'the two actors who play the sailor and Columbus should at the same time express, and without leaving their character, the element of water and the tossing force of the waves'.[132]

Bill Wallis, who performed in the London production of *Rabelais* described the requirements of performing in Barrault's 'total theatre':

as rehearsals progressed, one saw that the style of playing was implicit in this text; that the actors must be constantly ringing the changes on their identities. At different times within the same scene, they are miming objects or animals, speaking as themselves, acting as mouthpieces for some philosophical or religious movement – sometimes as characters, at other times taking part in a mass reaction. The 'total theatre' is not so much (for those in the play) the array of technical effects that are produced from an enormous range of theatrical resources both past and present, but this constant ranging through all the forms of dramatic action of which an actor is capable.[133]

However, Barrault used the actor as scenery overtly only when he felt the play could best be served by that staging.[134] For *Phaedra*, for example, he suggested that the true décor resides in the characters themselves. Although Venus presides over the action, her presence is felt through her influence upon Phaedra and Hippolytus. The bad omens, the flight of dark birds across the sky, the scent of heavy perfume – all these impressions are created by the character of Oenone. And so on.[135] Nonetheless, Barrault used scenery; he did not have actors play doors or waves or horses. For *Phaedra*, actors' creation of environment was subtle.

The catalysing object

Just as the actor may help to create environment, Barrault proposed that properties and scenery might participate in the action of the play and contribute to its meaning as characters do. Barrault called such an object the *signifying* or *catalysing object*. For example, in the third act of *Rhinoceros*, Dudard carried a cane with a handle in the shape of a rhinoceros horn. The actor usually held the cane with the handle level with his forehead, so when Dudard stood in profile, it looked as if the horn were growing out of his head.[136] This image projected a dual vision: an everyday object suddenly became a frightening metaphor for the mysterious transformation of men into rhinoceroses. Dudard's metamorphosis was also treated comically, by means of a little green plant upon which he occasionally munched.[137]

The décor for *Rhinoceros* (see Figure 2.2), as the play progressed, passed 'from the most reassuring realism to an apocalyptic chaos'.[138] In the third act, the back wall of Berenger's room gave way to a painted backdrop of the city filled with a horde of *rhinoceros*es. Rhinoceros horns poked through the side walls.[139] Thus, even the scenery seemed to metamorphose into beasts, leaving Berenger bereft of the security of everyday reality and totally, utterly alone.

A sock became a signifying object in *The Trial*, during the scene in which Joseph K.'s landlady discusses his arrest with him. She picks up a sock 'and pokes two fingers through the hole to simulate a puppet with which she will

FIGURE 2.2 *Jean-Louis Barrault staged Ionesco's* Rhinoceros *at the Odéon-Théâtre de France in 1960. Left to right: Jane Hummer, T. Arcanel, M.-H. Dasté, S. Valère, J.-L. Barrault, R. Lombard, J. Paredes and J. Martin. Photo by Lipnitzki/ Roget Viollet/Getty Images (Getty #55752535).*

play during the whole scene, through the everyday gestures of darning the socks'.[140] Darning the sock, sticking needles into it, became transposed into torture of the puppet. The ordinary sock's transformation into a puppet corresponded to Joseph K.'s transformation into a helpless victim tortured by forces he could not understand. Furthermore, the image created a double vision: at the same time, the audience could see the ordinary sock and a hapless puppet, superimposing Joseph K.'s nightmare world onto the world of everyday reality. Objects in *The Trial* sometimes appeared distorted in size and shape. For instance, the telephone through which Joseph K. received mysterious commands was oversized – eighteen inches long.[141] The settings for various scenes changed in sight of the audience, enhancing the dream-like impression of fluidity. Eric Bentley observed that 'Barrault's décor for

Le Procès is a perpetual transformation scene. From the first opening of the curtain, walls rise and fall. There are many broad, dark arches, many dark little rooms and eerie perspectives.'[142]

Some of Barrault's most striking uses of the catalysing object occurred when he developed an entire production around a central décor element, such as the sail in *Christopher Colombus* (1953):

> There were so many changes of place that any set was impossible. I had to hit on a catalyst, a magic object around which the slightest accessory would acquire life. The need for a screen for the cinematographic parts and the constant presence of the sea, the wind, and Columbus's caravel determined my choice of this symbol-object: the sail. Like the music, the sail in turn showed itself as human as ourselves. I wanted the whole theatre to be man: objects, notes of music, words.[143]

With the play of lights and shadows, colours and images, upon the sail, with its alternating positions, its white expanse soaring towards the sky like a great bird, the sail became a living symbol of the dove that Columbus's name suggests: the human spirit soaring upward in its aspiration towards that other world which, in Claudel's vision, was not only the geographical new world but the world of the spirit, of God. The humanity of the sail, along with the actors playing waves of the sea, helped to create the vision of the unity of all existence.

For his 1943 production of *The Satin Slipper* at the Comédie-Française, Barrault had used numerous settings which changed in sight of the audience. Inspired by the success of the sail in *Christopher Colombus*, Barrault sought a central catalysing object for his 1963 production of *The Satin Slipper* at the Théâtre de France (see Figure 2.3).

He decided upon a baroque altar like those he had seen in the Portuguese churches in Brazil. Dividing the altar into moveable set pieces not only allowed him to change locales quickly but metaphorically embodied what he viewed as the essential Claudelian conflict in the play: passion wrestling with the guardian angel.

> The altar is order. But if one breaks the altar one satisfies the disorder of passion. Therefore the altar (in the play) is made in several pieces. Sometimes the pieces are separated and the thrilling disorder is given its head. Sometimes the pieces are put together again and order is reconstituted.[144]

The setting, therefore, simultaneously represented the earthly space in which each scene took place and the divine space in which the drama of souls was enacted – another double vision. Furthermore, the breaking up and reconstituting of the altar visualized the disruption of the spiritual equilibrium by passion and the restoration of the balance.

FIGURE 2.3 *This scene from the 1980 revival of* The Satin Slipper, *directed by Jean-Louis Barrault (centre left), at the Théâtre d'Orsay, shows his use of masks and a catalysing object. Photo by Lipnitzki/Roger Viollet/Getty Images (Getty #56206987).*

Barrault chose a variety of catalysing objects and scenery to visualize the levels of reality in each play. Sometimes the settings were simple, but Barrault did not hesitate to use elaborate stage machinery, as in *The Trial*, when he felt the play required it.

Masks and costumes

The mask, Barrault believed, helps the actor achieve the transposition into another level of reality beyond everyday experience:

The mask opens upon both the visible and the invisible, the apparent and the absolute. ... This simultaneous expression of the inner and outer, of the apparent and the secret, of the relative and the absolute, of life and death, puts us in better touch with the occult.[145]

For the *Oresteia*, Barrault chose leather half-masks designed to evoke African tribes and primitive rituals rather than the masks of Greek tragedy.[146] The Furies' masks, for example, were topped with great twining snakes of hair. Imitation rubies flowed from their eyes like tears of blood.[147] By masking all characters, both men and gods, Barrault visualized the intimate relationship between the human and the divine. Similarly, he believed that the mask used for the mother in *As I Lay Dying* transformed the character into 'a kind of idol, like a "Totem," and elevated the subject from the level of drama to that of tragedy'.[148]

Barrault sometimes mixed masked and non-masked characters, as in *Rabelais*. For instance, the clerics on Ringing Island wore masks incorporating beak and tonsure or beak and hood.[149] Thus, they appeared simultaneously as priests, bishops, cardinals, etc., and as foolish birds, preening and fluttering in 'the "rich, luxurious cages" of the Vatican'.[150] *Rabelais* also used costume transformations to provide a double vision. Each company member appeared in a basic, dull-coloured set of work clothes, suggesting a band of strolling players. Character costumes, more elaborate, often followed the same colour scheme.[151] At times, however, the actors threw off their dull cloaks 'to transform into young, sparsely clad hippies'.[152] The outrageous, brightly coloured garments suggested the Rabelasian joy of life. In the militarist scene, 'Picrochole, the potential dictator, is black shirted, booted and trousered, whilst his henchmen are in garish parti-coloured tights and stiffened smocks.' Added to the clownish costumes was 'lead-coloured headgear, bulbous perversions of a cauldron, a saucepan, and a watering can – both ludicrous and harsh'.[153] The costumes contributed to the double vision of the dictators as modern totalitarian figures and as buffoons. Taken as a whole, the masks and costumes provided a kaleidoscopic vision in which one aspect of life was revealed after another – and the whole of life viewed as a marvellous theatrical show.

Lighting

Barrault suggested that lighting, like other theatrical elements, should 'act' in the production. He envisioned ostensibly realistic lighting for *Phaedra*, beginning at dawn and following the evolution of a single day towards night. Barrault's published *mise en scène*, however, indicates that he intended to visualize through contrasting light and shadow the characters' inner struggle with mysterious forces and their gradual immersion in darkness – death.[154]

Thus, he intended the lighting to affect the audience on a symbolic as well as a realistic level – a subtle transposition.

Shadows played a part in various Barrault productions. In *Christopher Colombus*, shadows projected on the sail represented inner voices, doubles, accusing Columbus of deserting those who loved him and setting out on a fool's voyage.[155] In *Rabelais*, Baby Gargantua's birth was portrayed by an actor who emerged from a trap and rose up beneath Gargamelle's 'long diaphanous gown, where his shadow mime of the child flailing and struggling to come into the world [could] be seen'.[156] Hamlet, the man passing through the labyrinth of doubt, half in this world and half in another, often appeared in shadow or as a silhouette.[157]

Barrault also used lighting for specific purposes, such as to help create the nightmare world of Joseph K. in *The Trial*. During the long march of K. and the chorus of accused through a maze of corridors, the lighting followed 'the undulating movements of the group in order to re-create the corridors simultaneously as they walk'.[158] Like the characters, the lighting moved through space. In *Rabelais*, the reflection of moving water on the ceiling combined with the sailors' mime, the canopy of ropes that descended from the ceiling and the music to give the impression of a ship at sea.[159] The Furies' masks in the *Oresteia* featured imitation rubies, like drops of blood, flowing from the eyes; light reflecting from the masks added to the terrifying impression created by the goddesses of vengeance.[160] Barrault designed the lighting for his productions himself, synthesizing lighting with movement, sound, colour and form, to create a theatrical experience of a world beyond that of everyday life.

The waking dream

This section describes a few examples of Barrault's synthesis of theatrical elements to conjure for the audience the waking dream, a trance-like state. Barrault said in reference to *Rabelais*, 'Since we can't get our audience drunk at every performance, we must evoke Dionysian abandon in a plastic way through movement, lights and music. We recreate upon the stage a state of trance.'[161] For example, when Panurge drank from the bottle of life in the final scene, an orgiastic dance ensued, accompanied by wild music. Along with their gaudy costumes, some actors wore coloured Chinese lanterns like hats. A female danced bare-breasted. Strobe lights and speeded-up movement added to the frenzy. Even conservative critic Jean-Jacques Gautier spoke enthusiastically about this scene, 'in which swirl a thousand flashes of light and colour indefinitely reflected and repeated by the imitation jewelry, the necklaces, the bracelets, the belts; the splashes of light briefly illuminate the passing faces and bodies tormented and carried away in the farandole and final ballet'.[162] Barrault interwove theatrical elements to provide simultaneous sensory stimulation: the music set the dancers in motion; the whirling of their costumes reflected a dizzying pattern of light which drove them – and the audience – deeper into abandon, into a celebration of the Dionysian joy of life.

The waking dream in *Hunger* gave the audience a physical experience of Tangen's famished delusions. Tangen sat on the bed in his cheap hotel room; his double sat in his shadow, whispering in his ear.[163] Drums provided the rhythm of his heartbeat; eerie sound effects represented the buzzing in his ears. Gradually, the murmur of voices became perceptible, grew louder and became distinct words. At the same time, the lights slowly faded up and revealed the chorus, playing furniture.[164] The shabby furniture came to life and danced 'a nightmarish circle dance'[165] around Tangen, chanting a rhythmic incantation evoking the physical sensations of hunger. At one point, the chant metamorphosed into nauseated retching sounds.[166] Periodically, a clock tolled to mark the passing of time. The rhythms of the chant became faster, and the sound effects more shrill and intense; the chorus intoned the Lord's Prayer, repeating the line 'give us our daily bread, give us our daily bread'. The buzzing in the ears became intolerable; the chant ended with 'and deliver us from flies'.[167] The lights faded; the drums slowed to represent the sleeping rhythm of Tangen's heart and only Tangen's breathing could be heard. Reality gradually reappeared with the far-off sounds of morning activity: running water, footsteps, the voice of the milkman.[168] Thus, Barrault interwove elements of total theatre – the double, the actor as scenery, lighting, choreographed movement, speech as incantation and physiological sounds – so the audience might experience the world as transformed by hunger.

Barrault described in his published *mise en scène* for *Phaedra* the acting of a waking dream. In Act 4, Scene 4, Phaedra learns that Hippolytus loves Aricia. The queen, left alone onstage (Scene 5), stands in silence, frozen in shock. Then, like a sleepwalker, she begins to speak. A slow transition builds to the climactic section. As Phaedra speaks of her husband, her crimes, her father, the lovers, she undergoes successive hallucinations. Her gestures become those of a madwoman. Her voice begins as a murmur and rises, placed in the head and nasal resonators. Her eyes fixed, and she advances towards the place at which, in her hallucination, she sees the lovers embracing. As she reaches them, the vision vanishes. She stops abruptly, puts her hands to her temples and slowly begins another build. Barrault described line 1268 as 'just one long, awful shiver, as if lightning were running up her spinal column. This discharge makes her spin in place like a top.'[169] Throughout the recitative, Phaedra undergoes constant changes of vocal placement, tempo and breathing. She trembles, her teeth chatter and she becomes, in Barrault's view, 'nothing but an electrical focus'.[170] At the end, Phaedra falls to the ground unconscious, appearing not to breathe.[171] In this scene, Barrault integrated rhythm, vocal placement, frenzied and trance-like movement, and respiration to create the waking dream – but here that hallucinatory world is created solely by the actor.

Conclusion

Barrault's critics often accused him of using the text as 'only an admirable pretext for the application of his scenic theories'.[172] One finds, however, opposing judgements, as in Lucien Descave's review of *Hunger*, that Barrault 'has not distorted in the slightest either the text or the author's intentions; on the contrary, he has translated them with the fidelity of a poodle'.[173] Critics also complained that Barrault overemphasized movement to the detriment of verbal expression. For example, Bertrand Poirot-Delpech, in his review of *The Trial*, attacked Barrault for 'adding ten gestures for one to the poor word'.[174] Michel Mohrt argued that the physical action in Barrault's productions of Molière 'deprives us of all the comedy depending on the words'.[175] Jean-Jacques Gautier took Barrault to task for 'transforming everything that he touches into a choreographic tragedy'.[176]

Harold Hobson, among others, came to Barrault's defence, arguing that disapproval of Barrault's use of movement was motivated by critics' suspicion that the director is usurping the power of the author.[177] When one examines some of the reviews, a critic's bias becomes obvious, as in André Ransan's critique of *The Trial*:

We had a novel called *The Trial*, and it was by Kafka.

We had this book and that was fully sufficient. For you and for me. But not for M. Jean-Louis Barrault, who quickly saw in it a pretext for a *mise en scène*. For, you will have observed, as I have, that M. Jean-Louis Barrault absolutely must have (as must all of his kind, the directors) 'pretexts' for the display of scenery, crowds, costumes, and lights.[178]

In French theatre, attention had been traditionally focused on the word and the actor's vocal expression. Hobson, however, argued that 'there is no man in France more sensitive than [Barrault] to the beauties and delicacies of speech', a talent which enabled Barrault to find a way to speak the poetic lines of Claudel's plays, which were previously considered unstageable.[179]

As a director, was Barrault a coldly calculating intellectual or an imaginative and intuitive artist? Extreme 'either/or' judgements can be misleading. Louis Cheronnet suggests a more complex description when he says Barrault's 'magnificent Romantic temperament is disciplined by the most classic intelligence'.[180] One certainly encounters Barrault's Romantic passion and imagination in his writings, but the precision with which he choreographed movement and communicated instructions to his collaborators demonstrates a disciplined mind.

Did Barrault practise fidelity to the text or sacrifice the play in order to apply his theories? Again, 'either/or' responses miss nuances. The critic Jacques Lemarchand, Barrault's personal friend, observed that for all of Barrault's productions, 'one knows why he loves the play'.[181] Directors choose to direct plays that speak to them on a deep level; Barrault was no exception. He saw poetic realism even in a Feydeau farce such as *Occupe-toi d'Amélie* (Look after Lulu).[182] The concept of poetic realism, however, is inherently flexible: theatre portrays the level of everyday life and a second level, but Barrault did not clearly define that second level. He could stay faithful to texts as different as *Hamlet, The Cherry Orchard* and *Look after Lulu*, while approaching them all as poetic realism, and save his more extreme total theatre experiments for plays which permit such an approach.

Yes, Barrault was eclectic. He borrowed from the whole range of theatrical styles and techniques to create the special world of each play. Barrault's eclecticism, however, was not haphazard, and his productions not careless jumbles of incompatible techniques. When Barrault juxtaposed in the same production mimed and real objects, masked and unmasked characters, clown costumes and Kabuki movement, he did so in order to expose more than one level of reality. In Barrault's view, life reveals multiple aspects according to the way one looks at it, and his productions portrayed the world as a rich and ever-changing mystery. When he said the emblem of the theatre is the kaleidoscope,[183] he gave an apt description of his own vision – a vision he sought to communicate as a director.

Ariane Mnouchkine

3

Ariane Mnouchkine and the Théâtre du Soleil: Towards a Utopian Vision

Helen Richardson

Utopia is not something which is impossible; it is something that has not been done yet. ... We are on the path to utopia. I accept that.[1]

Ariane Mnouchkine has been the artistic leader of the Théâtre du Soleil for over half a century, guiding it to international prominence and pursuing a culture within the company that is cosmopolitan in outlook, collaborative in its creative process, wide-ranging in its social engagement and theatrical aesthetics, while maintaining a rigorous ethos in its day-to-day functioning as a troupe. The Théâtre du Soleil is known for its collaboratively created productions that examine the social impact of political events, both contemporary and historical, and for its theatrically striking, emotionally evocative treatments of these issues, including its innovative approaches to classic plays by Aeschylus, Euripides, Shakespeare and Molière. Mnouchkine's compelling *mise en scène* is broadly influenced by popular traditional European theatre forms, such as the *commedia dell'arte* and puppetry, as well as Asian traditional theatre,

---

Unless otherwise indicated, all translations are by the author of this essay.

including *kabuki, bunraku* and *kathakali*. It is her admiration of popular theatre and, in particular, her resonance with melodrama, rarely covered in regards to the Théâtre du Soleil and to be discussed later, that give Mnouchkine's productions a particular utopian, somewhat Manichaean flavour that challenges the general sophistication of the contemporary avant-garde, while attracting a larger, more diverse audience than usually found at the theatres that see themselves functioning outside of the mainstream.

The Cartoucherie

For most of its years, the international troupe has resided at the Cartoucherie, a former ammunitions factory in the Bois de Vincennes on the periphery of Paris, secured by the troupe in 1970. This out-of-the way space provides Mnouchkine and her company a sanctuary in which to develop their epic creations and the stability necessary for a sustained approach to collaborative creation. The Théâtre du Soleil's process demands long, intensive rehearsals on works sweeping in content and dramaturgically complex, as well as rigorous discipline and stamina in the crafting of a characteristically physically demanding *mise en scène*. Contributions by actors, playwright, designers and musician are subject to continual development and adjustment during the rehearsal process. The Soleil, as it is often referred to by its members, has developed a global community within the precincts of the Cartoucherie: the company's participants are from various parts of the world and they often host international theatre companies; the audience is also international, both in Paris and through the company's extensive participation in international festivals.

What is compelling about the Théâtre du Soleil is the attention paid not only to the quality of the theatrical experience but to the exceptional ambiance that surrounds the troupe and its performance space. Pilgrimage to a Soleil performance begins with a trip to the Bois de Vincennes – a sprawling park at the south-eastern limits of Paris – via car, bus or the *navette* provided by the theatre, or on foot, going past the fortress-like Château de Vincennes and continuing along the route de la Pyramide, which is flanked by woods. Entering the Cartoucherie gates, one will find a complex that comprises the Soleil's hangar-sized performance space, with adjacent buildings for administrative and technical purposes, as well as the venues of several other alternative theatres residing in the Cartoucherie. This pastoral enclave offers respite from the hype of the usual commercial theatre district with its superstars and megahits. Decorative lights, strung through the trees and on the façade of the building, create a relaxed, festive atmosphere. The first stop may be at the ticket kiosk overseen by members of the Théâtre du Soleil administration, and it's very likely that Ariane

Mnouchkine will be there handling those visitors, often from abroad, who are hoping to get tickets to the sold-out performance. The queued audience is welcomed into the space an hour before performance time by three traditional knocks (*les trois coups*), performed by Mnouchkine herself, signalling that the house is about to open. The public, stepping into the vast, warmly lit Cartoucherie lobby, is likely to be confronted by an installation of maps and images painted on the walls, and hung posters and photos with explanatory text providing a background to the history and culture the audience will encounter in the performance. As well, there are tables to sit at where one can eat food from that region, purchased at the canteen and prepared and served by the company before the show and during intermission. One can also browse in the bookstore, manned by administrators of the Théâtre du Soleil. The anteroom, adjacent to the playing space, provides a window into the world of the actors as they ready themselves for performance. Before the audience enters, the troupe meets with Mnouchkine for a moment of dedication to the performance. Once the house is open, the audience is able to observe the performers in their final preparations, putting on their outer costumes and make-up before ascending the stage. The spectator is kept on the periphery through various scenic elements such as a diaphanous curtain or other barrier which preserve the actors' space and further the sense of sanctuary. Through this observance, through the pre-show atmosphere with its emphasis on welcoming the public through the attentive presence of the Soleil, the audience is given the opportunity to prepare itself, as well, for the contemporary morality play about to unfold.

During this pre-show activity, Mnouchkine is seen moving about the lobby, greeting friends of the Soleil and seeing to it that all is in order, as well as helping audience members to their seats, preventing latecomers from entering until the appropriate time, and in the past she would also serve up the meals. Mnouchkine's omnipresence at performances has become a trademark of the Théâtre du Soleil and exemplifies the unusual emphasis on community and on the Cartoucherie as the home of the troupe rather than just a venue. At the end of the show, the enthusiasm of the applause is as much a reflection of the connection forged between the audience and the company as it is for the spectacular *mise en scène*. Members of the audience often linger to greet actors or to speak with Mnouchkine herself, partaking in a last dose of the utopian community and its consecration to virtue as projected by Mnouchkine and her company.

Though this exceptional locus of the Cartoucherie has been fundamental to the development of the company's ethos, the space has thrived paradoxically because Ariane Mnouchkine is at heart nomadic. Cosmopolitan in her interests, she has travelled globally, from West to East, seeking theatrical forms and subject matter that could revitalize, what was to her, the moribund theatre of Europe, which has been losing its vitality through its reduction to realist aesthetics and presentation of life as absurd and meaningless. In this search, she has not been alone. Peter Brook, Jerzy Grotowski and Eugenio Barba, among others, also came to prominence in the 1960s, making similar journeys to the East. Mnouchkine has created, with her ensemble, works on China, France (both historical and contemporary), Germany, Cambodia, India, Tibet, Afghanistan, Eastern Europe, Iran, Patagonia and refugee camps. She is focused on global political realities, researching history and various nationalities to highlight the plight of the disenfranchised and the consequences of power politics and ethical choices on the lives of communities and individuals, while at the same time seeking to create a utopian vision that might continue to inspire the members of the Soleil community and audience towards civic engagement.

Mnouchkine's theatrical explorations have led to an ongoing transformation of the interior of the Cartoucherie into a panorama of vastly diverse geographies and epochs. Over the years, the scenic aspects of new productions have been much anticipated by the many Soleil faithful, with Mnouchkine insisting that these transformations be zealously guarded until opening night. In *1789* (1970), the troupe's first production at the Cartoucherie, the playing space was turned into the fairground of a marketplace in revolutionary Paris.

Open-air theatre performers moved across five large wooden platforms surrounding the audience (most of whom stood during the performance), parading through the audience, recounting the events of the French Revolution as it was unfolding, using song, pageant, puppets, commedia scenarios and other forms of street performance to tell the story and to enliven the public debates on the cause of 'the people' and the conflicts emerging among various factions on the eve of the French Revolution (see Figure 3.1). In *Les Atrides* (House of Atreus, 1990), the stage became a bullring: the chorus entered dramatically through large central stockade doors, performed exuberant dances of military precision and then perched on the walls in anticipation of witnessing – along with the audience – the destruction of the House of Atreus and the haunting of Orestes by the Furies. In the antechamber, next to the space where the actors prepare, the Théâtre du Soleil – inspired by the terracotta statues of warriors created for the tomb of the first emperor of China at Xi'an – dug a deep pit in which they placed larger-than-life statues resembling the characters of *House of Atreus*, as played by the actors of the Soleil, evoking the ancient history underlying the House of Atreus. In *L'Indiade ou l'Inde de leur rêves* (Indiade, or the India of Their Dreams, 1987), the space was agora-like: a place for the people and the political leaders of India to congregate and struggle for or against the partition of India into India and Pakistan, with large carpets periodically unfurled when the action moved indoors, to denote the households of the various leaders participating in the conflict over partition.

FIGURE 3.1 1789 *at the Cartoucherie de Vincennes. The platform stages are connected by runways, which are also used as playing areas. Most of the audience stands in the middle, although bleachers were set up on one side for those who could not stand.* © *Martine Franck/Magnum Photos (Magnum #PAR86941 FRM1 970040W02310/22A).*

Théâtre populaire

Mnouchkine strives for populist theatre that appeals to all generations, relating stories of historical events as told by the people for the people. Several of the Théâtre du Soleil productions, particularly those dealing with the ancient Greeks, Shakespeare and Asian political history, are in some measure reflective of traditional folk performances, with stunning costumes and physical athleticism, combining humour and pathos, inviting the audience to enjoy a more naive approach, asking actors and audience to see the world with the openness of a child. In this way Mnouchkine seeks to maintain her utopian vision, untrammelled by cynicism: 'Don't let the sarcasm and the cynicism win.'[2] At the same time, Mnouchkine's work reflects Brecht's epic vision and his notion of the Street Scene, in which the eyewitness man/woman in the street reports on local incidents. Dramaturgically, the Théâtre du Soleil's original creations, whether about the French Revolution or the plight of contemporary refuges, are structured around a series of consecutive scenes that portray the political realities of a community in which a people's misfortunes are examined and the audience is confronted with the consequence of society's indifference and power politics. However, rather than using Brechtian irony to stimulate an intellectual analysis of the scenes, Mnouchkine uses irony to create emotional awareness. In the production of *Indiade, or the India of Their Dreams*, a '*pousse pousse*' (a hand-pulled cart) is pulled onto the stage. Historically, the action occurs at the height of the conflict between the Hindus and Muslims over the partition of India. In the cart are the bodies of a Hindu and Muslim collected from the streets, killed in the fighting, lying in each other's arms, signifying the paradox that though divided in life, they are now united in death. Accentuated by quietly emotive music, the scene provides a visceral moment of recognition for the audience as to the futility of armed conflict. In Mnouchkine's version of *Richard II* (1981), Bolingbroke, the future Henry IV, cradles the body of Richard, whom he ordered assassinated, in his arms in the image of a *pietà*. A king commits the ultimate sacrilege against another king: regicide. In this gesture of the *pietà*, he both mourns and sanctifies the man who stood between himself and the throne.

Mnouchkine's use of stage imagery and extensive musical underscoring simultaneously enhances the irony and the pathos of human suffering in the scene. For Mnouchkine, realpolitik and human passions are intimately connected: 'the theatre is not supposed to represent psychology but passion, which is totally different. Its role is to represent the soul's different emotional states, and those of the mind, the world history'.[3] Mnouchkine often invokes the influence of Artaud, sharing his enthusiasm for the theatricality of Asian theatre forms: 'Artaud said "the theatre is oriental." I understand what he wanted to say. From the orient comes the specificity of theatre, which is the perpetual metaphor the actors produce – when they are capable of producing. That is what we do: try to understand the metaphors that an actor can employ.'[4] Mnouchkine's use of signifiers on the stage evoking 'universal truths' through compelling theatrical gestures suggests Artaud's concept of the actor 'signaling through the flames'.[5] Associated with the avant-garde, Mnouchkine's work is at core a renewal and evolution of certain popular theatre traditions, both secular and ceremonial: a reinvigoration of populist theatrical forms through an expansion of the melodramatic aesthetic via inspiration from *commedia dell'arte* and traditional Asian forms of performance, as well as other mechanics of the *mise en scène* influenced by the cinema.

This eclectic use of theatrical forms and belief in the universality of theatrical signs has opened Mnouchkine up to criticism as a theatre-maker who exploits non-Western forms and is naive in her quest for the universal (see Figure 3.2). The twentieth century has seen Western theatre-makers turn East for their inspiration, and theatre-makers from the East have looked West for inspiration as well. In some cases, influences have been borrowed naively, with admiration but little deep understanding of the cultural signifiers of the other. Mnouchkine has made a deep-seated effort in her work to understand the culture of others; however, her insistence on avoiding the traps of Realism, her reliance on diverse popular theatre forms,

FIGURE 3.2 *Mnouchkine is surrounded by* Twelfth Night *(La Nuit des rois) company members at the Festival of Avignon, where the production opened in 1982. The costumes reflect the layering of Asian on Elizabethan visual elements in a populist mix. Photo by Michele Laurent/Gamma-Rapho via Getty Images (Getty #459606770).*

her desire to avoid ambivalence and cynicism, and her interest in the larger political landscape tend to reduce many of her productions to what have been called 'storybook versions', which lack the nuance of a work that is focused more closely on the ambiguities of one's own culture and whose scope is narrower. As well, Mnouchkine is closer to Artaud in her inclination to expose the passions of conflict, which are less intellectual and rawer in their directness. Whereas Brecht used textual irony to question societal values, Mnouchkine favours the shock of overtly cruel human actions over the distancing of dispassionate observations on the realpolitik. This has led her to encourage text that is emotionally expressive as developed by the playwright-collaborator Hélène Cixous, thus enhancing the melodramatic effect of her productions.

Melodrama

Melodrama has a strong tradition in France, originating in the dramaturgical work of Jean-Jacques Rousseau, who experimented with the use of music in tandem with text to enhance the theatrical experience. According to Rousseau, music furthers a sense of moral sentiment that encourages the recognition of the other, stimulating sentiments of passion and ultimately compassion, resulting in a united will of the people.[6] Melodrama continued its evolution in response to the French Revolution with Robespierre, inspired by the work of Rousseau, using music and dramatic representations of the people's involvement in the revolution to inspire a new patriotism. Melodrama emerged as a major form in early-nineteenth-century France; it appealed to the moral sensibilities of the middle and lower classes through the use of populist forms of theatre, sensationalistic storylines in which good triumphs over evil and the development of character types representative of moral values, upending the heroic elite of classical tragedy, driven by hubris and fate, as well as bourgeois comedic characters, driven by personal love interests. Spectacular scenic imagery and dramatic music were used to underscore the pathos of the story. Exotic locations reflective of the imperialist politics of nineteenth-century France were part of the repertoire, and on civic holidays such performances were offered up free to the general populace. Eventually certain authors of melodrama used the form to criticize the exploitative social conditions resulting from those imperialistic ventures.[7]

The radical reorientation of structures of sovereignty in the post-revolutionary society of France demanded the articulation of a new value system in which *le peuple* were the main characters and social revolution the ultimate goal. Amid the contrary emotions of fervour for the rule of *the people* and ambivalence towards the rule of the mob, there was a need to find a new ethical centre focused on democratic sociopolitical economic values. At the same time there arose an essential occultism that empowered these values beyond day-to-day behavioural practices. Melodrama, rather than leaving religion and faith behind, reordered it into a metaphysical vision of character and individual choice, in which human virtue takes on a spiritual force (see Figure 3.3).

The Théâtre du Soleil seeks to embody this value system, spiritualizing the actions of *the people* and creating a theatre of social mission. Mnouchkine: 'I consider that the theatre must be political, and historical, and sacred, and contemporary, and mythological. It's only the proportions that change from production to production.'[8] The Soleil relies on many melodramatic conventions including the use of populist forms and of characters that are often defined by their social function and engaged in high-stakes political struggles of good versus evil. Dramatic music underscores the scenes, and Mnouchkine is renowned for her use of spectacular stage imagery.

Rather than starting with a crisis, as in tragedy, melodramas usually begin with a utopian environment that is marred by some mystery or enigma and soon threatened by a situation or person that subverts the idyllic situation, which in some melodramas is portrayed literally as a garden behind high walls or a cottage in the countryside. The Soleil embodies this manifestation of utopia in its very location in the Bois de Vincennes and in the Soleil's efforts at an idyllic collaborative community in contrast to the competitive commercial

FIGURE 3.3 *Mnouchkine rehearses* L'Indiade, or India of Their Dreams *by Hélène Cixous in January 1988. It is standard practice at the Théâtre du Soleil to rehearse in costume from the beginning. Photo by John van Hasselt/Corbis via Getty Images (Getty #542638032).*

values of establishment theatre and the pressures of modern life and politics. Through their productions, the company confronts the mystery of mankind's inhumanity and its potential to tear apart the fabric of society's and their own utopian strivings. Mnouchkine identifies herself as a world citizen, making the global struggles of the disenfranchised her own: participating in a hunger strike in protest of France's refusal to intervene in Bosnia; organizing protests over the years against abuses in Brazil, China, Europe, etc.; providing refuge for African émigrés threatened with deportation. In the summer of 2005, the Théâtre du Soleil was invited to conduct a workshop in Afghanistan by the Kabul-based Foundation for Culture and Civil Society. Since then, the company has supported the Theatre Aftaab (Aftaab means 'sun' in Dari), formed by Afghan theatre-makers who attended the workshop. This political engagement and protective mission defines the work of the company: treating issues of social inequity from the undermining of *the people's* revolution by the bourgeoisie in France to the terror exercised by the Cambodian Pol Pot regime over the Cambodian people; engaging in the world crisis of refugees forced to escape oppressive governments to helping a nascent theatre company in Afghanistan fulfil their mission.

Though melodrama is often seen as an inferior form of theatre, with its overt values and language, Peter Brooks in his book, *The Melodramatic*

Imagination, makes a convincing argument that melodrama is 'a central fact of the modern sensibility. ... in that modern art has typically felt itself to be constructed on, and over, the void, postulating meaning and symbolic systems which have no certain justification because they are backed by no theology and universally accepted social code'.[9] Melodrama seeks to counter ambivalence and terror as modern society faces the abyss of meaninglessness. Brooks characterizes melodrama as a 'Promethean search to illuminate man's quotidian existence by the reflected flame of the higher cosmic drama'[10] and that 'melodramatists refuse to allow that the world has been completely drained of transcendence; and they locate that transcendence in the struggle of the children of light with the children of darkness, in the ethical mind'.[11] Mnouchkine, and through her, the Soleil, embody this vision in their productions.

As nineteenth-century melodrama on the stage helped replace the church and the government as authority on the new morality after the revolutions, not only in France but in the United States and in Europe in general, it also extended into the twentieth century with film and television. In early French cinema, the French Revolution and the confrontation between the aristocracy and the people held a fascination. The Théâtre du Soleil's signature piece, which brought them international recognition, was their own production on the French Revolution, *1789*.

Elements typifying melodrama, the use of spectacular scenography and the underscoring of action and text with music dominate Mnouchkine's aesthetic. In *Le Dernier Caravansérail* (2003), about refuges attempting to escape conflict in their homeland, the *mise en scène* included, as an opening scene, Afghan refugees having to cross a rushing river in a moving basket suspended over the river. At the beginning of Act 2, refugees were shown crossing the sea in a small boat while overhead Australian soldiers descended ropes as if lowered from helicopters, forcing the boat people to turn back. These stage pictures of a rushing river and a vast ocean with the military descending from helicopters above are typical of Mnouchkine's passion for striking images on the stage.

The music of the Soleil is developed during rehearsals through improvisation and consultation between actor and company musician Jean-Jacques Lemêtre. This process helps the actor reach an *état* (state) of engagement, enhancing the emotions that underlie the scene as well as helping the actors define the nature of their characters down to the rhythms of their entrances, actions and speech. These musical improvisations become fixed as the rehearsals proceed and the actions become established. The narrative quality of Lemêtre's music is essential to the emotional through-line of the Soleil's productions, creating an operatic atmosphere, and the text, though spoken, is delivered with a musical resonance. As well, in the case of Asian-themed productions, Lemêtre has used over three hundred instruments in a performance, some native to the regions being evoked or created by himself, to provide a portal of access – for both performer and audience – atmospherically and emotionally, to the world of the *other*.

Mnouchkine's tendency towards the melodramatic has put her in conflict with theatre critics who question the literary value of the texts developed by her theatre company, as they expect a certain classical dramaturgical excellence to complement Mnouchkine's scenically powerful populist theatre. Paradoxically, though the Théâtre du Soleil has sought a populist audience and has taken melodrama and popular theatre to a high level, its audience and critics are in general sophisticated theatregoers, many of whom have the resources to travel great distances and the time to see the company's work and who, despite having questions about the strength of the Soleil's texts and portrayals of character, are enamoured of the *mise en scène* and politics. Over the years the Théâtre du Soleil has become a populist theatre for the intellectual elite as well as for the culturally inclined bourgeois theatregoer, who are hungry perhaps for a bit of utopian transcendence. Not that the productions of the Soleil are in any way naive about the violence of the world: in fact, Mnouchkine regularly depicts bloody violence on the stage worthy of the Grand Guignol, which sets her apart from her peers, such as Peter Brook who has developed a more understated approach over the years and Robert Wilson who is more abstract. Mnouchkine articulates an ongoing faith in the better intentions of the common man/woman and the need to recognize their anonymous efforts: projecting hope within a rather dark vision of humanity. At the same time, Mnouchkine struggles with the recognition that her political idealism is eroding, and her work has become more sombre, perhaps more fatalistic in the face of the seemingly never-ending tenacity necessary to pursue utopia.

The making of a director

In order to understand Mnouchkine's choices and evolution as a theatre artist, it's important to consider the political influences on her as a member of the sixties generation coming to maturity after the Second World War, seeing itself within a greater global context than previous generations. As well, it is important to consider her cultural influences, growing up in France as a cinephile, with a prominent film-producing father. The call for a populist theatre by French theatre luminaries such as Jacques Copeau, Charles Dullin and Jean Vilar, in the first half of the twentieth century; the influence of Bertolt Brecht's epic theatre; the metaphysical vision of Antonin Artaud; the popular cinema's use of music to underscore dramatic plots and create the atmosphere of epic vistas and exotic locations; the wanderlust of the sixties; the political realities of a bourgeoning China; the neocolonial politics emerging in Cambodia, India, Vietnam and other parts of the globe, all made their mark on Mnouchkine and her development as a theatre-maker.

Born on 3 March 1939, at Boulogne-sur-Seine, Paris, Mnouchkine is the daughter of a film producer of Russian origin, Alexandre Mnouchkine, famed for producing the films of Claude Lelouch and Philippe de Broca, among others. Her mother, Jane Hannen – an actress from a prominent English theatre family – left her husband when Mnouchkine was in her teens. Mnouchkine remained with her father, with whom she had a strong supportive relationship, while becoming estranged from her mother, with whom she reconciled only later in life. Though Mnouchkine was to take up the *métier* of theatre-maker, her early life was greatly influenced by film through her father's profession, as well as having grown up in a period of great cinema in France. Her favourite film-makers from the era are Marcel Carné, Jean Renoir and the American film-maker John Huston. The epic nature of their films, characters larger than life, melodramatic plots and lush music are reflected in Mnouchkine's approach to theatre-making. Her film experience – including her own film-making pursuits recreating the Soleil's productions on film, as well as an epic film on Molière – has inspired her to use film techniques to alienate (in the Brechtian sense) the theatre-viewer by incorporating the tracking shot into her staging: actors make their entrances and exits on wheeled platforms recreating the effect of a camera dolly shot in *Le Dernier Caravansérail*. As well, in *Les Ephémères* (2006), settings move onto the stage on large circular platforms that are pushed by actors and made to rotate slowly, allowing the audience to watch the scene from changing angles, as is possible with film.

Mnouchkine's grandparents, film-makers in Russia who emigrated to France after the October 1917 revolution, were deported as Jews to Auschwitz during the German occupation of France. However, Mnouchkine was not made aware of her Jewish background until she was seventeen, as her father chose not to speak of it. Mnouchkine, also, kept mostly silent about her childhood and private life until after the production of *Les Ephémères* in 2007, in which the company – in sharing family histories – chose to depict Mnouchkine's childhood as well as her efforts to know more, in her later years, about her grandparents and their deportation.

The Soleil has been both Mnouchkine's work and family: in her career of more than fifty years, she has never directed outside the company, and many members have worked with her long term, in some cases over thirty years. Her personal relationships have been with members of the company: actress Josephine Derenne, playwright Hélène Cixous and actress Juliana Carneiro da Cunha. As leader of the company, she projects the role of 'head of the family', mixing an authoritative oversight of company values with a sense of responsibility to nurture and protect the welfare of the troupe and, on a more global level, the disenfranchised within society. Mnouchkine's all-encompassing daily commitment to the troupe has been an essential factor in the longevity of the company.

Mnouchkine's turn towards the theatre began while she was a student of psychology at the Sorbonne and spent time at Oxford participating in productions of an amateur group directed by professionals. She says of that time: 'I was soon made aware of the artisanal character of theatre: it's to that which I have always wanted to be loyal, in the choices that I made since in the exercise of this profession.'[12] On returning to Paris in 1959, Mnouchkine and her friend Martine Franck – a future Magnum photographer who would document productions of the Théâtre du Soleil over a 48-year period – set about forming a university theatre group, l'ATEP (Association Théâtrale des Etudiants de Paris) with Roger Planchon, the French Brechtian director, as honorary president. The association organized courses in drama given by teachers from the Dullin and Lecoq schools and conferences – including one at which Jean-Paul Sartre spoke, condemning bourgeois theatre and evoking epic theatre as the alternative – all of which impacted the members of the group as they developed their own vision.

Genghis Khan

In 1961, Mnouchkine produced her first play as a director: *Genghis Khan* by Henri Bauchau, a friend and Belgian prize-winning poet. Mnouchkine, attracted to Eastern cultures, found in this epic work about the career of the great Khan 'all of China, to be staged'.[13] With a group of forty actors, both professional and amateur, Mnouchkine staged the play at an outdoor arena, Arènes Lutèce. Using toy soldiers to create the blocking, Mnouchkine had little concern for the acting. It was sufficient that the actors 'show their anger, show that they are content, that they can be heard'.[14] Inspired by her recent experience of seeing the Chinese Peking Opera in Paris, Mnouchkine worked towards creating an economy of visual signs and a beauty in the placement of the actors. Music was used to announce the appearance of various personages.[15]

The choice of *Genghis Khan* foreshadows many of Mnouchkine's preoccupations throughout her theatrical career: the Asian setting and theatrical forms, the historical emphasis and the portrait of an important figure in history – in this case a rather idealistic vision of Genghis Khan's evolution as a leader. The sense of excitement and adventure which surrounded the performance of this spectacle led to a consolidation of the group around the leadership of Mnouchkine.

Towards a collective

After *Genghis Khan*, Mnouchkine journeyed to the Far East, working for Japanese television and travelling through India. Denied a visa to enter China, she walked through Cambodia instead. These travels strengthened her interest in Asian theatre. In 1963, she returned to Paris to reconvene the ATEP. The ATEP, like many theatres of the time in France, took inspiration from the theatre innovator Jacques Copeau: 'Create a fellowship of actors. I sensed from the beginning that was the issue. Fellows living together, working together, playing together. But, I forgot this other condition which I must inevitably achieve: inventing theatre together.'[16] In 1913, Copeau formed Le Vieux-Colombier, a group dedicated to rediscovering the roots of theatre. Deploring the lack of good playwriting, Copeau suggested that theatre return to the works of Shakespeare and Molière to create a new theatre dominated by '*le Beau, le Bien* and *le Vrai*' (the Beautiful, the Good and the True).[17] Against the traditional Italianate theatre with its overly decorated interiors, Copeau created an austere theatrical space: a large empty stage and a series of simple stairs and levels in the background, putting the focus on the actor. He formed a school emphasizing rigorous physical and mental training of the actor as well as a collective responsibility for the good of the ensemble. *Commedia dell'arte* improvisations, work with masks and study of the classics were a fundamental part of the curriculum designed to form the 'total actor'.[18]

Charles Dullin, a leading actor at the Vieux-Colombier, created his own company, L'Atelier, a school and troupe influencing such prominent theatre artists as Jean-Louis Barrault, Antonin Artaud, Jean Vilar and Roger Blin. Dullin turned to the *commedia dell'arte* and Japanese theatre as models for the training of his actors. His troupe worked as an ensemble, living for a while in the countryside near Paris, where they shared in all the tasks of maintaining a community, from the domestic to the artistic. Dullin was convinced that the theatre had to broaden its social basis if it was to survive. After the war Jeanne Laurent, of the Ministry of Beaux-Arts, took the initiative to implement Dullin's proposal to establish several Centres Dramatiques Nationaux in the provinces. The directors of these centres were former disciples of Copeau and Dullin, dedicated to bringing theatre to the working class and to resurrecting popular theatre with its festival atmosphere. In 1951, Jean Vilar, founder of the Festival d'Avignon in 1947, was appointed director of the Théâtre National Populaire at the Palais de Chaillot in Paris. Vilar's goal was to encourage the working class of Paris and its nearby suburbs to attend the theatre; he did this through reduced ticket prices, early evening curtain times and making affordable pre-performance buffet meals available.

The Théâtre du Soleil grew up in this era dominated by the formation of ensemble companies, committed to rigorous training of actors through the exploration of populist and classic theatre forms, both European and Asian, with the purpose of bringing theatre to the people. As well, theatre in France was linked to the evolution of French intellectual history: Jean-Paul Sartre and Roland Barthes were fundamental to the political definition of French theatre. In 1953, Barthes helped form a theatre review called *Théâtre Populaire*, the purpose of which was to explore the possibilities of revitalizing French theatre by making it more responsive to the interests of a greater public: a theatre which would have the civic relevance of ancient Greek theatre. In 1954, Brecht's Berliner Ensemble visited Paris with *Mother Courage*, demonstrating to the editors of *Théâtre Populaire* a sophisticated handling of contemporary issues and offering a model for addressing the new political realities of post–Second World War France. The era of national unity that emerged in France out of the resistance against Nazi Germany was losing its momentum, replaced by a sense of alienation and disillusionment with post-war politics, which would soon spark social, political and economic divisions within France, culminating in the May 1968 uprisings of students and workers.

The Théâtre du Soleil established itself as a cross-fertilization between France's *théâtre populaire* movement and Brecht's epic theatre; it was committed to the vision of Copeau and his followers: an ensemble dedicated to popular theatre for the people and an epic theatre of social relevance, as evoked by Sartre in his address in 1959.[19] In 1964, Jean-Pierre Tailhade, Philippe Léotard, Jean-Claude Penchenat, Martine Franck, Françoise Tournafond, Myrrha Donzenac, Georges Donzenac, Gérard Hardy and Ariane Mnouchkine founded the Théâtre du Soleil. The choice of the name, Théâtre du Soleil, was in reaction to the fashion of the time to have names which were reduced down to initials, that is, TNP (Théâtre National Populaire), and was an homage to 'the filmmakers of light, of generosity and pleasure, such as Max Ophuls, Jean Renoir, Georges Cukor',[20] as well to the image of the sun, warm and illuminating, that could counter the cold-war bleakness that dominated the era.

Each member of the troupe contributed 900 francs and participated in various capacities in administrative, technical and performance roles. In the tradition of the Copeau and Dullin theatre schools, the group sought refuge in the countryside, intending to support themselves by raising sheep, working in tranquillity on their theatrical pieces, then taking the performances to Paris and other places when ready. In Ardèche, they soon discovered that raising sheep left them no time for creating theatre. Mnouchkine chose a play quickly, *Les Petits Bourgeois* (Common People) by Maxim Gorky, adapted by Arthur Adamov, which she thought would be a good starting point for actors with little experience. As well, the play confronted a way of life which the company, as children of bourgeois families, feared: the inability to risk, to surmount petty problems, to penetrate the communication gap between the generations.

Stanislavski

In Ardèche, the troupe shared tasks, taking turns cooking. At night there were long, ardent discussions about the future of theatre. Mnouchkine brought along a copy of the writings of Stanislavski; this began a new phase for her and the troupe in their methods, emphasizing the search for internal motivations through the extensive use of improvisation. Several of the newly joined actors left in disagreement with Mnouchkine's techniques. It seemed to them that all this improvisation meant that Mnouchkine did not know what she herself wanted. The décor of *Common People* was inspired by Mnouchkine's visit to the home of a peasant in Ardèche: all the furnishings were covered with lace. Mnouchkine imagined herself having lived all her childhood surrounded by macramé: 'that would have been worse than the bars of a prison'.[21] Costumes and make-up were worn for the last two months of rehearsal: 'It's essential that the costumes become one with the body.'[22] The importance of working with costumes from the start of the rehearsal process was to become a standard for the Soleil: actors are not allowed to rehearse in street clothes. Mnouchkine emphasizes that the actors must transform themselves in order to perform another person and that the costume is an essential part of that transformation.

Common People opened in November 1966 at the MJC de la Porte de Montreuil in the outskirts of Paris. The reviews, though few, were favourable: 'Success [of the production] is due to the totality of the team, which knew to offer a unified performance in spirit and diverse in its form.'[23] Photos of the production of *Common People* reflect none of the flamboyancy which was to eventually mark the style of the Soleil; rather they are reminiscent of Stanislavski's Moscow Art Theatre productions: moody, atmospheric, slice-of-life realism, with the *mise en scène* accentuating the ensemble nature of the acting.[24]

Commedia dell'arte

In response to the lassitude and death-like existence of the family in *Common People*, the next production of the Soleil was an adaptation of the novel *Le Capitaine Fracasse* (1965) by Théophile Gautier, about the escapades of a destitute baron who finds happiness by joining a traveling theatre troupe. The company began a demanding rehearsal process, improvising different scenes from the novel while Philippe Léotard and Mnouchkine took notes and then created the text from these improvisations. These texts were then reworked in rehearsal. The actors were trained by Georges Donzenac, a physical education teacher, to develop the athletic facility necessary for the physical gags and fight scenes in the story. *Le Capitaine Fracasse* signalled the Soleil's establishment of the exuberance, athleticism, theatricality and use of popular forms that offered a lively fairgrounds atmosphere appealing to the general public. The critiques of *Le Capitaine Fracasse* were for the most part favourable though Claude Olivier of *Les Lettres Françaises* questioned the quality of text. Gilles Sandier of *Arts and spectacles*, however, was charmed; he noted 'a youthfulness, a freshness, a delightfulness, a theatrical taste and intelligence that translates into a continual joy of invention'.[25] In this production, the troupe began to align themselves as a theatre of celebration against the mounting tide of a theatre of alienation.

La Cuisine, from Lecoq to the Living Theatre

In 1967, turning to contemporary themes, the Soleil presented *La Cuisine* (The Kitchen) by Arnold Wesker, a working-class British playwright of the late 1950s and part of the 'angry young men' movement. The play covers a day in the lives of a kitchen crew in a large London restaurant, focusing on one cook, Peter, a young German, lively and sensitive, who goes berserk under the competing pressures of his work, love life and aspirations; he slashes the gas lines of the kitchen's ovens and breaks dishes. Mnouchkine's utopian vision is reflected in her reasons for choosing to produce *The Kitchen*:

> It's not the dehumanization of people that interests me; on the contrary it's what remains in them as a desire to live. … And true popular theatre is that. In a person's life, there are at the base only two essential activities: work and love; failure in work is as serious as the impossibility of realizing love. Wesker said: 'Man has need of bread but also he has need of roses.' The roses in the piece is the dream.[26]

Feeling the necessity for further training, Mnouchkine attended the Lecoq school, assisting at courses during the day and imparting what she had learned to the company in the evenings. The Soleil did not begin rehearsal this time in the traditional manner by distributing the roles. They began by working on all the roles together, using an approach that was to become one of the basic developmental processes of the Soleil, through which casting evolves over time. Each actor has the possibility of attempting any role, and through rehearsals the role goes to whoever proves to be most effective in realizing the character. In this way characters can be built by the ensemble rather than by a single actor. This can be a very challenging process: an actor may have worked on a role for several months and then may see the role go to another who takes it further. Mnouchkine believes in an apprenticeship approach, similar to traditional Asian theatre training, in which the actors learn through observing the work of other members of the troupe. The entire cast is expected to be present at all rehearsals. In terms of collaborative creation, observing every rehearsal becomes essential to understanding the evolution of a piece as a whole.

Using Stanislavski as a base, the cast of *The Kitchen* invented the biographies of various characters, the schedule of their days and the tasks to be accomplished. They studied their parts by taking jobs in Paris restaurants in order to learn the skills, gestures and comportment of a kitchen staff. A professional cook gave them lessons. The stage designer, Roberto Moscoso, studied restaurant kitchens (see Figure 3.4).

A great deal of work was put into the miming of kitchen tasks since no real food was to be used. Ariane Mnouchkine said of the rehearsal process:

> It's this dialectic between total realism and the poetry of the gesture that impassions me. We arouse the imagination of the spectator and call it to completion. ... We always work in the situation. To warm up at the beginning, I created exercises; for example, I had a pile of dishes that I broke. I threw them to the women, telling them it's burning or it's cracked, you will cut yourself. The women became almost, in the end, like jugglers.[27]

FIGURE 3.4 *The Théâtre du Soleil got the attention of Paris audiences in 1967 with* The Kitchen *by Arnold Wesker. Photo by Lipnitzki/Roget Viollet/Getty Images (Getty #55757149).*

The Théâtre Récamier refused to house the play because the management considered it too vulgar. No other theatres were interested. The troupe was willing to perform anywhere: 'in a hangar, in a gymnasium, no matter where'.[28] Finally, Le Cirque Médrano de Montmartre offered itself; this abandoned circus site in Paris was slated for demolition.

The Kitchen opened on 5 April 1967. The precisely choreographed movements of the kitchen staff made a strong impression on critics and audience alike. As well, the focus on the quotidian world of the worker inspired unions to bring their members in significant numbers to the performance. The cadence of the movement and speech of the actors punctuated the increasingly hectic working pace. The open space of the Cirque Médrano (also known as Cirque de Montmartre) – with its spectators looking down at the action from the bleachers – gave the production the aspect of a sports arena; indeed, the audience watched a race for vocational survival. At the same time, it suggested the operating theatre of a hospital, showing the dissection of a social phenomenon: the rat race of life.

The Kitchen received rave reviews and large audiences, so the actors were able to quit their various part-time jobs and put all their attention into their craft. Pierre Marcabru in *Paris-Presse* lauded the *mise en scène* and the ensemble approach of the company:

> Is it a ballet? Is it an accelerated film? ... Is it the naturalism of father Antoine [André Antoine (1858–1943)]? In truth it is a bit of everything but it is also something else, very personal: the enthusiasm that the actors put into the characters without ever forcing their traits. They don't imitate life, they are life. ... They offer us perhaps for the first time in France, a stage of thirty-seven actors, in which all are up to the task.[29]

Workers' newspapers such as *Le Monde du travail*, *L'Hotellerie*, *La Cooperative de production* and *Populaire*, which generally had no interest in the world of theatre, covered the play. The production received the three major awards of the season: le prix de l'Association des Spectateurs, le prix du Syndicat de la Critique and le prix du Brigadier de l'Association des Régisseurs.

Through *The Kitchen*, the Soleil achieved a new level of craftsmanship: discovering the power of gesture, voice, mime, rhythm and choral work, both vocal and corporeal, reflective of the influence of the Lecoq training.[30] In three short years, the Soleil had worked through Stanislavski's psychological motivations, followed by forms of popular theatre and the training of Lecoq, to arrive in 1967 at the threshold of avant-garde theatre. This elicited comparisons with *The Brig*, which The Living Theatre (from New York) had performed in Paris the year before, influencing the Soleil with its creation of a highly formal, ritualized, yet at the same time hyper-real theatrical style.[31]

A Midsummer Night's Dream

During the run of *The Kitchen*, the Soleil began rehearsals for Shakespeare's *Le Songe d'une nuit d'été* (A Midsummer Night's Dream, 1968). Turning their backs on the traditionally more light-hearted interpretations of the play, the troupe saw the play as a descent into the nightmarish world of unfulfilled desires: 'A *Midsummer Night's Dream* is more savage, more violent than one can dream ... '[32] is how the programme notes began for the Soleil's production. The emphasis on the violence in *A Midsummer Night's Dream* may have been radical for its time but was not an isolated point of view. In 1964, Jan Kott, in his influential book *Shakespeare Our Contemporary*, suggested: 'For a long time theatres have been content to present the *Dream* as a Brothers Grimm fable, completely obliterating the pungency of the dialogue and the brutality of the situations.'[33] The return of the young aristocrats from the forest was compared in the programme notes to the morning after an orgy or drug party, each one disquieted over what the others might have discovered. On the other side of the forest, far away from the madness of unfulfilled desire, are the mechanicals who, though also impacted by the battle between Oberon and Titania, experience the gentle side of 'the demons'. Bottom – as an artisan earnest in his commitment to the mechanicals' theatrical effort – believes his enchantment to have been a marvellous dream: work is the antidote, offering protection from a world in the throes of a deep disruption.[34]

It was 1968 in France: students and workers were in revolt. Many theatre companies disbanded at the time, considering pure political action more effective than making theatre. Joining the masses who had taken over the Odéon, a symbol of establishment theatre in the minds of the younger generation (though the Odéon director Jean-Louis Barrault was one of France's theatrical innovators), the Soleil engaged in long debates over what direction to take. Ultimately, drawing on the inspiration of *Midsummer's* 'rude mechanicals', they chose to continue their work, believing that theatre itself was a process through which the alternative politics of 1968 could manifest. At night, they continued to perform *A Midsummer Night's Dream*. During the day, they performed *The Kitchen* at striking factories, followed by discussion with the workers.

Rehearsals for *A Midsummer Night's Dream* had begun with improvisations using masks in order to encourage a more theatrical approach to the play. Mask-work, as a process of purging an actor's slippage into the banality of Realism, stemmed from Mnouchkine's studies with Lecoq and is a process she continues to use liberally both in rehearsals and in workshops today.[35] She sees masks as fundamental in revealing an actor's lack of theatricality: 'the mask never lies'. The mask cannot be animated solely through interior psychological motives; it demands expressivity through corporeal engagement. For the parts of Oberon and Titania, Mnouchkine chose dancers, both from the Béjart ballet company, whom she felt could more easily create, through movement, the carnality of the characters.[36] During rehearsals Jacques Lasry composed music for the play, using various percussion and string instruments. The music was continuous, moving between bewitching melodies reminiscent of Indian music and very modern and disturbing sounds, as well as pop music.

Mnouchkine was searching for a soft and sensual environment for the set. A point arrived when she despaired of finding the right environment. Mnouchkine gave herself and designer Roberto Moscoso eight days in which to find a solution, or the play would have to be abandoned. On the fourth day, the answer came to them: a gigantic blanket of sheepskins to cover the whole playing area, which would create a world of softness, sensuality, animality, and would give the performers license to move with abandon and violence through the space. Moscoso added driftwood planks as part of the backdrop. Light penetrated the accentuated holes of the driftwood. The combination of the shadowy lighting and the floor of sheepskins gave the set the feeling of a lunar landscape. The image of the young boy desired by Oberon and conceived and born 'in the spiced Indian air' steered the production towards Indian-style costumes in combination with a 1960s hippy look. The mechanicals were clothed as nineteenth-century French working-class artisans.

On 15 February 1968, the Soleil opened *A Midsummer Night's Dream* at the Cirque Montmartre. As with *The Kitchen*, the reviews were favourable, and this time focused on the ingenuity of the production. Gilles Sandier wrote in *Elle*: 'Here at the Cirque Montmartre, *A Midsummer Night's Dream* passes through Antonin Artaud … here are Freud and Sade, two of today's gods, ruling in this beautiful Dionysian ceremony, realized with singular mastery and a great scenic richness of invention by Ariane Mnouchkine.'[37]

The crisis of May 1968 caused the cancellation of all summer festival events for the Théâtre du Soleil. The council general, which had originally invited the company to the Bourgogne festival, instead offered Ariane Mnouchkine and her troupe a large house in Salines d'Arc-et-Sénans – located in the Jura mountains – for the summer. Mnouchkine mentioned to the actors the possibility of joining her there if they had nothing better to do. She expected about five or six to come along; instead the whole troupe, families and all, elected to go together, about forty people. During the company's stay in Arc-et-Sénans, the townspeople requested that the troupe put on a show. The troupe set up a stage, some fair lights, and offered to do improvisations and to present some material they had been working on. To their delight, the improvisations worked. Their work on *commedia dell'arte* and clowning allowed them to 'express a personal discourse, transplanting it into a traditional figure that permitted the comedians to surpass themselves through a discipline both aesthetic and collective'.[38]

In September 1968, Jean Vilar invited the Théâtre du Soleil to participate in the next Avignon Festival, putting at their disposal a rehearsal room where they began their new creation. At Salines d'Arc-et-Sénans, the troupe had made a decision that *A Midsummer Night's Dream* was to be their last established text: in order to create a new relationship with the public, the troupe felt it would have to develop a new theatrical language. For the Soleil, it was not so much a rejection of the playwright as a desire to create their own playwriting along with Ariane Mnouchkine's faith in the actor as poet: 'to make writers arise, but from their own company'.[39]

Collaborative creation

Mnouchkine suggested that the actors themselves create their next piece and that it be based on characters the public could grasp directly. The company began with contemporary characters based on the popular theatre traditions, the *commedia* and the circus. Mnouchkine's role as director took on a new form: in order to allow the actors to achieve, through improvisation, their characters and situations, she renounced any incursion into the work. She took the role of observer, taking notes and commenting only on the form of the presentation. Over time it became clear that the clown type was the strongest form and the *commedia* characters disappeared: the inherent anarchy, energy and simplicity of the clown were unbeatable. Rather than engaging in professional clown training, the actors depended on their memories of circus experiences and their own explorations of voice, movement and costume. Traditional clown routines were soon abandoned for weightier themes such as religion, death, power, and domestic trials and tribulations. Creation of the scenes began with the basic premise:

> 'I would like to be ... '. Laïobule, the clown, wants to be Casanova and Monsieur Apollo wants to be Hitler: they engage in a merciless struggle over who will become the ruler of their island. A clown wants to go live in Paradise, but God won't let him unless he can bring him a magician. The clown finds the magician, but forgets about paradise as the magician reads his palm, and leads him away to drunkenness, stupidity and eventually death. Mademoiselle Scampouzi, reporter-photographer, interviews typical housewife, Madame Cleopatra, to find out what she looks forward to. The future seems bleak for Madame Cleopatra, who tries to keep up with the demands of her six children on roller-skates while kneading dough for bread. [40]

The clown acts were dependent on the association of ideas and play on words, as well as the ability to translate that into large gestures. Some actors excelled; others found the form impossible. Six of the twenty actors left the company. The form also encouraged individual development of character and text rather than a truly collective creativity, which took its toll on the company's sense of ensemble: the troupe had to take several steps back in order to have the actors develop their own, individual capacities, before they could go on to the next stage of collective creativity.

The Clowns opened on 25 April 1969.[41] Despite the technical virtuosity of the actors, the production received mixed reviews. The lack of a playwright, the lack of a unifying theme, a pessimistic vision, and clowns who seemed made neither for the world of the circus nor for the world of the theatre were the main criticisms. Critic Alfred Simon, however, saw the strengths of the Soleil's efforts in their continuing, rigorous exploration of theatrical forms, a form of resistance to the fashionable self-destruction of the avant-garde.[42] Mnouchkine – according to fellow company member Jean-Claude Penchenat – normally enthusiastic and tireless, was exhausted and irritable: a time of disillusionment and overwork had set in after an intense period of growth and discovery.[43] Actors, faced with little money and family responsibilities, and a demanding rehearsal schedule, in which they not only performed but created the piece, were stretched beyond their limit. Many had to leave due to financial burdens. The new phase of the Soleil took more resources than were on hand.

Mnouchkine started work on Brecht's *Baal* in hopes that the poetic language of Brecht might inspire, but she soon abandoned it. The challenge of creating contemporary theatre based on popular forms resonated with Mnouchkine's political and aesthetic sensibilities and much had been learned in the process of creating *Les Clowns*. She suggested that the troupe redouble its efforts by working on fairy tales, but soon it was determined that fairy tales had already become part of the literary canon. Mnouchkine was searching for a more theatrical form, which she had witnessed in her journey through Asia. The overcoming of psychological realism and its expectation of subtexts was an essential part of the Soleil's process in an attempt to leave behind a theatre that seemed to thrive on ambiguity and anti-theatricalism: the company saw psychological realism as serving a bourgeois and intellectual need to see their limited, often-calcified vision, celebrated on the stage. The troupe looked to the popular theatrical forms of the past in the hopes of making theatre a meaningful experience for *the people* again. The solution was to find a topic of interest to the public in general, which was, as Mnouchkine termed it, 'a communal heritage'. Mnouchkine suggested the French Revolution, a moment in history when all French citizens were linked together. According to Mnouchkine: 'From the moment that I made this proposition, the temperature of the troupe climbed.'[44]

1789

The French Revolution was a topic that every French citizen was familiar with, and the story had achieved a mythic or fairy tale status: 'Once upon a time there was a King and Queen.' But how to tell the story? The goal of the Soleil was to recreate the events from the point of view of the people who experienced the French Revolution, and for it to be a celebration in the spirit of *le quatorze juillet* (14 July, France's national holiday). At first, the troupe considered telling the story of a worker and his family, but that would have resulted in a tendency towards psychologizing the event, and the focus would have been too limited. Rather than telling the history, as was so often done, through the struggles of the key figures of the revolution, Mnouchkine suggested that the actors recreate the French Revolution as it might be told by those members of the masses whose role was to inform and dramatize the events of the time: as if a group of agitators, town criers, theatrical troupes and puppeteers had banded together in the marketplace to demonstrate to their fellow 'man/woman in the street' the highlights of the French Revolution that had just come to pass. Through this form of storytelling and acting out of their history, the hopes and wishes of *the people* could manifest the actual achievements of their revolution along with a critical evaluation of it. This method was ideal for the Soleil, using various forms of popular theatre to create the fairgrounds theatre, that is, puppets, *commedia*, juggling and tumbling, music, parades and celebration. It also meant a naturally naive approach to the history and text, in the sense that it was an opportunity to put the art of theatre back into the hands of the anonymous artisan whose ambition is not to write a masterpiece of theatre or create sophisticated arguments for a certain point of view but to tell a story that is pertinent, engaged in the politics of the people of its time, and entertaining to the spectator.

Naive was not synonymous with uninformed. The troupe began to take courses in the history of the French Revolution as well as to read histories and original texts of the time. Members of the troupe were surprised to discover how little they actually did know about the revolution and particularly about the economic and political realities that brought the revolution to an end with the bourgeoisie coming into power. The readings and lectures by experts provided substance to the troupe's ideological predisposition, identifying with the struggle of the people, the dispossessed, the poor. There was also the recent memory of the events of May 1968, with all those achievements and disillusionments, which influenced their view of the revolution of 1789. The full title of the Soleil's piece on the beginnings of the French Revolution became *1789: la révolution doit s'arrêter à la perfection du bonheur* (1789: The revolution must stop when complete happiness is achieved, 1970). The implication was that the revolution was still in fact going on or at least needed to be continued until happiness for all had been achieved. The troupe read the works of Michelet, Jaurès, Lefèbre, Soboul, Massin and the documents of the period. They saw popular films on the subject: the melodramas *La Marseillaise* by Jean Renoir, *Napoleon* by Abel Gance, *Orphans of the Storm* by D.W. Griffith. They worked on a variety of presentational forms: farce, debate, speechmaking, allegory, opera, marionettes. In July 1970, they began to rehearse at the Palace of Sports where the city of Paris rented them a space for a nominal fee, which was still, however, financially challenging, as the company was severely in debt at the time.

The troupe's process was to break into groups of four or five and work on various chosen moments of the revolution through improvisation, often all the diverse groups working on the same scene, which they would then present to each other for comparison. Members of the groups would rotate every few hours to keep the process fluid. Often, to begin with, a group would approach a theme as an elementary history book might or as a fabulous tale. From the first version, others would emerge. More than a thousand improvisations were recorded, though only a small percentage of the improvisations ever made it into the final performance. By performance time, it was impossible to say who had created which part. Final decisions on scenes were discussed collectively. In general, therefore, divisiveness was overcome and a new sense of collective adventure established.

The subject of the improvisation was usually suggested by Mnouchkine and then the groups would go off to work on the theme, using various forms such as fairy tales, *commedia dell'arte*, storytelling, clowning, puppets, etc., as inspiration in creating theatrical moments. Mnouchkine's role was to push the actors past their limits: stimulating their imaginations, pointing out where they fell into the traps of cliché or creating 'slice of life' rather than theatre, maintaining rigour in the process.

One scene, which was to become the highlight of *1789* when performed, gave the troupe the most difficulty in improvisation. The taking of the Bastille was fundamental to any telling of the story of the French Revolution by the people. In their first attempts, the troupe tried to re-enact the actual taking of the Bastille as a group of actor-acrobats might do at the fairgrounds; the goal was to find out who could tell the most terrifying version. The group soon realized that trying to illustrate the event seemed to trivialize it; something epic was needed. After several weeks of rehearsal and abortive attempts, a sense of defeat pervaded the troupe. Mnouchkine suggested that, as an exercise, the troupe divide into small groups of three or four and tell the story of the taking of the Bastille as if they were telling it to children, without any political interpretation. This exercise was then repeated as if they were telling the same story to adults, but keeping a clear simple approach. This method allowed the actors to feel the excitement of the people as they recounted the story: 'it is the first time that the people have overcome their fear, spoken up and felt their victory deeply'.[45]

The designer planned the dimensions of the set around the size and shape of a basketball court as *1789* could not be done in a conventional theatre space, and most towns had a basketball court, so it seemed logical that they would have no trouble finding a place to perform. As in previous productions, costumes were worn from day one of rehearsal while continuing to evolve. Actors created their costumes in conjunction with the design team. At performance time, the costumes had the natural look of clothes worn daily, accentuated by exaggerated details to emphasize the social, political or mythological aspects of the character; that is, the nobility wore larger than life, extravagantly plumed hats to accentuate their excess and decadence. The make-up was mask-like in intensity with most actors in whiteface as a base. The fiendish quality of the ruling classes was emphasized by giving them an almost vampire-like appearance: black around the eyes and blood red lips. Sometimes the aristocracy was portrayed with clownish faces suggesting stupidity or decadence. The poverty and hunger of the peasants was dramatized by dark accentuation under their eyes.

The troupe began improvisations in May 1970, and by August of that year, they had six hours of performable material. The decision was made to divide it into two different productions. *1789* began with the plight of the peasants and the List of Grievances of 8 August 1788 and ended with martial law and words from Marat. The later production, *1793* (1972) began with the fall of the monarchy in July 1792 and ended with prohibition of all direct democratic action on the part of the people by the Comité de Salut Public in 1793. That summer the troupe, in grave financial difficulty, was offered La Cartoucherie as a place to rehearse for a nominal fee. The troupe began looking for a place to perform and was surprised to find that no one seemed willing to take on this unorthodox project. Finally, Paolo Grassi, director of the Piccolo Theatre of Milan (where the Soleil had toured *The Kitchen* and *Les Clowns*), offered the troupe the possibility of putting on the production in Palalido, a giant sports arena in Milan.

1789 premiered in Milan on 12 November 1970 to exceptional reviews and an enthusiastic audience, numbering up to 2,000 per performance. On returning to Paris, the troupe was offered a three-year lease of the Cartoucherie and decided to present *1789* there. The actors set themselves to renovating the space to accommodate the production.[46] On 25 December 1970, a very cold winter day, *1789* opened at the unheated Cartoucherie. The production was a sensation, the audiences braving the freezing weather to stand for over two hours and relive the story of the French Revolution. A free performance for students led to a thirty-minute celebration by the audience at the scene of the taking of the Bastille.[47]

1789 was the culmination of a phase for the Soleil in its practice towards developing a populist theatre. It was Brechtian in form, with a series of episodes re-examining, through the eyes of *the people*, the French Revolution and its ultimate co-option by the bourgeoisie. It was Artaudian in its staging: an immersive experience with the action surrounding and moving through the audience. *1789* brought international prominence to the company, and the production toured to London, Berlin, Martinique, Lausanne and Belgrade as well as to several cities in France. Over 280,000 spectators saw *1789*. Critics were also, for the most part, highly enthusiastic. The general consensus was that the Théâtre du Soleil had succeeded in creating a genuine moment of popular theatre. One critic described *1789* as: 'The pleasure of participating in a great collective emotion',[48] and another as one of the few examples of contemporary '*théâtre populaire*'.[49]

However, not everyone was fully convinced. An article in *France Nouvelle* criticized the play as being without ambiguity and bewitching like a rock concert. It further stated that though it was artistically extraordinary, it should be condemned as 'hypnosis and collective intoxication'.[50] Georges Conchon agreed that *1789* was neither Georg Büchner nor Bertolt Brecht, but added in defence of the exuberant audience that 'the great talent of Ariane Mnouchkine is in making her public happy'.[51] Marc-Antoine Muret saw the production as biased towards a Maoist interpretation of the French Revolution.[52] *1789* became one of the major theatrical events to emerge from May 1968 and was under scrutiny not only for its theatrical value but also for its political stance. One of the major critiques haunting the Soleil yet again was the issue of the text. Alfred Simon saw the lack of quality text as the limit of collective creation.[53] The British playwright Arnold Wesker – author of *The Kitchen*, produced by the Soleil as *La Cuisine* in 1967 – took issue with the interpretation of the French Revolution by the troupe:

> This tendency for the left wing to oversimplify in the hope of commanding the greatest mass attention in the quickest possible way always boomeranged, and that in itself is why revolutions have failed. You can't teach the bourgeoisie is all bad and then expect people to trust or listen to intellectuals. Lenin, Castro, and Marx [Mnouchkine by implication] are products of the bourgeoisie.[54]

The critic Kenneth Tynan took issue with Wesker, saying that collective creation is what was needed to get away from the individualistic psychology that was the result of a single playwright.[55] Mnouchkine's response to Wesker: 'the bourgeois theatre has already done justice enough to the complexity of the situation and the good side of the bourgeoisie'. As to the simplicity of the play, Mnouchkine countered with: 'We made the play as simple as we could. We think it is not simple enough.'[56] She also acknowledged that the desire to reach the working class was an 'abstract ideal' but that it would not hurt for the bourgeoisie to witness the play. She emphasized that within the bourgeoisie there was a split between youth and their elders. The fact was that the audience for *1789* was mostly students and intellectuals from the bourgeois class. Mnouchkine had in the past already questioned the power of the theatre to inspire the working class, which was focused on its jobs, family and immediately accessible entertainment and sports provided by television and the cinema.[57] The issue of the playwright versus collective creation has continued to challenge the Soleil over the last forty years. And Mnouchkine has pursued her experiments with various dramaturgical and theatrical approaches, seeking in each production to find a method that will assure an effective theatricalization of the issues and stories while providing that ever elusive 'quality' text.

The search for an author: Collective creation, Shakespeare and Cixous

The next project, *L'Age d'or* (Golden Age, 1975), was a collaborative creation focused on the contemporary exploitation of émigré workers in France. *Commedia dell'arte* and Asian masks were used to theatricalize the piece. Various power dynamics within the troupe, the stress of the company's struggles to realize the work, both financially and collaboratively, resulted in a conflict-filled rehearsal process, and Mnouchkine briefly considered leaving the company. Though in general well attended and positively reviewed, *Golden Age*[58] faced similar critiques about the weakness of collaboratively created texts. Mnouchkine turned to a film project on Molière (1977)[59] to redirect the focus of the company and resorted to her own writing skills, which she continued with *Méphisto* (1979), an adaptation of Klaus Mann's novel about the impact of the rise of Hitler on German theatre-makers: a text that was more nuanced, complex and realist. But ultimately Mnouchkine was not content. She went 'back to school' by putting on a series of Shakespeare plays, which she translated, hoping to glean some insight into the poetic nature of his works. Mnouchkine turned to Asian theatrical traditions to overcome the tired approaches dominating Shakespeare productions, and the Soleil's international reputation for its outstanding *mise en scène* grew as their Shakespeare productions were universally admired for their athletic theatricality.[60]

Since the Shakespeares, Mnouchkine has engaged Hélène Cixous, the French feminist writer, to create various plays in collaboration with the company: *L'Histoire terrible mais inachevée de Norodom Sihanouk, roi de Cambodge* (The Terrible but Unfinished Story of Norodom Sihanouk, King of Cambodia, 1985), *Indiade, or the India of Their Dreams* (1987),[61] *Tambours sur la digue* (Drums on the Dike, 1999), and *Les Naufragés du Fol Espoir* (The Castaways of the Fol Espoir, 2010), among other pieces. The hope was that Cixous's style would enhance the literary quality of their collaborative efforts. Cixous's lyrical texts, often descriptive and sometimes tending towards the didactic – when supported by Mnouchkine's bold visuals and Lemêtre's underscoring – intensified the melodramatic nature of the work. Cixous shares Mnouchkine's valuing of emotions in the moral evolution of the human being and provides strong moments such as Gandhi's conversation with his deceased wife Kasturbai in *L'Indiade*, in which the power of his grief leads to renewed action. Cixous excels at intimate expressions. However, Cixous's poetic verbal embellishment, when paired with the style of delivery by the actors, with its emphasis on the passions, tends to keep the text at a singularly intense level, preventing nuanced poetic sensibilities from showing through. Though the language of previous texts by the Soleil had been dismissed by critics as too pedestrian, their simplicity and rawness was perhaps more suited to the overt visual and musical theatricality of Mnouchkine's staging and its populist flavour. Whereas understatement can be as powerful as overt assertions, as demonstrated in the work of Brecht, Mnouchkine's favouring of *les grandes passions* categorically eliminates subtleties.

The classics and the contemporary

Mnouchkine takes up the classics, intermittently, as a way of renewing her understanding of the principles of theatre. In 1992, the Soleil performed its highly successful productions of Euripides' *Iphigenia at Aulis* (see Figure 3.5) and the three tragedies of Aeschylus' *Oresteia* as a cycle under the umbrella title *House of Atreus*.[62]

In these, Mnouchkine was able to focus her prodigious energies on the *mise en scène*, using the full force of Jean-Jacques Lemêtre's musical talents to capture the emotional fervour of the choral dances, so often tepidly performed in contemporary productions. The athleticism, passionate energy and synchronous quality of the dances brought the Greek plays to life but strained the abilities of the actors, forcing Mnouchkine to add dancers to the company.

Mnouchkine then set her sights on contemporary issues with *La Ville parjure ou le réveil des Erinyes* (The Perjured City, or The Awakening of the Furies, 1994) about the infamous incident in France where

FIGURE 3.5 *The Théâtre du Soleil presented* Iphigénie at Aulis *by Euripides in 1990 as a prelude to Aeschylus'* Oresteia *trilogy. Elements of Asian theatre are evident in the chorus costumes and dance movements. © Martine Franck/Magnum Photos (Magnum PAR87407).*

AIDS-contaminated blood was knowingly distributed in transfusions to haemophiliacs. Mnouchkine's staging was unusually monochrome with a cemetery/necropolis at the centre of the play. The focus on the Furies (a holdover from *Les Euménides* of *House of Atreus*) and on characters that were grotesque stereotypes seemed more Grand Guignol than melodrama or civic theatre. Cixous's text included a lengthy trial scene, which felt interminable. It was the first time that the Théâtre du Soleil received across-the-board weak reviews and low audience attendance as compared to previous productions. Mnouchkine and Cixous's efforts at political theatre were characterized as 'pomposity, caricature and emotional manipulation' by John Rockwell of the *New York Times*.[63]

Mnouchkine returned to the classics with Molière's *Tartuffe* (1995) set in an Islamic household, which brought the audience back to the Cartoucherie. This was followed by *Et soudais des nuits d'éveil* (And Suddenly, Nights of Awakening, 1997) about Tibetan refugees. Mnouchkine seemed to be moving from one political issue to another, relying on her theatrical virtuosity to enliven what was seen as yet another production one critic termed 'heavy handed didacticism'.[64]

Coup de théâtre: Drums on the Dike

It was with the production of *Drums on the Dike* in 1999 that Mnouchkine discovered a new radical approach to the *mise en scène*, a *coup de théâtre* that led to a new masterpiece. Cixous wrote a parable on human avarice and environmental destruction set in a town in ancient China threatened by flooding, based on the environmental disaster of China's Three Gorges Dam. In rehearsal Mnouchkine suggested that the actors, as an exercise, play it as puppets in order to 'escape realism' at the start of the process. It became clear to the company that this technique helped the actors avoid 'mundane, prosaic gestures' allowing for greater poetry and theatricality.[65] And so the company determined to perform the piece as if the actors were *bunraku* puppets supported by other actors in the roles of the puppeteers. This approach suggested a people moved about by forces beyond their control. The physical virtuosity, the precision of gestures achieved by the actors creating the movement of *bunraku* puppets, as well as the aesthetic realization of the *bunraku*-styled costumes – in which the facial masks strikingly enhanced the illusion that the audience was watching puppets – were outstanding.[66] This melodramatic parable with its didactic storytelling suited the ingenuous quality of the puppet format. Traditional Korean drumming by puppet-actors, serving as a warning system heralding the upcoming floods, enhanced the dramatic power of the story, while the scenic use of water – both through the employment of fabric and then, at the end, using real water in the tradition of Vietnamese water puppets – provided memorable images. Naive appropriation of another culture's forms? For Mnouchkine, her understanding of traditional art forms and her embrace of learning traditions in Asian theatre put a premium on imitation as a path towards mastery of the craft. Asian theatre scholars and artists have had varying responses from appreciation to dismay with regard to such imitations. Mnouchkine is no different from most artists of her calibre: highly intelligent, rigorous and interested in the culture of the other, yet aware of the difference between admiration and mastery. However, she is not immune to making assumptions and applying her Franco-Western values onto the other. Mnouchkine embodies the intersection of Modernism and Postmodernism; she thinks in terms of universal values but creates work that continually forces her, and us for that matter, to confront the limits of those values. There are always liabilities in replicating the cultural heritage of the other, no matter how brilliant, and yet there is always the potential for greater understanding of the other and ultimately for some degree of self-transcendence in the effort.

Looking for utopia

Four years later, after extensive touring and making a film of *Drums on the Dike*, the Soleil created *Le Dernier Caravansérail* (2003) based on interviews with political refugees. *Le Dernier Caravansérail* demonstrated how the utopian hopes and aspirations of those seeking a better existence were continually crushed by the brutality of ruthless politics and unending poverty. *Le Dernier Caravansérail*[67] is a relentless depiction of human suffering as men, women and children endure oppressive governments, wars, the dangers surrounding attempts at escape, including falling into new bondage through the sex trade, continuing poverty, and the no man's land of refugee camps, effectively bringing to light the lives of millions across the globe who have been forced to leave their homes. Performed in 2003, it turned out to be a prescient warning about the political realities of Europe in 2015. The scenic device in *Le Dernier Caravansérail*, that of having the actors make their entrances and exits standing on small dollies pushed by fellow actors, continued the theme of the characters' vulnerability to the political realities over which they have no control, as portrayed in *Drums on the Dike*.

In their next creation, *Les Ephémères* (2006),[68] the Soleil turned inward and created their most intimate production yet, based on personal stories of encounters and tragedies told by members of the troupe. The audience sat on both sides of the stage area, on steep risers, as if in a medical theatre observing an autopsy, easily visible to one another. The actors and scenes were brought in on revolving platforms which were pushed on and off through side curtains by other actors who would slowly and continuously revolve the scene before the audience, providing changing perspectives. The music was contemporary, and the Soleil again found a passionate international audience.

The Soleil's 2010 production of *The Castaways of the Fol Espoir*[69] examines the struggle between obsession for material wealth and humanity's aspirations towards a socialist-inspired utopia. It was adapted from a posthumously published novel by Jules Verne, concerning an anarchist doctor who lives in self-imposed exile among indigenous people at the ends of the earth in Tierra del Fuego and his encounter with a group of Europeans who become shipwrecked on a nearby island. The Soleil's text, written by Hélène Cixous in collaboration with the actors, focuses on a group of socialist film-makers on the eve of the First World War, trying to finish a film based on the members of the shipwreck comprised of migrants, utopian socialists, convicts and a magnate obsessed with wealth, whose weak brother and opera-singer wife join him on this ill-fated journey.

Encounters between the indigenous inhabitants, preyed upon by bounty hunters, and Europeans, who try to help them, form the core of the story, told in a fairy tale manner through the silent movie by the socialist film-makers. The play suggests nostalgia for a time before the First World War, when the world was full of idealism; however, as soon as the shipwrecked party tries to establish a utopian society, the fabric of the community begins to unwind. The final image rests on a European hero standing in a boat paddled by his seated indigenous friend, leading the remaining idealists to a more hopeful future and reciting the following text: 'In these dark days, we have a mission to bring to vessels, adrift in the night, the unrelenting glimmer of a lighthouse.' For postcolonial observers, this image is dismaying and reminiscent of the imperialist concept of the 'white man's burden'. This is something that Mnouchkine, in her own mission to save the oppressed of the world, tends to cultivate, albeit unconsciously, as she holds to a confidence in her own guardianship of the disenfranchised, a confidence that has undeniably allowed her to bring a real degree of sustenance to those touched by her humanitarian vision.

The Soleil's next project continues Mnouchkine's nomadic wanderings. This time the Soleil returns to India for inspiration; according to the promotional blurb by Hélène Cixous, the theme concerns a poor theatre troupe that despairs of achieving their goal to be 'resolutely contemporary and political'[70] in the face of seemingly insurmountable upheavals. Mnouchkine is now seventy-seven years old and continues, unfazed, her quest in partnership with the Soleil, for that elusive utopia that fuels the engine of her aspirations and imagination.

4

Ariane Mnouchkine's Théâtre du Soleil: Inside-Out

Emilie Gruat

August 2002, 9.00 am. The sun was already high above Paris, while about 500 theatre artists gathered at the Théâtre du Soleil to attend a fifteen-day workshop offered by Ariane Mnouchkine. A kind of curiosity, mingled with some awe and perhaps a little excitement, filled the air: how would this great director proceed to have everyone participate? Which 'tools' would be used? How to make sure that 'She' noticed such and such? How to be 'brilliant'?

On the second day of the workshop, it was clear: Ariane already knew everyone's first names, and the focus was not on 'succeeding' but on entering the stage, and on 'trying'; that is, on trying to approach the truth and to reveal, through one's acting, *something* about the world we lived in, about humanness, about humanity as a whole and about human beings as individuals.

During the workshop, Ariane proposed that we work from newspapers on contemporary issues, and from books, either provided by the company or by us. No pre-given dramatic texts were used to rehearse; in fact, there were no rehearsals, but discussions with other actors, in groups, on 'visions' (ideas for improvisations) which each group would then improvise together on stage before Ariane. Beyond that: nothing. Nothing was provided as the

---

All translations are by the author of this article.

right tools and skills for us to 'go on stage, enter, and try'. Nothing, except one's breath, awareness and others.

'God is in details,' Ariane kept repeating. 'Come on, come on, be still inside, put your ego aside, just receive, and if you don't feel anything, then, keep still, and do nothing ... breathe! Just be, all right?' Simple: to *just be*'. On stage. After entering. Indeed, at the Théâtre du Soleil, to enter the stage – which was, and still is, regarded and approached as a sacred space watched over by 'the Gods of theatre' – meant everything. So entering was like passing through fire. Besides, Ariane made it clear when one failed to do so: a distinct 'out!' echoed from the tiers, from where she saw everything. So how to prepare well in order to enter and pass through that 'fire'?

After discussing the terms of a vision and its improvised canvas with other actors in groups, each of us had to find the proper costume(s) and make-up. Hundreds of costumes were at hand, and costume designers were present to advise us. As for make-up, some permanent actors of the company helped us and, if necessary, made us up. Then, we each had to talk with the musician to give him an idea of the canvas of the improvisation at stake, so he too might improvise along with the actors.

During the workshop, some actors jumped or shouted on stage, because they wanted to make sure that 'She' noticed their talent. But 'Her' reaction to that was:

> Who do you think you are? You're doing nothing here, you just show me how well you play the actor. But that's not the point here. You don't get it. I don't care about what you think you know, I want to see some part of the unknown. Come on, don't make us lose our precious time. A thousand eyes are watching you and waiting to get their turn on stage, so cut out any attempt at making some effect, or having success.

Inside the company

Late summer 2002. A letter from the Théâtre du Soleil: 'Please come back at this date in October. You are one of the seventy actors that Ariane wants to work with again, for another workshop/audition.' It was my dream to enter the company, but I had never thought that, in fact, the workshop in August was an early audition. Of course, I went back to the Théâtre du Soleil in October, as invited by the letter. I didn't know what I was expected to do, or what role I would eventually perform. Ariane wanted to see how she could integrate new actors into the company, so she paid attention to our acting and to how we interacted with other team members and actors. This audition process lasted for about a month. At the end of each week, she received us – the seventy she had selected – one by one in the kitchen of the theatre, and she either said 'goodbye' or explained what she needed to see during the following week. Finally, her words, at the very end of the last week: 'Welcome to the Théâtre du Soleil.'

On the first official day of the rehearsal of *Le Dernier Caravansérail* (The Last Caravanserai), Ariane's new project, the company was finally constituted, welcoming eleven new members carefully selected during the workshop. However, to start to rehearse meant first to 'honour' and please 'the gods of theatre', so they might grant auspiciousness and success to the project at hand. Consequently, the first four days of rehearsal were actually days of deep and intense cleaning of the entire theatre: from the tiers to the kitchen, from the 'room of the Buddha' – left from a past production, where the walls were covered with painted Buddhas, and where the future performance was to be set – to the offices. Cleaning was also carried out from the costume warehouse to the crafting and design studio; and from what would become the 'hosting' room – the foyer where the public ate and chatted together with the artists after the performance – to the stage. Nothing was left unpolished. Then, the entire company gathered again to prepare the spirit of the whole company with a short time of togetherness and hopeful celebration: Ariane, the actors, the cooks, the people in the offices, the technicians, the lighting designers, the costume designers and the painters.

At that meeting, Ariane announced the theme of *The Last Caravanserai* in detail: what was at the time called 'the refugees crisis' in the media, which in fact was a worldwide, ever-flowing movement of people trying to escape war zones and save their lives. This situation started in France in 2001, where large numbers of people in need of help and shelter arrived and where, at times, racism and prejudices prevailed over kindness and compassion. With the information offered by Ariane, the actors could know and respect their improvisational frameworks, fields of investigations and improvised propositions on stage.

Ariane asked the actors to prepare and propose as many improvisations as possible. Their work had to investigate and try to answer the following questions: Who exactly were these people? What did their lives look like in their home countries? How to help them and integrate them at best? How to ease the rising local and patriotic tensions? Then, what was the nature of the latter? To what extent did it affect the overall mindset of Western Europeans? Was there any possible way out? Since, at the Théâtre du Soleil, theatre was the 'Art of the Present' and of Compassion, how to use everyone's creativity to reveal and shed light on, and learn from, this particular moment in human history? How to incarnate and become on stage the refugees?

Discovering true stories

While some members of the company went on preparing the space, others travelled to a refugee camp in Sangatte, in northern France, where most of the refugees – mainly coming from Africa, Eastern Europe or the Middle East – had settled and tried to reach England through local smugglers.

Meetings and interviews with the smugglers, the refugees, the volunteers and doctors took place to collect comprehensive and accurate material for the rehearsal. A year before, Ariane and Shaghayegh Beheshti, one of the actors, had also carried out some interviews and taken pictures in Sydney, Auckland and Mataram, in Lombok, Indonesia. *The Last Caravanserai* was born out of all these stories, which may be regarded as 'heroic myths of our times' and were used as sources of inspiration. Sometimes, they were adapted to respect and preserve the identity of their owners by the actors when developing their improvisations. The following are some examples of characters created by the actors:

Hapali, *an Indonesian sailor, who transported refugees towards Australia aboard his tiny craft.*

Olia, *a young Russian refugee arrived in Sangatte with her mother, who prostituted Olia to get a place in Timour's cabin. Timour was a refugee from Kurdistan. Olia reached England without her mother, who sacrificed herself to let her daughter travel first.*

Parviz, *an Iranian refugee in Sangatte, who had one of his legs caught and cut in half by a train when he tried to jump aboard a train towards England.*

Julia, *a prostitute at a bus stop in Sangatte, who had arrived from Serbia after being kidnapped during her sister's wedding (in fact, a fake one) and transported inside a merchandise truck for trafficking. She was under the authority and good will of Yosco and Misha, both of them pimps, smugglers and dealers, respectively from Serbia and Russia, who constantly argued and fought over their 'properties' and 'territories' until Misha 'got rid' of Yosco. Julia firmly decided to break off her situation and to try her chance to get to England. Thanks to the help and friendship of Kourosh, an Iranian refugee, she succeeded.*

'Baba-Jun', *an Afghan film-lover, who had left his country, travelled with, and took care of, Leyli, the daughter of his best friend Azizulah. The latter was shot by the Taliban for watching* The Night of the Hunter *with Leyli.*

Solange, *a nurse in Sangatte, whose infirmary was in a small cabin, inside the refugee camp, and who worked days and nights with Chantal, her colleague, and various team members, some volunteers, others not, such as Dalia. Refugees came and went to and from Solange's office for all kinds of reasons: to get injuries treated, to obtain medicines, to chat, to confide in one of the members of the crew, to share memories or even to get an arbitrator or a mediator to lessen a conflict.*

Fawad and Azadeh, *Afghan lovers, whose relationship was violently broken by the Taliban: they kidnapped Azadeh and later hanged her.*

Michele and her colleagues, *security agents at Eurotunnel:*[1] *in charge of checking the railroad tracks and the tunnel's surroundings. They had to look for refugees who were ready to grasp onto the bottom of a train or a truck, or to hide inside the latter. When they found someone, they pulled that person out of the tracks, violently if necessary, and brought him or her back to the camp.*

A female refugee from Nigeria, *removed from a plane ready to take off, and mistreated and asphyxiated by agents at a French airport.*

Moussa, *an amateur smuggler, in Sangatte, who knew all the tricks to avoid spending money, such as using a teaspoon instead of a telephone card at a phone booth. He regularly sent money to his family in Africa.*

Lieutenant Duffy, *an Australian flight agent working in a harness fastened to the bottom of a helicopter, who was in charge of preventing the refugees' boats from reaching the coast, while allegedly making sure that no one was hurt.*

Some books[2] and materials were also collected. Poems or words written on the walls of the camp or elsewhere were regarded as precious poetic and societal 'symptoms' reflecting the crisis of the early twenty-first century. They served the creation and provided a wide imaginary dramaturgical landscape to the actors and the team working on *The Last Caravanserai*. The following exemplifies some of this written data:

'Many countries pretended that it was not allowed for their citizens to leave the country where they were born by chance. Clearly, the meaning of this law is: this country is bad and so poorly governed, that it's forbidden to any individual to leave, for fear that everyone else might leave too. Do better: provide all your subjects with the desire to remain at home, and all foreigners with the desire to come.'[3]

'What is to love?
It is to give up oneself.
It is to reveal, without any words, the secret of the two worlds.
It is, as a butterfly faced with the fire of Love,
To express one's manifest state
Through a secret gesture.'[4]

'My dear mother, please forgive me for abandoning you. I took all my desires with me and I left you all my pains.'[5]

'This is not my home.'[6]

'Is this the longest night? (Winter Solstice) Far from you, my eyes are without light.'[7]

'I arrived in Callas until the day of Tuesday 12/13/2001. I was here, four times, I tried to pass, I have succeeded not. With Abdullah, I wish you well, your brother, I am from village.'[8]

'When will I pass?'[9]

'Oh! (or alas!) we made a mistake, we set a trap for ourselves
We lost ourselves
We destroyed our house with our hands
We became griefs for our mothers, our fathers, our relatives.'[10]

'In August [2001], 438 people, mostly Afghan, were the first among more than 2,500 to be forbidden their right to seek asylum in Australia. They were rescued by the crew of the Norwegian freighter *Tampa* off the coast of the Australian Island Christmas, while the Indonesian boat which transported them was sinking. The Indonesian and the Australian authorities forbade them to draw alongside, and they spent eight days aboard *Tampa* in dire conditions [despite Captain Ronin's efforts]. The Australian government prohibited access on-board to a medical crew sent by Doctors Without Borders to provide humanitarian care. After launching a distress signal because of the rescued ones' health problems – some of whom were threatening to throw themselves overboard if they were sent back to Indonesia – then, *Tampa* ... headed towards Christmas Island, without any authorization from Australia. Members of the Australian armed forces went on board, before transferring the shipwrecked to an improvised detention center in Nauru, a remote insular State in South Pacific. In October, 131 of these people flew to New Zealand, which had offered the right of residency to the ones considered as refugees.'[11]

'You will abandon all the things you like the most: that's the first sting you get in exile. You will taste how bitter the others' bread is, and how hard the way which leads you to go up and down the stairs of others.'[12]

'Only now, the exiled may choose to become the gravedigger of lost ages. Then, he may say anything he wants about calamities, because no one is interested by the chant of epic poems, and by birds landing after the Deluge.'[13]

'That's Spring. Here, leaves grow on branches; but in my country, the trees have lost theirs under the hail of the enemies' bullets.'
'You were hidden behind the door; I was massaging my naked breast, and you caught sight of me.'[14]

'I am coming back from the land which is indifferent to thoughts, words, and sounds; and this land resembles the nests of snakes; and this land is full of the noise of the steps of those, who, while they kiss you, weave the future rope of your hanging in their mind.'[15]

'Such as caravans on roads, accidents, slavery, the misfortunes of nations will come and go; the world is a garden set apart, people are flowers; Oh, how many violets and roses will come and go.'[16]

Shaping the production

Hélène Cixous didn't write the final text of this creation, but she wrote many essays about its theme, attended some rehearsals, gave recommendations to actors and listened to them, and as already mentioned, she helped shape and create the final programme of *The Last Caravanserai*. Sometimes, she also came about twenty minutes before the beginning of the performance for a ritual usually held by Ariane at the very back of the dressing room, where actors were all gathered together. There, as Ariane would do, she talked to them, sometimes about political issues, sometimes about social ones, or sometimes she even read a poem or two, or a text, or even a philosophical essay – to stir and set the actors' concentration, engagement and focus.

Which form to use to transcribe best the trajectories and various paths and movements of refugees? How to also include the worldwide aspect of these cultural, societal and political transitions and mutations? Indeed, some of the refugees had travelled as long as six years before reaching France: leaving Afghanistan, then heading to Russia, and passing through Austria, Germany or Italy. They took risks and lived in dire conditions. They never settled; they always remained on the lookout, ready to flee, to hide and, at times, to die, in order not to return to their native lands.

Ariane had envisioned a way to keep the kinetic energy and flow at stake: she summoned the company and explained that the actors would not put a step on the stage, but instead, would enter, act and leave the stage standing on rolling platforms – later called 'chariots' (trolleys), resembling skateboards – and that they would be pushed and propelled forward by other actors. As for the sets, she also insisted that they be built on larger platforms – manipulated by actors – which would mirror well the movement of coming and going of the refugees and of never remaining in one place for an extended amount of time. These larger rolling platforms would act a bit like catalysts, or atoms, pulling in and drawing out living and vibrating particles and fragments of energy: the refugees/actors/characters.

The rehearsal period lasted about eight months. In the early phase of the work, the schedule spread over four or five days a week, from Monday to Thursday or Friday; after four months, over seven days a week. Every day, the company gathered at 8.30 am in the kitchen of the Théâtre du Soleil for a quick breakfast meeting during which the exact organization of the day was set. Usually, mornings were devoted to doing gentle breathing and stretching exercises, and crafting and preparing some propositions for improvisations. Lunch took place sometime between noon and 2.30 pm and never lasted more than forty-five minutes. Then, after deciding the order of the improvisations, about two hours were devoted to putting on costume(s) and make-up, to finalize/build the set needed, to find the right trolleys, to find available pushers and to talk to the musician. During the rest of the afternoon, Ariane watched the improvisations and either started to finesse specific points and validate (momentarily, or not) the scene or rejected it. By 6.00 or 7.00 pm, if it was clear that the day wouldn't end before 11.00 pm or midnight, everyone took a short snack/rest time, after which more improvisations were presented to the rest of the actors – who also gave feedback – and Ariane, and reworked or not.

During the rehearsal period, as soon as a team of actors came up with a potential scene, they joined the technicians either to give them a design of how they saw their set or perhaps to simply build it. Usually, the technicians built the cabin and trolleys, and the actors shaped the latter as they needed, according to the content of their improvisations. Of course, because *The Last Caravanserai* was inspired by and grounded in the real world, much attention was given to detail, so the sets would seem to be almost perfect reproductions of reality. For instance, when the set represented a refugees' cabin at Sangatte, technicians and actors would use pictures of real ones and try to copy the aspect of a real cabin precisely: Which pictures to hang on walls? Was/were there (a) mirror(s)? What did the bed(s) look like? Was it a mixed or unisex cabin? Were there various nationalities living together? Was there a 'dominant' person 'ruling' a cabin? What was the colour of the sheets, blankets and curtains? Were there bags under the beds? Would the refugees hide things somewhere? Was the cabin clean? Eventually, when seeing and working on an improvisation, Ariane suggested or asked to design/put more elements in the set – for instance, in Timour's cabin, where Olia is prostituted, an old radio set.

Refining the performance

When the second phase of rehearsals began, the scenes were chosen and put together. Then, it became a matter of precisely refining them, so they would seem real, true and revelatory. Each movement (the actors and the trolleys) of a given scene was reviewed by Ariane, who asked us to let go of how we had first imagined the action of our scenes. For instance, for one of the scenes of the prostitute Julia in the bus stop in Sangatte, a role I played among others, Ariane asked me to avoid crying or acting fully the harshness of the situation (see Figure 4.1).

Indeed, Ariane insisted on the strength of Julia's character. I had to be very careful not to let myself be drawn by emotion; I had to play something counterbalancing and hopeful to make sure that the revelatory aspect of the scene would remain – she knew that the scene was already hard in itself and that the public would receive it with deep emotion anyway. She also felt that the scene would become more powerful if there were more characters coming in and out of the bus stop. Consequently, she asked two actors and one actress to propose some characters, and that's how – on top of the pimps, the man trying to make a phone call, and Julia – Cathy (the wandering woman), Moussa and Kourosh were created.

Moreover, we were also advised and trained by a team of physiotherapists, who taught us how to stand and move smoothly on the rolling platforms, especially on the individual ones, where it was hard, at first, to find balance and to remain centred enough to act. They taught us specific exercises of strength training (abdominal, flexibility of the knees and ankles, deep breathing) and of core stabilization. Eventually, actors pushing and manoeuvring the sets were called 'pushers', and before proposing their scenes, actors involved on stage carefully shared with them the specific canvas of their improvisation(s), so 'pushers' could turn, move onward and backward or leave the stage when needed, and feel and pick a pace in agreement with the action at stake.

During the second phase of the rehearsals, Ariane directed the pushers too: she gave them very precise and meticulous movements, as if their trolleys were film cameras – which added another layer and perspective to *The Last Caravanserai*. The 'pushers' were also coached by physiotherapists, who taught them specific stretching and neck exercises to make sure that they wouldn't hurt themselves (their backs, knees, necks or fingers/hands, which were close to the wheels of the platforms). Consequently, they pushed the platforms with choreographic grace and full attention to the actor(s)/characters on stage and to what was going on in the scene. In fact, very much like a chorus in Greek tragedy, the pushers became mute watchmen of the actor(s)/character(s) and of the action(s).

Furthermore, it was decided that the stage and curtains would also have meaning and participate in the performance: curtains opening and closing a scene, as well as the ones at the very back of the stage, or even the curtains on each side, would be in a dark-blue silk, on which to project, before their opening and in white light, the specific dates and names of the locations of each scene. It is to be noted that the curtains were always opened according to the style of the scene they introduced: for instance, dynamically, while running, in a shaky way, or with calm and authority. These elements allowed for powerful creative freedom. In *The Last Caravanserai*, time and space weren't approached through a chronological or linear lens. What connected scenes together were the characters themselves, weaving their webs and trajectories, circulating around the world, to and through, and towards somewhere. Thus, this fragmented, brisk, rapid and fluid tempo found its unity in evasiveness and ephemerality; and silk was the ideal fabric to mirror these elements.

Sometimes, between scenes, a poem, a sort of mantra or actual texts of refugees would appear on the curtains and were echoed by a voice off-stage (either a recording of a refugee, met previously, or Ariane, or of one of the actors or team members of the company) – a bit like interludes in musical pieces to refresh the audience's attention, to layer the performance or to simply change its tone and break its rhythm. All these projections were developed through time, along with the rehearsals, and once the order of the scenes was set, their order and content were finally shaped and organized too. The projections were not meant to illustrate the actions or to break the overall intensity of the subject: even when providing a sense of lightness to the performance, they had to add a very subtle and fine layer of information, thought and truth to *The Last Caravanserai*. In any case, a sense of emergency had to prevail. This might explain perhaps the rather 'raw' aspect of the performance as when actors/characters, pushers or any team members would cross the stage running between scenes, or dancing, or even grabbing something left on stage – something having a dramaturgical meaning such as Julia's garland of flowers after the scene 'Reminiscences, Serbia'.

Silk was also used during scenes in which the action took place on the sea or on a river: actors or team members manipulated the fabric from all sides of the stage or/and from underneath by making movements resembling waves and/or by jumping, moving or dancing. The same process was used to create wind: for example, when there was wind in a scene, pushers or another team member used invisible fishing yarn to move the costumes, flags or any piece of fabric at stake. For scenes with soil or sand, the real material was used, and for snow, just sections of cotton, mingled with a bit of dirt to make it look real, or some confetti for falling snow. When needed, there was real water, quickly swept away during the interludes, or a false fire (created by a specific accessory, a light effect and real wood). Last but not least, the entire stage was painted with a silvery metallic colour, and to add an overall sense of danger and the unknown, traces or sprayings of golden orange, white and/or yellow were made here and there.

The culmination and 'birth'

How, without understanding each other by words, understanding one another by heart? How not to appropriate the others' anxiety while making theater? ... How to be as close as possible to the other's situation, without taking it? ... How to become human, that is, never enough, nor never too much? ... How to be the actor of a character, and not its master? How to let oneself be a refuge for the foreigner? How not to play any role? ... What if we don't make it? That's the refugee's question during his journey.[17]

As a company, we struggled to find a way to keep telling these stories without falling into clichés; for instance, for the actors, how to work without

FIGURE 4.1 *Emilie Gruat and Serge Nicolai in* The Last Caravanserai. © *Martine Franck/Magnum Photos (Magnum PAR243289 FRM1003005W00005/20A).*

using our regular acting skills? How to let go of what one thinks he 'has' or 'knows'? Indeed, it was quite a challenge for everyone at the Théâtre du Soleil to become almost transparent, that is, to drop all the projections or ideas we had about what was really happening in France. Our disappointment or anger about the overall social and political situation, and what it meant, about France – the alleged country of Liberty, Equality, and Freedom – as well as about the world at large, had to be entirely muted and compressed and then channelled and used to enhance the matter at stake and serve the creative process best.

Furthermore, as actors, it was quite tough not to let ourselves be haunted or overwhelmed by our characters. Their lives and concerns became ours, but at the same time, for the sake of the creation, the company and the audience, we had to ensure that, once outside the Théâtre du Soleil, we distanced ourselves enough – if possible – from them. Even if we kept thinking about them, documenting ourselves, or travelling in their countries (during time off) to learn more about their origins, it was mandatory for everyone to keep closer to sanity and hope than rage or despair.

Since *The Last Caravanserai* was created out of improvisations, Ariane insisted that very minimal language be used. The stress was put on *sensing*, rather than emoting – which systematically allowed one to speak out and express before even feeling and receiving any sensations. Whenever an actor entered the stage 'in his mind', or already full of emotion, Ariane either asked that person to get out and breathe or she guided him on stage, so he might let his ego fall and connect with his sense of universality and of humanness: 'listen inside … shush … be quiet! … if you don't feel anything, then, breathe, do nothing, *just sense*. Let *it* come, muffle your ideas on the character. Let the character talk to you and penetrate your entire self … let go of yourself.'

Moreover, while rehearsing *The Last Caravanserai*, actors totally transformed themselves. Again, attention was given to details or 'symptoms', allowing each of us to truly know our character: did the character have scars? Did he or she have obsessive compulsive disorder? How did he or she breathe? What was the colour of his or her eyes? What was his or her linguistic tone? How many times per week did he shave? What did his or her nose precisely look like? The costume designers had found and prepared many racks of casual clothes, so we could totally look like the refugees, and also work clothes such as suits or dresses. When needed, they helped the actors soil or tear an item. Specific and 'rare' items were given to the theatre. For example, an Afghan woman who lived in England came to the Théâtre du Soleil and brought burkas. She also taught all the actresses who performed Afghan characters to properly wear and move with burkas. In the end, thanks to the richness of the material at hand, while preparing and putting on make-up, we really metamorphosed into our characters; we received and let them penetrate our skins and beings too, every night or matinee, for almost three years during which *The Last Caravanserai* toured worldwide.

Since the refugees were always on the go and under pressure, the characters mostly spoke only when really needed, so, for most of the time, talking was an action moving them onwards, almost a (re-)assertion of their trajectories and destination. As a consequence, the actors remained silent as much as possible, and their bodies and faces expressed more than their voices. Words supported and propelled the overall action of the scene at stake; they were not the action itself. If there was idle conversation, Ariane would advise one to 'get out!'

In order to express the universal quality of *The Last Caravanserai*, actors had to learn a variety of bits of languages, specific words or full sentences in foreign languages. Indeed, most of the scenes were not solely in French, but in Kurdish, Dâri, Serbian, Russian, English or Persian. When on tour or when needed, translation was provided for the audience on a screen at the front of the stage. Otherwise, a blank screen would leave the audience feeling insecure, as if in a foreign land. Last but not least, live music gave rhythm to each scene and added to the atmosphere, and sometimes the musician created specific soundtracks or isolated sounds, such as a car crashing or pouring rain, to increase a feeling of reality and exactness.

At the Théâtre du Soleil, music is never used as an element of entertainment; indeed, music is always considered an element on equal standing with the actors and as a key agent of a given performance. That's why, in any creation, actors had to talk with the musician during the rehearsal, first without Ariane, to make sure to listen to each other and that neither element – the acting or the music – was more present than the other. All the key ingredients of a scene had to be and to progress in sync with one another. Even during the run of the performance, sometimes, actors and the musician discussed precise moments of the scenes and refined their relationship and interaction.

Of course, once she had seen all the scenes, reworked some and designed the shape of the overall performance, Ariane became a total conductor of both the actors and the music. For instance, she asked the musician if he could play more of one instrument and less of another, and the actors to lessen their urge to talk at a given moment of their scene. At Théâtre du Soleil, music was a partner and a language in itself, hence Ariane's incentive to speak very little on stage, to listen to music, to 'receive' it inside and to be nourished and feel supported by it, so they might give their very best to their character(s) and to each performance.

Needless to say, the work of the Théâtre du Soleil impacted and still impacts the worldwide theatre arena. *The Last Caravanserai* toured from Athens to Buenos Aires, from Taipei to New York, and from Berlin to Melbourne. Touring was always an extraordinary adventure. It involved the energy and work of 90 per cent of the company: the cooks, the technicians, some people from the office and administration, the actors, the wardrobe crew, the musician and Ariane. From the opening to the final and last performance of *The Last Caravanserai*, Ariane continued responding to the work and gave notes to everyone – about the acting, the music, the organization of the day, a specific issue/change to adapt to in a specific touring place. In fact, her notes warned never to let the transparent intensity and quality of the matter fade away.

The effect of the work of Théâtre du Soleil didn't/doesn't 'only' spread on a horizontal and contemporary scale, but on a vertical one too: through history. Indeed, the Théâtre du Soleil belongs to the worldwide sphere of history of theatre: created in 1964, it has never stopped radiating since then. Each creation is a world in itself, for which the company constantly reinvents a specific form and sets high artistic stakes: 'Remember that tonight may be the first or last time that someone attends a show ... We are here to crack hearts open ... perhaps to change one's life.' Ariane's vision and the unique quality of the work of the company seem never to stop growing and maturing. However, although many books have been written on the Théâtre du Soleil in French, too few have been translated into English, German, Spanish or any other language.

Peter Stein

5

Peter Stein: Life, Work, Art

William Grange

Peter Stein (b. 1937) is among the most honoured of German theatre directors. Over the past four decades, he has received more than thirty awards and citations for his work, including the Grand Service Cross of the Federal Republic of Germany, a Knighthood in the Legion of Honor from the French Republic, and in 2011, the French government's highest civilian honour, the Order *Pour le Mérite*. Eighteen of his productions have been invited to the Berliner Festspiele (Berlin Theatre Festival, popularly known as the *Theatertreffen* or 'theatre gathering').

Stein made his reputation as an innovative iconoclast, beginning with his first productions in Munich, followed by several noteworthy productions in Bremen, Zurich and Berlin, where the public began to identify him with a new dispensation sweeping through the rather stolid West German theatre establishment. 'The German theatre of the 1950s was just dreadful,' he once told an interviewer. 'Stupid in every sense of the word.'[1] In the late 1960s, he developed an ensemble of actors, designers, dramaturges and technicians; in 1970, he accepted the position of artistic director at the Schaubühne am Halleschen Ufer, a former workers' recreation hall in the West Berlin borough of Kreuzberg. Several observers at the time likened Stein's arrival to the blast of an oracular trumpet heralding a new age. It was not that stupendous, but with fiscal assistance from the West Berlin Senate, Stein with his colleagues opened a far more intellectual chapter in the German theatre's history.[2] With a comparatively lavish subsidy of 1.8 million Deutschmarks in 1970 (about $480,000 at the time), the Schaubühne became a destination for intellectuals, theatre devotees and culture connoisseurs throughout what was then West

Germany – and in the process cast East Berlin into the shadows. The superb theatre life of East Berlin, thanks to Bertolt Brecht (1898–1956) and his Berliner Ensemble, had been an embarrassment for West Berlin since 1954. In that year, Brecht and his productions had gained worldwide prominence by virtue of prize-winning productions. The Schaubühne by the mid-1970s became so illustrious that it far outpaced anything the East German regime could offer.

After leading the Schaubühne to its new location in the upscale Berlin borough of Wilmersdorf in 1980, Stein resigned as artistic director in 1985. He continued working at the Schaubühne as a freelance director, while winning praise and encomia for productions at the Salzburg Festival and at numerous opera houses and theatres in Europe, Great Britain, Japan, Russia and North America. Now in his eighties, Stein contents himself with occasional opera directing as well as cultivating olives, fruits, vegetables and wines on his small farm near San Pancrazio, Italy, where he has resided since the early 1990s.

Peter Stein is unusual among most German directors in that his approach to theatre and drama was fiercely intellectual and speculative. He had previously given little thought to theatre directing as a professional goal until age twenty-eight, when he began working part-time at the Munich Kammerspiele. He had enjoyed travelling throughout Europe to see certain productions, and he found Peter Brook's work in London and Giorgio Strehler's in Milan intriguing. The city whose theatre impressed him most was Paris,[3] largely because he spoke fluent French, a result of his turbulent boyhood during and after the Second World War.

Stein's early formation

Born in Berlin in 1937, Stein moved with his family in the autumn of 1945 to a village near Frankfurt, where Stein's paternal grandmother lived. Soon after their arrival, American military officials arrested Stein's father Herbert for complicity in the war effort. Though he had not been a member of the Nazi Party, a military tribunal officially designated Herbert Stein as a collaborator and sentenced him to hard labour for one year on a work gang. Peter and his mother moved to the French occupation sector near Freiburg, which allowed him finally to start school (at age nine). School officials discovered that his reading and writing abilities were already well developed, far ahead of the other pupils. At age ten, he enrolled in high school, where most of his classes were in French. At age fifteen, he transferred to the Lessing School in Frankfurt, where he found himself in classes with German army veterans in their mid- to late twenties. He rose to the top of his class and graduated in 1956 with highest honours, winning the school's Lessing Prize for best thesis by a graduating student.

Peter Stein lived at home with his parents for two unhappy years while attending university classes in Frankfurt. When he transferred in 1958 to Ludwig-Maximilian University in Munich, he fell in with a disreputable theatre crowd that, like Stein, found the study of drama a rewarding escape from what Stein described as the 'claustrophobia' of the 1950s. During those years, West Germany was devoted to rebuilding, conformity and creating 'Prosperity for All', in the jargon of Chancellor Konrad Adenauer (1876–1967) and his Economics Minster Ludwig Erhard (1897–1977). In the 1950s, Stein said, 'An open shirt collar without a necktie was an outrage, and an unclosed buttonhole the next button down signaled revolutionary tendencies.'[4] Among the fellow students whom Stein counted as friends in Munich was Dieter Giesing (b. 1934), later to become an accomplished director in Bochum, Cologne and Vienna. Giesing got Stein a job at the Munich Kammerspiele as a director's assistant in 1964, and there Stein began working with Therese Giehse and Fritz Kortner.

Therese Giehse and Fritz Kortner

Both Giehse and Kortner were German Jews who had spent the Nazi years in exile, Giehse in Switzerland and Kortner in the United States. Therese Giehse (1898–1975) settled in Zurich by 1937 as a regular member of the Zurich Schauspielhaus company, where she played the title role in the world premiere of Bertolt Brecht's *Mother Courage* in 1941. She alternated between Munich and Zurich for the rest of her career, and her successes in Zurich in the premieres of plays by Friedrich Dürrenmatt (1921–90) prompted many observers to believe she was one of the greatest actresses the German theatre had ever produced; few other actresses matched the heights Giehse attained while creating the leading roles in plays that later became famous worldwide. Her career in some ways resembled Fritz Kortner's, since both performers experienced the losses of exile, followed by triumphal rebounds in the post-war years.

Fritz Kortner (1892–1970) was among the most accomplished actors in German theatre and film during the 1920s, and in 1949, he had settled in Munich, where he began directing at the Kammerspiele. Working with him, Stein absorbed Kortner's compulsion to reform German acting. Kortner believed the Nazis had corrupted German acting almost beyond repair, noting that they encouraged *heroische Sachlichkeit* (heroic matter-of-factness) in the theatre because Adolf Hitler 'was preoccupied with heroism'.[5] Kortner observed that many actors in the Nazi years had approached 'style' completely in terms that were superficial, perhaps because Nazi ideology selectively embraced modernist tendencics such as spare stage decoration, abstract lighting and symbolic use of colour. Kortner insisted that 'Nazi theatre' may have looked modern, but it was essentially a throwback to the affectations of the court theatres, particularly in plays such as Kleist's *Der Prinz von Homburg* (The Prince of Homburg), Schiller's *Kabale und Liebe* (Intrigue and Love), and Goethe's *Faust* – plays which Stein later directed to noteworthy effect. With other student assistants, Stein found himself at the Munich Kammerspiele in a kind of three-year master class, working with both Kortner and Giehse on several productions. Among the most significant lessons he learned in those years was how to work on language with actors. 'Stage German' has been a topic to which scholars and critics have often returned in an attempt to explicate what it means, so herewith follows a brief analysis of it as a kind of *lingua franca* among German actors, much like the Meissen court usage which Martin Luther (1483–1546) selected for his translation of the New Testament in 1522. Luther believed that Meissen usage was accessible to most German speakers, many of whom could not understand each other. That difficulty continued up through the eighteenth century, when Gotthold Ephraim Lessing (1729–81), Johann Christoph Gottsched (1700–66), Karoline Neuber (1697–1760), Konrad Ernst Ackermann (1710–71) and other 'reformers' insisted on a 'supra-regional' stage idiom comprehensible among speakers of German. The result was beneficial in terms of theatricality, but 'stage German' was highly idiosyncratic. Only on the stage, many believed, did audiences encounter it; only in performance did actors use it. It was a vernacular that automatically signalled one's presence in a playhouse; under the Nazis, it decayed into a species of extravagant bombast.[6] Kortner believed that the tendency to speak lines from Goethe, Schiller, Kleist or Shakespeare (in the Schlegel-Tieck translations) as though they formed some kind of sacred text demanded mistrust, precisely because the text was considered sacred.[7]

Stein claimed that Kortner's influence on his own work as a student of directing was of paramount importance, and he especially absorbed Kortner's approach to a play's text with reverence, yet paradoxically with concomitant scepticism. Stein once said that some plays were so difficult that 'one needed a can opener to get into them',[8] and he came to realize that paradox was in fact a crucially important aspect of any director's work – especially when approaching Aeschylus, Sophocles, Euripides, Shakespeare, Goethe, Schiller, Kleist or Chekhov. Kortner taught Stein that the best way to understand and stage a play was to proceed 'from sentence to sentence', rendering every phrase more plausible, insisting that actors come to the stage with pictures in their minds' eyes, thoughts in their heads and inner responses focused on the playwright's words.[9] Critics often mistook Kortner's work as 'embellishment' of the text, but it was nothing of the kind. It was instead a revolution with Kortner himself at its forefront, 'a pioneer in the cause of a new, meaningful realism'.[10] The remainder of this chapter will address Stein's approach to and fascination with the use of language in selected productions by Aeschylus, Shakespeare, Goethe, Schiller, Heinrich von Kleist, Henrik Ibsen, Eugène Labiche, Maxim Gorky, Vsevolod Vishnevsky and Edward Bond.

Edward Bond's *Saved* in 1967

Peter Stein was Kortner's heir, and the legacy of meticulousness that Kortner bequeathed to Stein was first apparent in Stein's debut production in 1967, *Saved* by the English playwright Edward Bond (b. 1934) at the Munich Kammerspiele. Stein enhanced his endowment from Kortner by virtue of fluency in several languages, which included English. Bond's *Saved*, however, presented several problems to any director – including the man who attempted to stage its world premiere in London, William Gaskill, at the Royal Court Theatre. The Lord Chamberlain's office had banned *Saved* from both public and private performance, and the play was still forbidden in the UK when Stein's production opened in Munich. When Bond learned of Stein's plans for his play, he stated that Munich audiences would clearly understand, as their counterparts in the English government could not, and that the spectacle of stoning a baby to death in a London park during the first act was merely an example of 'typical English understatement'.[11]

Stein got permission from Kammerspiele artistic and general manager August Everding (1928–99) to commission Martin Sperr[12] (1944–2002) to translate Bond's East End patois into a comparable Bavarian vernacular, and the results won general acclaim among Munich critics and audiences. The Munich *Merkur* newspaper believed Stein's production offered 'relevance' to the anti-war, long-haired, blue-jeaned generation which was beginning to make its presence felt in West Germany. This play had nothing to do with denim fabric nor with long hair, Stein noted – though by 1967 he wore his hair shoulder-length and usually dressed in denim. 'It is simply a fantastic and magnificent play,' he said. 'And for the beginning of my career, it's a good play to do. Who else gets a chance like this? … When people complain it's all so exaggerated and serves only to show sadism and cruelty on the stage, you can always point to the real reality outside the theatre, which is much worse.'[13] The *Bayrische Staatszeitung* of Munich waxed euphoric, praising Stein's eye for detail and his 'silent tension'[14] in reference to a technique which Stein had developed in rehearsal, one which subsequently appeared in several Stein productions through the 1970s: the silent stage picture.

As Michael Patterson has pointed out, Bond wrote *Saved* with only one line of dialogue in the final scene ('Fetch me a hammer'), and Stein found staging an entire ten-minute scene around one line of dialogue irresistible.[15] It also embodied Stein's growing curiosity about how language actually functions in the theatre, and how silence is a distinctively important part of language. He began to realize that if actors spoke dialogue with unprecedented discipline, the audience would often remain solemn in anticipation, as one line unfolded from the other, and scenes grew from one to the next. The profession's monthly *Theater heute* heaped praise upon the production, its editors somewhat grandiloquently proclaiming Stein the director whom all of German theatre had awaited since the end of the Second World War. Other critics designated him as the first director to represent a generational change in German theatre. *Theater heute* also named *Saved* as its 'Production of the Year' for 1967; the Berlin *Theatertreffen* invited Stein and the show's actors to its nationwide showcase.

Stein resisted descriptions of himself as a member of a 'youth movement', but he nevertheless resolved to work only with young actors who, as he did, enjoyed rehearsing for months to refine every gesture and every utterance. Stein stated that he desired to work from 'the ground up' in the hopes of achieving a 'second natural state' when opening night arrived. Brecht had worked in a similar way, spending months in rehearsal, working with actors until he had them on the stage 'behaving like real human beings, without a trace of "acting" in their performance', said Carl Weber, one of Brecht's assistants. 'The economy of the set, of every prop used, was absolutely overwhelming to one who had seen until then only run-of-the mill and sometimes even the best German theatre. ... Brecht encouraged actors to try a multitude of little bits of business, and one actor tried thirty different ways of falling off a table.'[16] But Brecht always had a political motive in mind in his work with actors.

Schiller's *Intrigue and Love* in 1967

Soon after *Saved*, artistic and general manager of Theater Bremen Kurt Hübner (1916–2007) invited Stein to stage Schiller's *Intrigue and Love* with a relatively generous budget. It was a flattering offer, the like of which few inexperienced directors receive. The production opened in November of 1967, and the collaboration with Bremen actors proved to be fateful for all parties concerned for the next dozen years. In this production of *Intrigue and Love*, Stein began working with Edith Clever (b. 1940), Bruno Ganz (b. 1941), Michael König (b. 1947) and the actress with whom Stein became most closely associated (both professionally and personally), Jutta Lampe (b. 1943). With them, Stein discovered that there was less political intrigue than is apparent in the play's title. It is a 'middle-class tragedy' involving class distinctions between aristocrats and the middle-class courtiers who serve them. Schiller's is a realistic treatment, featuring dialogue characteristic of the eighteenth-century German middle class. The central conflict is the love of the aristocratic Ferdinand for Luise Miller, daughter of a bourgeois court musician; the elder Miller's attempts to stifle the relationship result in numerous silent *contretemps* between Luise and Ferdinand, based on their knowledge of what perils would lie ahead for their relationship. There also ensue numerous intrigues between Ferdinand's father (called simply 'President') and his unappealing courtier Wurm to arrange a marriage between Ferdinand and the President's mistress, Lady Milford. Milford herself is on the side of young love and promises Ferdinand her assistance. Ferdinand pleads with Luise to run away with him, but she refuses to 'overturn the order of society'. Meanwhile the President and Wurm convince Luise to write a letter to Ferdinand, falsely confessing her infidelity. When Ferdinand confronts her, she maintains that she does not love him. Ferdinand then poisons her, and in her dying gasps, she confesses her true feelings for him and discloses what his father and Wurm forced her to do. Ferdinand likewise takes poison and, as he dies, accuses his father of murdering them both. Botho Strauss, who at the time was a critic for *Theater heute*, praised Stein for 'jettisoning Ferdinand's metaphysical pallor and overheated egocentrism. The actual centerpiece of the play appears to be the damaged relationship between Ferdinand and Luisa. Stein also dispensed with the eschatological "Storm and Stress" fidgetiness'.[17] Nor did Stein accommodate the play's 'social grouchiness', that is, its critique of class differences. He was convinced that love, and only love, lay at the heart of its tragedy.

Strauss described the exactitude of speech and the organic gestures of the actors as the major strength of the staging: 'If Stein wanted to present introversion, he had the actors speak slowly and quietly, without appearing to be mannered. Introversion is not self-indulgence, but it will always attempt to manifest itself, then become something else. It works almost at a level of "psychomotorized mechanism." The language places pressure on the body which one can relieve only through movement or gesturing.'[18] With such analysis, Strauss matched Stein's own willingness to probe far beyond the obvious in sacred texts such as *Intrigue and Love*. Strauss seemed as searching as were Stein and the actors.

Strauss also praised Stein's revelation of Lady Milford as a loving and lovable figure. Stein saw her as the third figure in a chaste *ménage à trois* between Ferdinand (Michael König) and Luisa (Edith Clever). But Stein had Jutta Lampe play Lady Milford not as a disenchanted courtesan but as a surprisingly young woman who has finally had enough of elegant whoring at court. Lampe later stated that playing Lady Milford under Stein's direction was her 'liberation' from her previous work with autocratic theatre directors.

'This production was my joyful birth as an actress,' she said. 'Working with other directors, I always had the feeling that I had to do something, I had to "play," which I really couldn't understand. In the work with Stein it was important above everything else to understand the words, the text, the situation, the playwright, the playwright's time period. And what the playwright wanted to do with the play. It was necessary to understand the character in her sense of outsiderness, her feelings, her world. And then we went on stage in an effort to find the right means to express those things. Only with the help of a director who can see what kind of people are supposed to be on that stage is that possible. And this was the time I learned to "be" on the stage, to "live" on the stage, as I had always dreamed of doing.'[19]

Bruno Ganz stated that Hübner, with whom Ganz had been working since 1960, wanted Stein for *Intrigue and Love* in Bremen because Stein's star was rising quickly in the German theatrical firmament.[20] Hübner wanted some stardust to rub off on everybody in Bremen. The city had already developed a substantial reputation in West Germany, and the actors there noticed immediately that Stein was working up to Hübner's standards, which had earned Bremen two *Theatertreffen* invitations already (in 1964 and 1966, with two Peter Zadek productions). Hübner wanted another invitation, and soon. He had to wait, however, until 1969 for Stein to deliver, which he did with his production of Goethe's *Torquato Tasso*.

Goethe's *Torquato Tasso* in 1969

Torquato Tasso has an inconsistent production history, largely because of its literary reputation and its eponymous hero. Johann Wolfgang Goethe (1749–1832) based the character on Torquato Tasso (1544–95), a poet in the ducal court of Ferarra, who died shortly before Pope Clement VIII was to crown him 'King of Poets'. Goethe found in Tasso's life the subject matter he sought for writing a play focused on Romantic suffering, which he structured within the confines of outdated neoclassicism. Goethe accordingly adhered to the unities of time, place and action, but he wrote the dialogue in unconstrained, somewhat lugubrious verse; he was also meditating on his supererogatory role in the ducal court of Weimar. In rehearsals, Stein realized the paradox that Goethe wanted to ponder: the privileges of court life contrasted with the superfluity of being a court poet. Stein's production cast a spotlight in odd but convincing ways on the duality Tasso experienced. Susanne Raschig's costumes, for example, depicted eighteenth-century Germany rather than Renaissance Italy; designer Wilfried Minks (b. 1930) placed a bust of Goethe onstage, whereas Goethe had called for a bust of Ludovico Ariosto (1474–1533), likewise a court poet in Ferrara. Minks's stage design was extraordinary: he covered the stage floor with green carpeting, which was to contrast with the gilt embellishments and damask walls of the court. Then he set transparent Plexiglas panels in front of the walls, at once degrading the opulence of the court while suggesting a 'fishbowl existence' in which courtiers were on display.

Stein then set about cutting Goethe's text. His rearrangements marked the beginning of a vogue in *Regietheater*, according to many critics, enabling directors arbitrarily to cut, paste, rearrange and ultimately transform the original play into something of the director's own creation. The idea of 'theater dominated by the director' was nothing new, however. It had its origins in the mid-nineteenth-century writings of composer Richard Wagner (1813–83) and in the early-twentieth-century musings of Edward Gordon Craig (1872–1966), both of whom recognized the need for a dominant personality in a theatre practice which at the time was becoming transfigured by technology. Leopold Jessner (1878–1945) was among the first directors to move beyond presentation to reinterpretation, assigning political implications and innuendoes. Later directors agreed with Peter Brook (b. 1925), who claimed that the director's work 'paralleled' that of the playwright and allowed the director a wide berth for 'rethinking' a play. Stein's Bremen colleague Peter Zadek embraced a directorial approach that was essentially epistemological, by which the director exposed a play's cognitive constituents, allowing him to bring forth a 'renewed' vision of a play.

Such approaches often disregarded what the playwright may have intended – but since nobody can ever really know what the playwright's intention was (according to Peter Brook, not even the playwright himself knew what he intended), why bother with remaining 'true' to the text? Text did remain a significant part of this production, however. By the time *Torquato Tasso* opened in Bremen on 20 March 1969, the language remained atop Stein's 'reigning offer of meaning'[21] in theatre performance. Thus, he felt free to append a prologue, allowing each character to present him- or herself to the audience, dispensing with Goethe's carefully wrought exposition.

Stein also cut major portions of Tasso's lines, while keeping all the characters onstage to maintain the irony of their presence when other characters talked about them. The production was no longer Goethe's *Torquato Tasso* but Stein's meditation on Goethe (see Figure 5.1). It outraged some critics; Joachim Kaiser stated flatly that he had travelled to Bremen to see a play by Goethe, not by Peter Stein, no matter how ingenious Stein's manipulation of the text had been, pronouncing it 'neither good, nor meaningful, nor enlightening, and certainly not true'.[22] Kaiser spoke for many Goethe devotees, accusing Stein of transforming Goethe's characters into amalgams of 'lunacy and doltishness'.

The director whom Stein had most closely emulated in this production was paradoxically Goethe himself. As a theatre director in Weimar from 1791 to 1817, Goethe espoused a kind of 'classicism' which had little to do with classical Greek models and even less with the staging of works in the classical Greek manner. Instead he was concerned with a clarity in performance (particularly in *Torquato Tasso*, which he completed in 1790) that enabled audiences to see more distinctly the implications of significant patterns of action taking place on the stage. 'The actor must realize that he should not only imitate Nature,' according to one of his *Rules for Actors* but 'present it in an idealized form, thereby uniting the true with the beautiful in his performance', he wrote. He also laid down other rules aimed at eliminating discrepancies in proper enunciation, regionalisms in pronunciation, idiosyncrasies in their movement, and most humorously in 'avoiding bad habits: "The actor should never allow his handkerchief to be seen on stage, still less should he blow his nose in it, still less spit in it. It is disgusting for audiences to be reminded of such bodily functions in

FIGURE 5.1 *Bruno Ganz played the title role in* Torquato Tasso *by Johann Wolfgang von Goethe at the Schaubühne am Hallescgeb Ufer in 1970. Wilfrid Minks designed the sets. Photo by Ludwig Binder/ullstein bild via Getty Images (Getty#549718161).*

a work of art.""[23] With his concern for clarity, Goethe moved vigorously against contemporary currents running through the German stage, the same currents he had helped set in motion. Many of the characteristics mentioned earlier closely resembled those of Stein.

Critics who from their school days had learned to revere Goethe considered Stein's production of *Torquato Tasso* a conscious act of monument desecration, almost on the order of blasphemy. Ivan Nagel and Botho Strauss, however, countered that the production set a precedent, prophesying (correctly, as it turned out) that Stein's staging of 'the most thoughtful and exciting production in Germany for years' would affect productions of the German classics in years to come.[24] The most important of the critics were the ones who served on the jury from the *Theatertreffen* in Berlin; they voted – though not unanimously – to invite the production to the festival in May 1970. Critical response in Berlin was likewise split; one critic referred to the production as 'Tasso in Plexiglas', while another titled his review 'Silkworms and Butterflies', asserting that Stein and designer Minks had gone a few steps too far in setting the play 'on a poisonous green carpet between two transparent plastic walls. It was no longer a court garden in Ferrara during the late sixteenth century, but a paradigmatic Nowhere and Everywhere at the same time'.[25]

'How else are you supposed to get into this play?', protested Jutta Lampe, providing a refreshing viewpoint from the perspective of an articulate and talented performer in the production.

> Everything was so foreign, so beautiful, and so immensely remote. ... Tasso's problems appeared to me, at least, so exclusively to be Goethe's problems as well, or maybe the problems of a genius on the order of Goethe or Tasso. For Stein, the problem was neither of Goethe nor of genius but the problem of the artist within his society – in other words, the problems Tasso was wrestling with were exactly the same problems which we as artists encounter.[26]

Stein agreed, saying that the process had nothing to do with 'an "artist in a gilded cage syndrome," something or someone whom cultural bureaucrats could exploit. That was a point of reference, however, which gave us a basic emotional presupposition for our performance'. Neither he nor the actors were interested in 'realizing the play' and certainly not in bringing its themes 'up to date'. They wanted instead 'to subject its historical conflicts to intensive investigation, to entice them into speech. Thus was *Torquato Tasso*, Goethe's text and performance, brought into being as *Torquato Tasso*, text and performance about Goethe'.[27] Patterson agreed that Stein had no desire to 'reconstruct' Tasso, but the intent to 'tear away the veil of classical perfection' was obvious. Stein revealed certain aspects of Goethe's verse that apparently had gone unnoticed for decades. 'Seldom is a word uttered on stage that does not belong to the original, but speeches or whole scenes he rearranged, giving lines of one character to another. Stein believed that Goethe's original play was too long and too decorative.'[28]

Hübner was pleased with the outcome, which was not only an invitation to the *Theatertreffen* but also an invitation to the Venice Biennale Teatro;

Torquato Tasso then went on tour to numerous cities. By then its reputation as a harbinger of novelty preceded it. At the *experimenta* Festival in Frankfurt, young audiences laughed hysterically, welcoming what they considered an iconoclastic take on an old master their teachers had forced them to read in school. Not only did Hübner get the *Theatertreffen* invitation he desired; his cash flow increased measurably from the income earned on the tours. Hübner wanted to offer Stein a full-time directing position in Bremen, but soon after *Torquato Tasso* opened at the *Theatertreffen*, the Berlin Senate made Stein the offer of a lifetime, which he accepted.

At the Schaubühne am Halleschen Ufer

Before he accepted the Berlin Senate's offer, however, Stein agreed to stage three productions in Zurich, the Swiss city where the only free German-language theatre anywhere in the world existed from 1938 to 1945, as under the directorship of Oskar Wälterlin (1895–1961), the Zurich Schauspielhaus developed a repertoire of anti-Nazi plays. By 1945, Wälterlin had staged over sixty world premieres by expatriate German-language playwrights. In the post-war period, he presented numerous world premieres of plays by Max Frisch and Friedrich Dürrenmatt. In Zurich, Stein staged Edward Bond's *Early Morning*, the Jacobean tragedy *The Changeling* by Thomas Middleton (1580–1627) and William Rowley (1585–1626), and *Cock-a-Doodle-Dandy* by Sean O'Casey (1880–1964). All three productions were flops, but they gave Stein a chance to work intensively with the actors he had come to know in Bremen. Stein also accepted the failure of the productions as necessary, because 'there are some plays you need a can opener to get into. Some are so tightly constructed and have such a formidable architecture' that few directors and actors can get at the material inside the can. Most actor training, he observed, was insufficient for opening the can, too. 'It has to do with the actor's approach, and with his viewpoint. If an actor feels the play is closed to him, he's unlikely to pursue it successfully.'[29] Actors Bruno Ganz, Jutta Lampe, Michael König, Dieter Laser, Werner Rehm, Sabine Andreas, Tilo Prückner and Otto Sander agreed; they also agreed to work with Stein in forming a theatre collective at the Schaubühne, an enterprise that became so successful that it marked them and Stein for the rest of their careers. A good measure of their success is a string of invitations to the *Theatertreffen* that ran for ten consecutive years, a record of accomplishment no German theatre has yet matched.

The history of the Schaubühne am Halleschen Ufer began in 1962 when former theatre students at the Free University of Berlin – Jürgen Schitthelm (b. 1939), Dieter Sturm (b. 1936) and Klaus Weiffenbach (b. 1939) – took over a multipurpose room in a building owned by the Workers' Welfare Association (*Arbeiterwohlfahrt*, or AWO, a not-for-profit organization). They formed an amateur theatre with the intention of running a 'socially engaged' theatre with a distinctly left-wing political bias. It was moribund until the student riots of 1968 energized West German politics, bringing the Social Democratic Party (SPD) into the national government. The SPD privileged efforts throughout the German economy aimed at *Mitbestimmung* (literally 'co-determination', but perhaps a better understood translation is 'collective agency'), giving the term a currency it had not hitherto enjoyed. Collective agency in theatre work has always been necessary to a certain degree; but Stein and his colleagues wanted *Mitbestimmung* to go beyond the SPD's sloganeering that brought labour union officials onto boards of corporate directors. Stein had by 1970 developed a highly intellectualized conceptualization of how *Mitbestimmung* might have beneficial aesthetic effects. As Stein stated in 1970, 'when actors on stage know what they want to communicate, their performances will gain tremendously in conviction'.[30] That statement reflects Stein's quixotic idealism, because there is little evidence that actors who speak with conviction are any more effective than those who speak without it. Stein's idealism, however, gained credibility through his aesthetic intellectualizing. While Berlin itself had evinced strong leftist leanings since the founding of the Social Democratic Workers' Party in 1869 (a result of large numbers of labour unions and manufacturing operations in Berlin), West Berlin identified itself as a free-market outpost in the midst of a hostile Marxist reality called the German Democratic Republic. The new West German socialist government was intent on something its chancellor, Willy Brandt (1913–92), called *Ostpolitik*. It was a new approach to dealing with Soviet-dominated East Germany, yet it did not diminish the desire among West Germans to maintain West Berlin as a showplace of Western freedoms while literally walled in by an East German regime intent on isolating the city from the rest of West Germany. West German governments, as a result, subsidized all manner of cultural activity in West Berlin to the tune of approximately 170 million Deutschmarks (about $57 million at the time),[31] including eight theatres.[32]

Peter Iden believes that Stein saw his role as the Schaubühne's artistic director as a kind of catalyst who promoted interaction. He realized that a theatre ensemble is nothing like a musical ensemble such as a string quartet, a brass quintet or even a chamber orchestra. Theatre ensembles require a complete command of performance skills, but they also require an abundance of conceit, presumption and narcissism – qualities not usually associated with successful ensemble work. One should remember, as Iden notes, that the Schaubühne group was not an ordinary ensemble, and Stein was no ordinary artistic director. Under his directorship, the Schaubühne was an attempt to study certain aspects of culture, human behaviour and politics with strong programmatic objectives. To this attempt Stein brought to bear certain characteristics which members came to respect: an insistence of self-discipline, company loyalty, devotion to the endeavour at hand and a willingness to work eighteen hours per day. He somehow figured out ways to make political differences within the group function as a glue that held everything together. He also realized that the group was not a commune, such as the Living Theatre in America.

Members of the group drew up a set of bylaws which were not intended as 'Goethean' set of rules or code of conduct. They were more like a collection of 'mission statements' in which participating individuals set forth idealistic goals, towards which they mutually pledged themselves to strive in the spirit of Mao Zedong, who urged his followers to 'serve the people'.[33] Using a quotation from Mao Zedong is a good example of just how utopian some of Stein's colleagues were prepared to be in following a set of principles based on class consciousness, the study of imperialism, the place of the actor within a bourgeois society, the development of an historical consciousness, the history of revolutions, the international workers' movement, liberation movements among the oppressed in the Third World, the international student movement, etc. 'And the whole thing should be a lot of fun!' they concluded. Stein disagreed, but he did not distance himself from the 'consensus' of such utopian idealism among his colleagues – and this was a chief characteristic of his leadership talent. He rarely allowed political considerations to interpose themselves between him and his sense of theatre art. The Schaubühne bylaws seemed initially to function fairly well, much like the way the Group Theater in America cohered as a unit for a few years in the 1930s. The Schaubühne, like the Group, was a thoughtful, self-critical and unsentimental collection of artists dedicated to pursuing experiments in theatre, not as an exercise in 'self-realization' but as serious investigators undertaking examinations of human behaviour using theatrical means.[34] Some members of the West Berlin Senate claimed the Schaubühne was a Communist-front organization, which was understandable after word leaked out that cadres of the German Communist Party were attending rehearsals and holding meetings with actors to 'raise class consciousness'. After a while, the cadres stopped coming and efforts aimed at obvious political targets tapered off. The Senate briefly cancelled all funding for the Schaubühne, but it was restored after a Senate investigation cleared Stein and everyone else of wrongdoing.

Therese Giehse (whom Stein had contracted to play the title role in the Schaubühne's initial offering, Brecht's *The Mother*) was one of Stein's ardent champions.

Stein is a great revitalizer, a kind of poetic rejuvenator. Imaginative, honest, and meticulous – by no means a dilettante. With him, everything is revisable, renewable. He is so curious that he dismantles every play, tears it completely apart, dissects it into its tiniest component parts. Only when he has all the parts in front of him is he ready to bring it to life. And he is gentle. He makes things simple, as if you are discovering things so easily. Rehearsals are loose, everybody is laughing. Nobody sweats. Stein learned a lot from Brecht, whose way of working was similar.[35]

Such observations did nothing to win over the hearts and minds of the West Berlin Senate, but *The Mother* proved to have a beneficial effect. The production was among the first indications that Stein was not a communist, nor even a confirmed socialist.

Stein's production of *Die Mutter* (The Mother) opened in early October of 1970. Brecht had based his script on a 1906 novel titled *The Mother: Life of the Revolutionary Pelagea Vlassova from Tver* by Maxim Gorky (1868–1936), and Stein found it an intriguing examination of events that led up to the Russian revolution. Brecht had visualized it as an agitprop[36] piece, but Stein's production switched emphasis from the angry young revolutionaries to the 65-year-old Pelagea Vlassova. In doing so, Stein hoped to revive an acting tradition he had witnessed in Kortner and in Giehse herself. He also hoped that working directly with Giehse would teach him more about a tradition that had generally disappeared. Work with Giehse, Stein believed, could help him to rediscover what German acting had once been like. He believed nobody really knew anymore, because most West German actors and directors in the 1950s and 1960s were intent first of all on rehabilitation, not renewal. Stein's position was one of curiosity. He disliked what he considered the 'bourgeois standards' of acting in West Germany, but he was dubious of Brecht's methods in East Germany; he therefore sought to discover what he hoped would be the source of what may have been 'authentic' German acting before the Nazi takeover. He did the same with a companion piece to *The Mother*, namely *Optimistiche Tragödie* (Optimistic Tragedy) by Vsevolod Vitalievich Vishnevsky (1950–1), opening at the Schaubühne on 18 April 1972. Its run (twenty-seven performances) was briefer than *The Mother*'s sixty-eight performances, but it expanded Stein's inquiries into the Russian Revolution. Its characters belonged to a marine regiment stationed in Kronstadt, the main seaport of St. Petersburg, home to the Imperial Russian Admiralty and the Imperial Russian Baltic Fleet. In the story, based on an actual event in 1919, members of the regiment were ready to fight anti-revolutionary forces, but Bolshevik leaders V.I. Lenin (1870–1924) and Leon Trotsky (1879–1940) felt the regiment needed additional indoctrination. They sent a young female commissar named Larissa Reissner (1895–1926) to whip them into shape, enabling them to enter combat with the appropriate consciousness of class conflict. The play premiered in 1932 as Stalin's tyranny was beginning to sink into depths of unprecedented depravity; the 'Stalin-approved' version was the last of three different versions, but Stein used the original 1930 version, which explored personal conflicts among members of the regiment.

Stein had become fond of stage pictures as a result of his success with the dumbshow gambit in *Saved*. He thus sought in *Optimistic Tragedy* to create 'living posters' that embodied a certain viewpoint. He staged several static, silent moments to 'illustrate history', perhaps hoping to make history 'come alive' for audiences. But he was not attempting to 'distance' events onstage in the Brechtian manner; neither did he stage history as an end in itself. He instead sought to expose power relations. *Optimistic Tragedy* is a play with obvious political preoccupations, but Stein used it to explore less obvious, but no less vital preoccupations Vishnevsky had in mind: sexuality and betrayal.

Vsevolod Vitalievich Vishnevsky had been a student of sexuality, often praising the Institute for Sexual Research in Berlin for gathering interviews from thousands of people whose sexual practices Soviet leader Joseph Stalin (1878–1953) considered perverse or depraved. The characters in *Optimistic Tragedy* suffered implicitly from various forms of suppressed desire, perhaps a reflection of Stalinist prudery, which became part of state policy after 1930. Stein saw an opportunity to address contemporary German sexuality in light of the 'sexual revolution' that had started in 1961 with the introduction of the birth control pill in West Germany. By 1968, in both West and East Germany, the pill had revolutionized Stein's generation, perhaps not so differently from the ways in which the Russian revolution has occasioned massive changes in sexual behaviour among young Russians. Characters in *Optimistic Tragedy* manifested sexual tension in other ways, Stein believed. Although direct references to sex are minor and superficial, behind those manifestations lurk various perspectives, based on shame, voyeurism, promiscuity, exhibitionism, salaciousness, carnality and many others. In combination, these perspectives served to increase the production's overall vitality, since each character seemed to have a particular sexual preoccupation.

In the role of the Bolshevik commissar sent to organize the regiment into a class-conscious fighting force, Elke Petri emphasized the character's sexual frustrations. The character thinks she has found a substitute for orgasm in political advocacy and party discipline, but her opponents counter with demands for absolute freedom – including the freedom to have sex with partners of their choice. The result in Elke Petri's character was what critic Hellmuth Karasek called a 'Joan of Arc complex'.[37] As a result, each character in the play mistrusts others for various reasons, and each feels betrayed by someone else. Stein saw the sexual angle as directly relevant to the 1968 student upheavals in West Germany and believed he had discovered Vishnevsky's original intent: his *Optimistic Tragedy* became a tragedy of optimism. The revolutionary cause to which all the characters seemed at first devoted, like the devotion among student activists in 1968, was merely a façade.

In 1974, Stein continued his inquiries into the causes of revolution with *Sommergäste* (*Dachniki*/Summerfolk) by Gorky, a 1904 play depicting a group of indolent Russians in a *dacha* colony.[38] Gorky depicts it as privileged territory, watched over by hired guards. These Russians are a coarser breed than the ones who inhabit Chekhov's plays, perhaps the kind Stein and the cast encountered when they visited the Soviet Union in the autumn of 1974 to research the places and people Gorky had studiously imitated. Gorky presented twenty-six characters, about twice the number that appear in Chekhov's plays. Like Chekhov, however, Gorky presented them with interwoven backgrounds, with little in the way of plot. They philosophize with one another, play the piano, flirt with one another, play chess, eat, drink, put on playlets, attempt to quiet their nerves, recite poetry, expose their insecurities and go on a picnic in a birch forest. Some confess feelings of love to each other in the forest, one tries unsuccessfully to commit suicide and most of them disappoint each other. The point of the play is to depict a pre-revolutionary bourgeois milieu; the point of the production was to present the work of four months' rehearsal, which had resulted in unprecedented clarity and meticulousness.

Summerfolk was distinctive by virtue of Maria Lvovna (Jutta Lampe), who resembled the commissar in *Optimistic Tragedy*. Maria Lvovna is a middle-aged, middle-class licensed physician. Her diagnosis of indolence among the *dachniki* carries echoes of Chekhov's plays, but the character portrayed by Jutta Lampe is far more straightforward than her less outspoken Chekhovian cognates. She exhorts her fellow *dachniki* to 'change, and change utterly. Who are we, anyway? We are the children of housemaids, cooks, workers. And here we die of boredom! It's not right. There are so many of us who have come from the masses. Have we forgotten the drudgery of their lives? How they almost suffocated darkness and wallowed in filth? They are our blood relations!' She is the prototype of the 'new woman' when the 'new Russia' becomes a reality. But Stein was not interested in that kind of reality (see Figure 5.2). As Patterson has noted, Edith Clever as Varvara (the young wife of Basov, in and around whose *dacha* the play takes place) turned to face the audience in her rebuttal, which turned out to be timid and self-pitying: 'I don't know what I'm saying. Perhaps this is wrong and I shouldn't speak this way, but I am struggling like a fly that beats against the glass. I long for liberty and … yes, I am also a helpless, pitiable creature. I know it. I knew it long ago.'[39]

The production programme likewise noted a clear departure from Gorky's propagandistic intent and set forth Stein's staging as a kind of ontogenesis within a specific environment. In Stein's conception, the play was less a sequence and more of an unfolding, an exploration of both inner and external circumstances. Throughout the production, all the actors were onstage – not because of some directorial conceit as had been the case of *Torquato Tasso*. They were instead there because they simply couldn't separate from one another, so integrated was their dialogue. Bradby and Williams have observed that Stein was using naturalist assumptions against middle-class perspectives. The meticulousness Stein had pursued for 'a totally realistic, imitative performance was so perfect that it stood clearly revealed as a kind of fetishistic navel-gazing. The trees were too real and too many, the characters too convincing and too relentlessly present'.[40] The result was like watching something take shape under a microscope, allowing the pettiness of behaviour to unfold into a set of interwoven entanglements which meant nothing, but from which there was no escape.

FIGURE 5.2 *Wolf Redl and Edith Clever in* Summerfolk *by Maxim Gorky sit in front of the real trees that were incorporated into Karl-Ernst Herrmann's setting for the 1974 production. Photo by Bionder/ullstein bild via Getty Images (Getty #548133047).*

In an effort to make all utterances on stage as seamless as possible, dramaturge Botho Strauss spent weeks with the actors as they 'extemporized' their lines and the situations in which they found themselves; he took detailed notes of what they said and how they spoke. He and Stein then spent hours going over how best to get the most out of line readings. They had no desire to use the line readings to create a 'stage realism' but to allow interactions to reveal themselves. Such a procedure allowed Stein to 'perceive' what goes on between two actors or among a larger group. Stein was a sensitive listener and tolerated no 'jargonizing' among actors.

He disliked intensely the 'door opens, scene starts' technique Gorky had used as scene breaks and was determined to allow much of the action to take place outdoors. He felt that outdoor settings facilitated spatial relationships between audience and performers because exteriors conveyed a sense of sharing the same reality. It also facilitated the flow of scenes from one to another with greater subtlety and more fluidity

Some German critics found Gorky's language coarser in quality than Chekhov's, and Stein's knowledge of Russian allowed him to take liberties with Gorky's dialogue and provide a colour and musicality that was obviously a façade – but it became an essential quality of the ensemble. The characters then became part of a panorama, rather than components of a story. The 'panoramic' quality of *Summerfolk* lent a kind of historicity Stein was looking for that went beyond mere reflections of empirical presentation. Stein's characters became more resonant than the ones Gorky had created, because Stein's were portraits, not stage figures. Stein's had stronger outlines; they spoke from within themselves and not from Gorky's ideological typewriter. To achieve that kind of portraiture required actors to engage in a kind of tightrope walk between identifying too much with the characters they played – as director and actor Konstantin Stanislavski (1863–1938) would have had insisted – while avoiding critical distance from the characters which Brecht would have demanded.

Most critics found much to like in *Summerfolk*. It ran in repertoire with other productions at the Schaubühne through 1975, received an invitation to the *Theatertreffen*, and then went on tour to Switzerland, Yugoslavia, France, Belgium, Finland and Russia. It also appeared for a two-week run at the National Theatre in London, the first foreign-language staging the National had presented. Stein's insistence on meticulousness included selecting birch saplings from local parks and nurseries. British stagehands under Stein's direct supervision then replanted the saplings onstage and watered them according to his specifications.

New explorations

Having completed his inquiries into the ramifications of revolution (though the production of *Summerfolk* had also opened new avenues of subsequent inquiry into the plays of Chekhov), Stein returned to pursue an aspect of theatrical presentation he had already begun in 1971 with Henrik Ibsen's *Peer Gynt*: the extravaganza. Karl-Ernst Herrmann's design for *Peer Gynt* had been a kind of anthropological diorama rather than a stage composition. It provided space for the various stations which Peer

Gynt visits throughout his life. The original idea behind the choice of a *Peer Gynt* production at the Schaubühne lay in conceiving it as an examination of the nineteenth century's fascination with exoticism, historicism and trivial entertainment. At a discussion of the play, Stein uttered his much cited quote about the 'nineteenth century as a grandfather whom we recognize, but ultimately he remains a stranger'.[41] At the centre of Stein's deliberations was the preoccupation with the ephemeral presupposition of individualism's importance. Individualism was supposed to contrast with Marxist collectivism, but as dramaturge Strauss noted, an examination of such abstractions was an old-fashioned pursuit of 'consciousness raising', and like peeling an onion, it became 'an exercise in wishful thinking'.[42] Stein wanted to parody the false goal of individualism, and his success lay in the way he found ways to make the production far more than the sum of its numerous parts. 'Out of the swarm of polished details, finely wrought gestures of speech and movement, there emerged a sense of ensemble,' Ivan Nagel wrote, 'which the German theatre had witnessed only sporadically in the productions of Otto Brahm or Bertolt Brecht'.[43]

Critic Volker Canaris wrote that Stein and the ensemble had created a new kind of performance style; for example, Stein cast six actors in the title role. Canaris called it 'a way of playing a character while subjecting him simultaneously to criticism' – which was in fact not new at all, since Brecht had accomplished it two decades earlier. But Stein's company had 'turned on its head the bourgeois theatre aesthetic of acting as embodiment; it became a dialectical-critical aestheticism, an aesthetic method of recognition'.[44] What Canaris may have meant is that the company's realism achieved a dimension that called attention to its own imperfections, thus making it recognizable and accessible in a totally new way. 'Stein did not wish to imitate reality but to criticize it, not to accept it as a done deal but to show it as alterable.'[45]

Stein continued his interest in fixations on individualism when he staged *Das Sparschwein* (*La Cagnotte*/The Piggy Bank, 1864) by Eugène Labiche (1815–88) in 1973; it ran for 133 performances. As in *Optimistic Tragedy* (and to a lesser extent, *Summerfolk*), the main character is a group of people. They reside in a provincial town called La Ferté-sous-Jouarre, all members of the *petit-bourgeois* property-owning class. They include a pensioner named Champbourcy, his sister 'the aged virgin' Leonida, his marriageable daughter Blanche, a young lawyer named Gaston in amorous pursuit of Blanche, the farmer Colladan and a pharmacist named Cordenbois. They meet socially once a week to play cards and have collectively agreed to deposit their winnings in a porcelain piggy bank (whence the original French title). While they have agreed to spend the money collectively when the piggy bank is full, each has a secret: they have all cheated at cards during their social functions, and each feels entitled to the lion's share of the money (see Figure 5.3).

They all agree they should spend the money on a trip to Paris, but the trip falls apart on their first day in Paris when they unwittingly spend the entire

FIGURE 5.3 *Otto Sander, Jutta Lampe, Werner Rehm and Wolf Redl played nineteenth-century bourgeois characters in Stein's 1975 production of* The Piggy Bank *by Eugène Labiche. Photo by Binder/ullstein bild via Getty Images (Getty #545733451).*

pot of money on dinner at a mediocre Parisian restaurant. After numerous plot twists, they end up broke, under arrest and completely perplexed. They appeal to every possible authority for recognition of their rights as French citizens, yet they sink ever deeper into the quicksand of bureaucratic obstinacy and governmental jargon. Then, as if on cue, the young lawyer Gaston, Blanche's hopeful suitor, arrives from Ferté-sous-Jouarre. He pays their fines, gets them out of trouble and loads them onto a train back home. In the play's original ending, they find themselves back home in their comfortable little world of pensions, ownership of small plots of land or businesses, and government jobs.

Stein gave the play a new ending. Instead of being rescued, their travails continue and they find themselves setting up barricades in the street, fighting the police and shooting at members of the Parisian working class. It was pure farce, until events took a tragic turn: young Gaston enters, but instead of coming to their aid and rescuing his beloved Blanche, he ignores them all. The audience is left to presume they suffered violent death at the hands of the courts. They had become, according to one critic, 'desperados, anarchists against their wills, marauders up to their necks in trouble'.[46] Another critic praised the production for exposing how much anxiety, anarchy and pure terror lurked behind French popular farces, their ingenious plotting and appealing characterizations notwithstanding.[47] Stein himself described the production as 'an orgy of comic realism', set in 'a greenhouse of unfettered capitalism',[48] noting that the *petit-bourgeois* were just as likely as the proletariat to fight for and start revolutions. In other words, *The Piggy Bank* was an extravaganza of misperception, of poseurs in regalia, a ludicrous chronicle of empty-headed conviction.

Stein's production of Heinrich von Kleist's *The Prince of Homburg* (*Prinz Friedrich von Homburg*) shared qualities with *The Piggy Bank* – though none was at first obvious. The young Prussian nobleman of the title disobeys orders from his military superiors yet emerges victorious in the 1675 Battle of Fehrbellin. Despite the Prince's heroic and successful action on the field, his superiors arrest Prince Friedrich and sentence him to death for insubordination. He finds himself terrified at the thought of death and pleads to the Elector of Brandenburg for mercy; the Elector will grant him amnesty if he will attest that the army's decision to execute him is unjust. Prince Friedrich's sense of Prussian honour, however, forbids arguing against his superiors' judgement. He thus finds inner peace and governs himself calmly in preparation for the firing squad. Then, as if on cue, the Elector frees him, convinced that Prince Friedrich's honour is intact, and hails him as the hero of Fehrbellin. As the curtain falls, the Prince nevertheless wonders if he has not, in fact, dreamed the whole episode.

It was characteristic of Stein to uncover hitherto overlooked aspects in the text and then emphasize them to the point of creating an altogether new play – as he had done in *The Piggy Bank*. In *The Prince of Homburg*, he discovered that somnambulism was the root of the Prince's dilemma. In fact, Stein retitled the play *Kleist's Dream of the Homburg Prince* (*Kleists Traum vom Prinzen Homburg*). Again Stein insisted on a large open space for the performance, a space in which Bruno Ganz as the Prince could roam about freely – though eccentrically – at key moments in the performance. The production opened with a scene in moonlight, as Ganz wandered about as if he were under glass, recalling Caspar David Friedrich's painting *The Monk by the Sea*, created shortly before Kleist's 1811 suicide on the shores of Lake Wannsee near Berlin. The painting depicts a solitary figure almost obscured by fog, merely standing in the vastness of the space around him. The difference between Bruno Ganz and the Monk, of course, was movement. But Ganz based his movement on the study of *tai chi*, a Chinese martial art which endowed him with a balance that made his abrupt starts, stops and turns so convincing that viewers gasped at his ability to avoid collisions with objects and other actors.

Stein and Botho Strauss determined to reject any notion of interpreting the play as a chronicle of Prussian heroism and chose instead to view it as an emanation from somewhere deep within Kleist (the playwright was, like the

Prince of Homburg, a scion of Prussian military aristocrats). The production was a display of how Kleist's dreaming had rendered the playwright insecure; Stein placed his main emphasis on dream sequences, which reflected inner torment. Ganz's remarkable somnambulation demonstrated a unique kind of surety as he moved about the stage, shifting his weight fluidly, breathing deeply, eyes wide open but fixed on nothing in particular, knees unbent but loose, shoulders released, upper torso fully relaxed and unaffected by movement of the legs. Ganz could shift directions in ways that looked extremely complicated to audiences, as if the prince had a 'sixth sense' of the space around him. Strauss stated in the production's published programme, 'Everything in this play is a dream. It was a dream the unfortunate Heinrich von Kleist had about the fortunate Prince of Homburg who, tenuously and powerfully, under sentence of death, asserts his great longing and wishful thinking against the forces which oppose him, and ultimately, miraculously, realizes delectable fulfillment.'[49] In a virtuosic display of Ganz's movement, Stein saw a way to explore the empty-headed convictions of Prussian dreams of glory.

Directing as research: Shakespeare and Greek classics

Stein later described his process of directing as

> bringing to expression what the playwright was thinking under social, historical, and religious situations different from our own. When I really like a playwright, who let us say, was a devout Catholic, I want to show that fact. That's why the emphasis of dreaming was so strong in *The Prince of Homburg* – but in retrospect I find it completely superfluous and altogether uncomfortable.[50]

Stein also dismissed his earlier efforts at extravagant staging, indulging a curious tendency towards frank self-criticism. He indulged other tendencies as he became more widely known and praised, particularly the tendency to over-rehearse and overanalyse the plays he was directing. His 'research projects' for Shakespeare's *As You Like It* and *The Oresteia* by Aeschylus are the best examples. The project created as preparation for *As You Like It* he titled *Shakespeare's Memory*; it was a kind of kaleidoscopic diorama of the Elizabethan world. When Stein's production of *Wie es euch gefällt* (As You Like It) finally opened in 1977 and ran for 117 performances, it incorporated many of the conceits developed in *Shakespeare's Memory*. Both were staged in the CCC Film Studios. For *As You Like It*, Stein completely reordered the sequence of scenes, presenting court scenes in one sound stage and Forest of Arden scenes in another. He also used the 'dioramic juxtaposition' device from *Peer Gynt*, intercutting scenes in cinematic fashion. One actor or group of actors spoke a few lines and then remained static while a passage from another scene began elsewhere in the sound stage. The effect was to abandon linearity for the sake of montage effect, but woe betide the spectator who was not already intensely familiar with the play.

Transferring the audience from the 'world of the court' to the Forest of Arden began with sounds of barking hounds and hunting horns that led characters and audience members into a kind of cavern, past Elizabethan craft guild installations and into the Forest left over from *Shakespeare's Memory*. It was a sylvan vista, where audiences seated themselves among bird songs from hidden loudspeakers, and warm light filtered through abundant tree leaves. Some critics invented metaphors for the Forest of Arden, imagining it to be an escape analogous to the municipal parks of West Berlin; Stein's view, however, was less metaphorical and more paradoxical. He viewed the Forest of Arden as an example of the mistaken notions which many people have about Nature. The so-called freedom one experiences in forests and mountains is an illusion, he asserted, since Nature operates under inflexible, immutable laws. It may be valuable to escape urban environments and glimpse an imaginary utopia once in a while, but no politician can control or direct the creation of utopias.[51]

Stein later said that the reason he chose *As You Like It* as a means to investigate utopianism was the infrequency of *As You Like It* productions on German stages in the twentieth century. Though Otto Falckenberg (1873–1947) had presented it dozens of times in Munich and Max Reinhardt (1873–1943) over 180 times in Berlin, there had been far fewer in the Weimar Republic,[52] only forty-one productions of it in the Third Reich, and in post-war West Germany, the numbers were even smaller. No production of the play had ever received an invitation to the *Theatertreffen*. 'But this play had something I was interested in,' Stein said. 'The human relationship with utopianism, the utopia of love, the utopia of living freely in harmony with Nature, the utopia of the good ruler, the utopia of making the world a better place through melancholia – they all make an appearance in *As You Like It*. That is something that strikes [in me] an immediate chord.'[53]

In numerous interviews, Stein had maintained that he was most interested in the ancient Greeks, Shakespeare and Chekhov, because they are 'the pillars of the western theatre tradition'. He staged his first investigation of the Greeks in 1974, a kaleidoscopic panorama of the Helladic world titled *Antikenprojekt* (Antiquity Project), from which he later drew when he worked directly with the text of Aeschylus' *Oresteia* in 1980. On the preliminary research project, Stein worked with his Schaubühne directorial colleague Klaus-Michael Grüber (1941–2008), who was directing *The Bacchae* by Euripides, featuring Schaubühne actors Michael König as Dionysos, Bruno Ganz as Pentheus and Edith Clever as Agave. Their preparation involved a chartered boat trip to the Mediterranean, where the actors studied the Palaeolithic prehistory of the Greeks and the origins of despotism and slavery in the Mediterranean basin. They watched educational films about demonology in Tibet, demon possession among tribes in West Africa, animal sacrifices in East Africa, tribes such as the Aztecs who practised human sacrifice, the meaning of the bar-mitzvah among Jewish tribes and the ceremonies common among Roman Catholic priests. They listened to the rhythms of tribes practising sacrificial dances as clues to how the Greeks used rhythm in their verse forms; they read scholarly treatises on cults, rituals and myths, and other texts. Their endeavours manifested Stein's growing obsession with detail, having led members of the Schaubühne company into their own obsessions with such things. Their endeavours were also signs of the serious commitment among company members who used their own money and vacation time to remain together and continue communal studies. They immersed themselves in all kinds of exercises and improvisations, but in contrast to groups like the Living Theatre in the United States, they presented their work with no particular agenda in mind. They had no intention of experiencing some quasi-religious venture in which they expected the audience to take part.

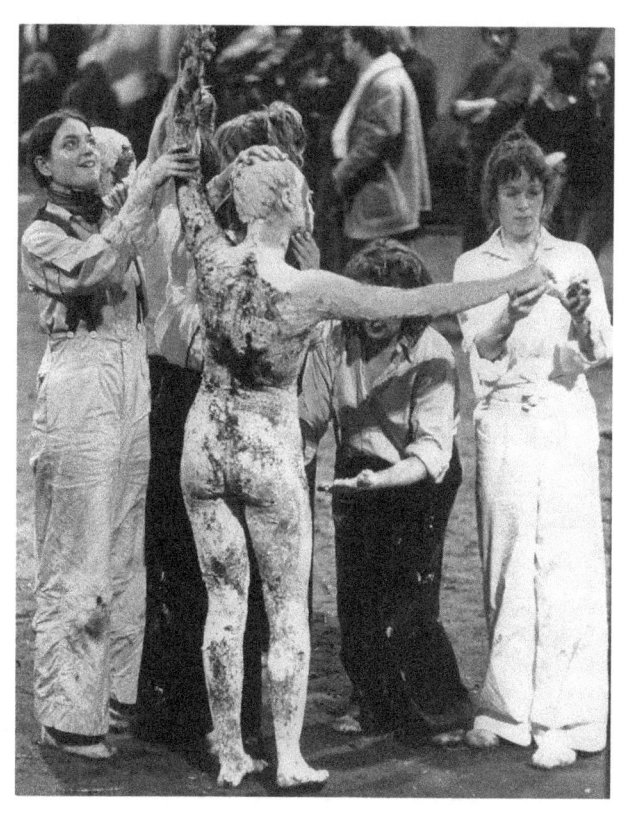

FIGURE 5.4 *In 1974, Stein staged* Antikenprojekt *(Antiquity Project), based upon the research the company had done for Klaus-Michael Grüber's production of* The Bacchae *by Euripides. This work further served as a basis for Stein's* Oresteia *by Aeschylus in 1980. Photo by Kneidl/ullstein bild via Getty Images (Getty #542933583).*

Audiences flocked to the presentations of the *Antiquity Project*, which included a sequence in which the audience was divided into male and female attendees. Three actors stood before male audiences, three actresses before female audiences; the performers were stripped naked, beaten, tortured, ceremonially killed and then buried. Ten other performers dug up their bodies (covered with kaolin clay), painted masks on their faces and brought them back to life. Like newborns, the performers had to learn how to stand up, walk, grasp and see anew (see Figure 5.4).

Gradually the resurrected performers rejoined the group of the living and participated in their activities. Reaction to such exercises was lukewarm; though the *Theatertreffen* jury invited the staging to its festival, many critics dismissed it.

In 1980, Stein returned to the project for his staging of *The Oresteia* with Clever as Clytemnestra, Jutta Lampe as Athena and Udo Samel as Orestes. By the time Stein's *Oresteia* got off the ground on 18 October 1980, the chorus wore three-piece suits, bowler hats, and carried fancy walking sticks. Their speech was an amalgam of broken verse, hummed ritual chants and a wide range of tonalities. They spoke at times in falsetto flutterings, at others in basso profundities, sometimes interrupting each other, sometimes yammering, grumbling or howling. They even spoke some lines in the original Greek. The chorus became a phonic sounding board: characters verbally bounced off it, bashed into it or were embraced by it. Critics praised the vocal work of the chorus, especially when Stein allowed 'ancient tones of lamentation and vehement lyricism to mix and mingle with murmurings that sounded like discussions at a nearby café or the babbling one hears in an Italian piazza'.[54] The chorus was most effective, Ivan Nagel said, when speaking in fear and anxiety about the dictatorship of Clytemnestra and her consort Aegisthus. Of pivotal importance to Stein in *The Oresteia* was the mother–son conflict between Orestes and Clytemnestra. In begging for her life at the conclusion of *The Libation Bearers*, Clever exposed her left breast to Samel, who then slowly placed the tip of his sword on her nipple. She pushed her naked breast towards the sword, enveloping it. Orestes (Udo Samel) was so overcome with primordial memories of nursing at her breast that he let his sword fall. But prompted by Pylades (Gregor Hansen), he picked it up and plunged it into her naked breast.

This staging was exemplary, some critics maintained, in showing Stein's insistence that patriarchal order must surmount chthonic attempts to displace it. Stein's production featured Furies who were, as Aeschylus intended, the embodiments of the anarchic, dark and hysterical viewpoint. The Furies are personifications of the irrational and impulsive, spreading terror wherever they go. As Goethe described them in *Faust II*, 'half-humans, the plague of states and cities', but Stein's Furies, in the costumes of Moidele Bickel (1937–2016), resembled the half-women/half-serpent creatures in Circle Five of Dante's *Inferno*, shrieking and howling. As a chorus, 'They wound in and around each other, slimy, black, and dissonant scarecrows, making audiences think of charred bodies at the site of an airliner crash.'[55] Stein believed, fifteen years later, that he had captured for modern audiences what Aeschylus had provided 2,500 years earlier: a sense of sheer terror, which to Stein was both miraculous and mystical.[56] In the Aeschylean view, the only thing standing between such irrational forces and their embrace of chaos is the order and stability of patriarchy. Thus, Athene (Jutta Lampe) confronted an inevitability: she must transform the Furies by means of cultural appropriation – and the process furthermore needed to be irreversible. Were it not final and beyond recall, the reappearance of matriarchy's chaos and terror would remain under the surface, threatening to break through and attempt another destructive challenge to patriarchy.

The concluding tableau included the now-favourite Stein device, namely a silent picture. The back wall flew out and the Furies become caryatids upholding the pedestal of governmental authority, giving the whole thing a human face. Justice became embedded within the Greek system, making the democratic process stronger because of the tension divinely built into it. Stein himself created most of the prose dialogue in German from several German translations. The purpose above all, he said, was to make Aeschylus' text as clear as possible. The translation became a bestseller in Germany with over 20,000 copies sold soon after the production's premiere.[57]

As noted earlier, Stein often disparaged his earlier productions, but *The Oresteia* remained fond in his memory. 'I regard that production as the only reasonable effort on my part that I accomplished in those days. Everything I was interested in at the time – archeology, philology, anthropology – I was able to put into practice. The Greek theatre operated with quasi-ritualistic elements, yet carried with it at the same time an appeal to the rational mind and to rationality.' Stein concluded at the end of his Greek inquiries that theatre is not, as many believe, a ritual endeavour. In fact,

> it is structurally opposed to any form of ritualization. It is also opposed to myth. In a certain sense, theatre actually kills myth. After World War II, there was a sense that Greek tragedy was a kind of festival in honor of Dionysos. That is complete nonsense. What actually happens is the destruction of religion through the theatricalization of the sacred. If you really analyze Greek tragedy, then you understand everything you need to know about the theatre. It is the *sine qua non* of all theatre study.[58]

The Oresteia was not only invited to the 1981 Theatertreffen; it toured to several other European theatre festivals in France, Spain, Italy, Poland and Greece, where the hosts built a site-specific theatre for the production accommodating 3,500 spectators per performance. Fourteen years later, on 29 January 1994, Stein staged the production in Russian at the Red Army Theatre in Moscow. It then toured to many Russian cities.

Stein's Chekhov productions

Stein's relationship with the Russian theatre and with the plays of Anton Pavlovich Chekhov (1860–1904) was remarkable. He told an interviewer from the Russian-German Friendship Association of the Soviet Union that there was no rational explanation for it. He recalled pictures of himself as a child in a Russian shirt like the ones Tolstoy wore, with a belt around the waist. He also said that many Russians, when he visited the Soviet Union in 1975, may have thought that he was ethnically Russian, given his high cheek bones and narrow Tatar-like eyes. He spent generous amounts of time during 1975 as a guest of the Russian-German Friendship Association, visiting Moscow, St Petersburg, towns and cities in Siberia, Archangel, and the Solovetsky Islands. Bruno Ganz noticed that Stein had always had a preference for Russia and none whatsoever for America. He believed that the plays of Anton Pavlovich Chekhov became a channel for Stein's devotion to Russia and that his love of the Russian language came from the fact that West German children, unlike their East German counterparts, were never forced to learn Russian in school. Stein claimed to have learned the language entirely on his own. When he determined to direct Chekhov's *Drei Schwestern* (Three Sisters, 1984) in the new Schaubühne in Wilmersdorf, he once again set about discovering overlooked aspects of the play and dedicated himself to what he considered the essential metaphysics contained within Chekhov's dialogue.

Stein found Chekhov's dialogue somehow irresistible, because it contained neither technical brilliance nor richness of poetic metaphor. Its riches lay elsewhere, he believed. How it works in performance onstage is similar to what Vladimir Nabokov (1899–1977) described as 'keeping all his words in the same dim light and the same exact tint of gray, a tint between the color of an old fence and that of a low cloud'. There is little evidence that Stein had read much of Nabokov, but his work with actors on Chekhov's dialogue reveals startling parallels with Nabokov's thinking. 'The variety of Chekhov's moods', wrote Nabokov, 'the flicker of his charming wit, the deeply artistic economy of characterization, the vivid detail, and the fade-out of human life – all the peculiar Chekhovian features – are enhanced by being suffused and surrounded by a faintly iridescent verbal haziness'.[59] Stein's concentration on actors' line delivery in *Three Sisters* (and in a later production of *The Cherry Orchard*) mirrors Nabokov's thinking. The 'haziness' of the characters as protagonists in the plays was another factor that figured into Stein's fascination with Chekhov's dialogue. Both the imprecision of traditional dramaturgical functions for the characters and the near absence of plot in his plays heighten the significance of acting Chekhov's plays. Actors must move and speak according to the extraordinarily subtle relationships their characters have with one another. Unlike Stanislavski, however, Stein had little interest in a character's 'inner life'. Though he consulted Stanislavski's promptbooks and even used some of the Russian director's staging he found there, he felt that many of Stanislavski's techniques for actors were unsuitable for the Schaubühne actors. They were unsuitable because Stein wanted to create a realism that went beyond Stanislavski, a kind of realism which in the subsequent opinion of many critics surpassed normal expectations of what 'reality' onstage actually was. Stein had often stated his scepticism of 'reality' onstage, because the stage is further removed from reality than anyone suspects. The very act of speaking onstage is an act of alienation, so why pretend otherwise? True, Brecht had insisted on performances that 'distanced' the audience, which he termed *Verfremdung*, a term that limned his political agenda. Stein's rejection of both Stanislavski's sense of realism commensurate with his rejection of Brecht's politics resulted in acts of utterance onstage with unprecedented calibration in tonality, phraseology and cadence. *Three Sisters* won another *Theatertreffen* invitation (the seventeenth of Stein's career) and *Theater heute*'s 'Production of the Year' award. The most astonishing facet of this production took place when Stein took it to Moscow and staged it in Stanislavski's Moscow Art Theatre in German without subtitles or simultaneous translation.

Most Russian audiences were familiar with *Three Sisters*, but familiarity alone does not explain the rapture with which they greeted every performance. What enthralled Russian audiences was Stein's understanding of what Nabokov had termed Chekhov's creation of the most admirable among the laws of Nature: 'the survival of the weakest'. Nabokov said that Chekhov took a special artistic pleasure in the creation of characters whose major attribute was dreaming of a distant utopia. 'They broke their own lives and the lives of others, they were silly, weak, futile, hysterical; but as Chekhov suggests, blessed be the country which produces such a person. They missed opportunities, they shunned action, they spent sleepless nights in planning worlds they could not build.'[60] They were a particular Russian species of idealist, weak in determination, pure in spirit, strong in desire for moral elevation. That Stein was able to uncover such a species and exhibit it on stage in German before Russian audiences was to many observers nothing short of miraculous.

Stein recapitulated his Chekhovian success with *Der Kirschgarten* (The Cherry Orchard) in 1989. In contrast to his treatment of the characters in *Three Sisters*, however, Stein's *Cherry Orchard* had a protagonist: the cherry orchard itself. Around the orchard, human characters served as a chorus to comment on, manipulate and ultimately destroy the orchard. The principal chorus member in this sense was Mme. Lyubov Andreievna Ranevskaya (Jutta Lampe), owner of the heavily mortgaged ancestral estate on which the cherry orchard stands. As creditors close in on her, she refuses throughout the play to convert the orchard into subdivided lots that would save the whole estate, which is located near the new train station. Doing so would bring all manner of *dachniki* in search of respite from the summer heat; such people Mme. Ranevskaya cannot accept. She runs an emotional gantlet of exhaustion, hysteria, eccentric emotionality, regret, self-pity, volatile outbursts, renunciation, weeping, promises kept and unfulfilled – all of them manifestations of a debilitated Russian, one whose soul is 'hunchbacked', as Gorky describes such individuals in *Summerfolk*. Through such twisted debilitation, the orchard will be transformed into vulgar *dachas* like the one presented in *Summerfolk*. Chekhov leaves in doubt the twisted fate of Mme. Ranevskaya as she sinks deeper and deeper into the swamps of her existence – her misfortune in love, her hopeless incapacity at everything she tries to do, a good person who brings no good to anybody. Her constant faltering and floundering causes her always to hope something will turn up to save her. She has shattered her own life and the lives of others so that in the final scene she is forced to listen to the sounds of the woodsmen cutting down her orchard. To accompany those sounds, Stein used a scenic device he had employed to great effect for *Saved* nearly two decades earlier: silence. Everyone was packed and ready to depart the estate. They all just sat there in immobile stillness. It is a common Russian practice to sit mute for a moment to bid farewell before a journey. After all have said their farewells and exited the stage, the peasant Firs emerges, wondering where everyone has gone and whether they have forgotten him. It's a shocking moment, the abandonment of Firs after his long years of service to the family. He stumbles around and then lies down on the sofa. Suddenly a huge cherry tree limb (no doubt the largest in the orchard) crashes through the window, sending splinters of glass and wood everywhere. Firs lies motionless on the sofa, presumably dead of a broken heart.

Conclusion

Critics were nearly unanimous in their praise for *The Cherry Orchard*. It was Stein's last critical triumph in Germany, making the farewell scene in the production a kind of symbolic valedictory departure. Stein had realized that he and his colleagues at the Schaubühne were drifting apart a few years earlier when he had surgery in a nearby hospital and required a week's convalescence. None of his colleagues visited him, not even Jutta Lampe, his colleague and companion for nearly twenty years. He had resigned from his post as artistic director in 1985 and returned occasionally through 1990. After 1990, he embarked on a 'freelance' directing career that included opera productions in North America, Europe, Great Britain and Russia. The theatre directorship of the Salzburg Festival featured both opera and theatre stagings, which included numerous Shakespeare stagings and premieres of works by Botho Strauss.[61] Among Stein's most sensational stagings after his departure from the Schaubühne were Goethe's entire text of *Faust I* and *II* staged for the 2000 Hanover World Expo and the entire *Wallenstein Trilogy* by Friedrich Schiller in 2007.

Stein's production of *Faust I* and *II* premiered in Hanover, but it had lengthy runs thereafter in Berlin and Vienna. As was his usual practice even in the early days of the Schaubühne, he oversaw the conversion of enormously large spaces into eighteen different stage and seating arrangements at a cost of 24 million Deutschmarks (about $18.5 million at the time). At one point, the audience joined in the staging while they sat at banquet tables, sharing dinner with the performers. In Hanover, one of the performers was supposed to have been one of Stein's long-time colleagues, Bruno Ganz, playing the elder Faust. But midway through rehearsals, Ganz fell from a platform and broke his pelvis; he rejoined the production when it transferred to Berlin. Stein himself suffered a severed finger after a severe injury in Hanover. He, the cast and crew had by that time dedicated over two years to the project, rehearsing for eighteen months in Hall 23 on the Expo grounds in Hanover to create what Stein hoped would be the most perfectly spoken production of *Faust* in German theatre history.[62] Stein promised no new interpretations, no quips and cranks, no wanton wiles, no nods nor becks, no wreathed smiles, just fifteen hours and all 12,111 lines of the complete play. He stated that he would privilege the play's text, paying meticulous attention to hidden details for effective stage presentation. He also insisted on musicality in line delivery. Intonation, gestures, movement and text were all to complement each other together. At the same time, actors were to 'speak against' the musical accompaniment Stein had commissioned from composer Arturo Annecchino (b. 1954).[63]

Every line was letter perfect, prompting furious denunciation from many critics. They accused Stein of being a 'text fetishist' in the belief that no one could possibly understand a text-true performance without reference to contemporary concerns such as environmental degradation, overpopulation, the spread of poverty throughout the Third World, etc. Some critics stated that without such references, Stein had actually limited the audience's imagination. Stein's approach, apparently, did not limit audience attendance. Most of the performances in Berlin and Vienna subsequent to the premiere in Hanover were sold out weeks in advance. The eleven-hour production of Schiller's *Wallenstein Trilogy* of 2007 was likewise an exercise in fidelity to the text. Again Stein reaped the scorn of critics, who ridiculed him as a kind of cleric holding church services in the classics. *Wallenstein* also featured a star actor in the leading role: Klaus Maria Brandauer (b. 1943), who played the Thirty Years' War field marshal plagued by doubt. He was an insomniac believing in his destiny yet troubled by indecipherable astrological omens. Staged in a refurbished fermentation hall and cold storage warehouse of a defunct brewery in Berlin, it cost about €6 million (about $8 million at the time) and attracted film and television stars, major government officials, sports stars and serious theatregoers from all over the country. Audiences knew what kind of arduous ordeal lay ahead of them: witnessing three plays on narrow metal seats, broken up by four intermissions. But for many it was worth hearing the cast declaim some of Schiller's most elevated language and frequently quoted aphorisms: 'The dictates of the heart are the voice of fate'; 'War is an unseemly, forceful handiwork'; 'I know my boys from Pappenheim!' or 'When the wine goes in, strange things come out.'

Prior to the premiere, several cultural watchdogs in Germany had begun accusing Stein of trying to execute a publicity stunt rather than direct a classic of the German stage. Others accused him and fellow director Claus Peymann (whose Berliner Ensemble functioned as co-producer, providing salaries for many of the actors, their costumes and most of the production's publicity) of foisting show business values on considerations of both art and cultural integrity. What business did the Berlin Senate have in subsidizing a star turn and for an ageing star who was Austrian to boot?

In response to such questions, Stein stated that his production of Schiller's classic was in fact a noteworthy description of political confusion. At the core of his directorial intention was Schiller's conception of Europe, which in the trilogy's second play *The Piccolomini* takes pride of place. In the long discursive deliberations of Wallenstein's lieutenant general Octavio Piccolomini, Europe is an idea. It could become 'the culmination', Piccolomini states. Yet aggrandizement combined with superstition consumes nearly the whole of *The Piccolomini* and most of the trilogy's third play, *Wallenstein's, Death* before Irish agents assassinate Wallenstein; by that time, all striving has ceased; Octavio's son Max and Wallenstein's daughter Thekla are casualties of the conflict. In between have rained torrents of words, which often threatened to drown out the stage picture. The design of Ferdinand Wögerbauer (with whom Stein had begun working in 1996 and who had designed *Faust I* for Hanover Expo) was reminiscent of several Stein extravaganzas, dating all the way back to those of Wilfred Minks in the late 1960s and Karl-Ernst Herrmann in the 1970s. It was stunning, emplaced on the entirety of the purpose-built stage, measuring approximately 130 feet wide by about 80 feet deep. Technical director Uwe Arsand's stage crew made over twenty complicated major scene changes (as they had also done for *Faust I* and *II*) executed in relatively brief periods of time over what sometimes seemed like vast distances. The enormous stage space, combined with Schiller's poetic idiom, the lofty ideas he attempts to place in historical context, and the sheer weight and number of words – all made for a marathon that compared favourably with Stein's other lengthy productions.

Stein's legacy, however, will not consist predominantly of his extravaganzas. Historians will remember Stein mostly for the work he did at the Schaubühne in both Kreuzberg and Wilmersdorf, winning invitations year after year to the *Theatertreffen* and in effect changing the course of German theatre history. Working with a company of actors, designers and technicians who remained loyal to him for a term longer than most German directors can expect, Peter Stein enjoyed a reputation for innovation comparable perhaps only to that of Max Reinhardt. Stein was also instrumental in refocusing theatrical attention on West Berlin during the Cold War period. Berlin had been the unquestioned 'Theatre Metropolis' of the German-speaking world from the 1870s to 1944, the peak of the theatrical pyramid, the professional goal of nearly every theatre artist. In the wake of Berlin's destruction after 1945, most of its former leading directors were either dead, in jail or scattered elsewhere. West German theatre became decentralized in various cities until 1989, with the fortunes of some rising and others falling from time to time in Bremen, Bochum, Cologne, Düsseldorf, Darmstadt, Frankfurt, Hamburg, Munich or Stuttgart. Stein changed all that in the 1970s.

Unlike other outstanding German stage directors who preceded him, Stein found himself completely ostracized among his contemporaries about twenty years after his emergence as the most significant director since the end of the Second World War. By the mid-1980s, he unknowingly and unwittingly became caught in the cogwheels of a complicated cultural wrangle called the *Historikerstreit* (Historians' Dispute) that began in 1986. One of the leading participants in the dispute, Michael Stürmer, stated that 'in a land without history, the future is controlled by those who determine the content of memory, coin the concepts, and interpret the past'. Many believed that Stein was, or at least should have been, in the business of controlling that future. At the very least, his critics believed, he was in a position to have consciously influenced the direction German theatre should take. He had, after all, completely reinterpreted and given new meanings to several German texts over the past twenty years; he had opened unfamiliar windows and allowed fresh breezes of perception to clear the air inside the German theatre for a whole new generation of audiences.

The problem, however, was that Stein had absolutely no interest in coining new concepts or in disputes about what was soon to become postmodernist reinterpretations of interpretations. Many accused him of betraying the 'cause' of refiguring cherished texts in an effort to make them vehicles of political agenda-formation, social improvement and even *Vergangenheitsbewältigung* ('coming to grips with the past'). Stein dismissed most of the 'interpreted' texts as 'assholes', in his estimation, both stupid and uninformed. He refused even to consider working with the newer generation of directors, in many of whom he found 'authoritarian remnants of the German Democratic Republic'. What about working with some of the new women directors? 'Women should not be directors,' he concluded.[64]

6

Peter Stein: Politics in Art

K. Scott Baker

Peter Stein impressed theatre critics and audiences with his professional directorial debut, Edward Bond's *Saved* at the Munich Kammerspiele in 1967. Several elemental preoccupations found throughout his work already characterized this staging – a focus on the actors, a simple and open theatrical space, and a demonstrated commitment to the text as the source of the performance. These principles have manifested themselves differently over the course of Stein's career but underlie his practices even into the twenty-first century. Clearly, these are not radical deviations from or innovations in the traditions of theatrical performance. The splash he made derived primarily from the ways in which he made texts, primarily canonical but also contemporaneous, relevant for the politically volatile post-1968 Germany. That is, his political, socially critical orientation provided the framework for his renditions of plays on stage.

Stein's early projects thus require a closer analysis in order to identify how he established himself so quickly and so prominently in the West German theatre milieu. Although he has consistently distanced himself from any particular political group, the choice of plays, theatrical adaptations of the texts, and the kinds of contextualizing materials that were used to inform the performers (historical and textual research) and the audiences (programme notes), all bore the imprints of a leftist orientation. In no way does this political cast imply a pandering to the audience, which, in retrospect,

---

Unless otherwise noted, all translations are by the author.

might be assumed to have mirrored this orientation. In actuality, theatre audiences, at least at the time of his premiere, tended to prefer productions that could be perceived as a close representation of the authorial position on the subject matter at the heart of the given play. Instead, Stein's take on the plays he chose and brought to performance challenged mainstream conventions from a socially critical position that, by the time he began establishing himself in Berlin in 1970, could be culturally understood and artistically appreciated by West German theatregoers beyond the issues of an individual's personal politics and even beyond the troupe's clearly Marxist position. Looking at Stein's beginnings in Munich provides examples of how his productions could be both identifiably leftist and yet appealing as theatrical performances.

Three stagings in particular illustrate how Stein's preoccupation with theatrical methods coincided with the ostensible political context of the productions. By the time Stein's migration from Munich to Berlin (via Bremen) had culminated in a celebrated production of Ibsen's *Peer Gynt* in 1971, he had shaped an ensemble organization that extended beyond just the actors to include the entire professional cadre of the theatre. This ensemble – and not just the director(s) – was responsible for the artistic decisions of every performance. This democratic collective structurally mirrored the leftist political sentiments that already informed Stein's earlier development in Munich. Each of the three stagings with which he transitioned to Berlin reflects a particular problem that their theatre could mediate effectively: Goethe's *Torquato Tasso* and the problem of the artist when art is defined by moneyed interests; Brecht's *Die Mutter* (The Mother) and the problem of the individual response to a society tolerant of the state's use of repressive policies; and *Peer Gynt*, whose title character exemplifies unfettered individuality in disregard of his impact on others.

These three stagings also bridge into Stein's position as the leader of the Schaubühne in West Berlin. This stage, which was originally located at the Hallisches Ufer in a less-desirable neighbourhood of West Berlin (because of its proximity to the Berlin Wall), became synonymous with Stein's name and practices from his arrival in 1970. He was also the most important agitator for its relocation to Lehniner Platz in a technologically cutting-edge new theatre building in 1981. The organizational structure of the Schaubühne, and the transformations it underwent that led to Stein's departure in 1984, reveal some of the most important aspects of his impact on theatre.

Since leaving the Schaubühne, Stein has taken on a variety of projects in several countries beyond Germany, and he continues to work as a guest director.[1] These projects show new interests in Stein's theatrical endeavours but are largely irrelevant for understanding his contributions to theatrical practices. In fact, his productions at the Schaubühne after *Peer Gynt*, and elsewhere after his departure from the Schaubühne, compel only cursory attention as he and his group become increasingly transfixed by aesthetic issues that are primarily internal to the theatre. His staging of Goethe's *Faust* in 2000 provides a capstone to his career and summarizes how political relevancy gave way to aesthetic preoccupations.

Munich in the 1960s

Stein was studying German and art history when he transferred from the university at Frankfurt to Munich in 1958. Even as he worked towards a dissertation that combined these two interests in an examination of pictorial representations in the literary works of E.T.A. Hoffmann (1776–1822), he invested more time and energy on his interest in theatre. On the one hand, this took the form of theatre tourism with travel in the late 1950s and early 1960s to Milan, Paris, London and Berlin in order to attend performances, and on the other hand, an active participation in student theatre in which he alternately acted, directed or played the role of intendant.[2] In this milieu, he made contacts with people who worked for professional theatres in Munich, and ultimately he abandoned his dissertation in order to work at the Kammerspiele.

Beginning in 1964, Stein embarked on a journeyman-type education in this theatre, one of Munich's most important. Through the intercession of a friend from the theatre group, he began doing 'free-lance' work as an assistant to the dramaturgical and directorial staff. As Michael Patterson has pointed out, this kind of position in the German theatre industry is rather menial, comprising 'trivial tasks that the director cannot be troubled with'.[3] And yet within three years, Stein was allowed to direct the premier of *Gerettet* (Saved, 1967), a controversial and disturbing play by Edward Bond, a contemporary British playwright whose work had yet to be performed in West Germany. Stein had clearly made an impression on those above him, and not simply because of his work ethic or his willingness to be a patsy in case the play proved too controversial.[4] Stein had already developed principles that made his staging of *Saved* the performance of the year for the influential theatre monthly *Theater Heute* (Theater Today).

Stein drew on competencies from his university studies and applied them in personally creative ways to the theatre. Art history gave him a background in historically contextualizing works of art according to the modes of production and aesthetic norms of the period in which they were created. Stein was particularly interested in architecture, a focus that cultivated skills beyond historical appreciation and interpretation. There are obvious connections between studying the space and design of buildings and the design of theatrical stages and settings, yet Stein has rarely commented on this overlap. In his own assessment, and in that of several acquaintances, his architectural studies oriented him to the relationships between the small supporting parts of a structure and their role in the construction of the whole.[5] This dialectical mode of thinking and analysing predominates in German universities and only to a lesser extent in the artistic technical schools.

The same practices informed Stein's approach to textual interpretation and dramatization as well. He is especially known for his painstaking approach in working with actors line by line, and even word by word, as they develop their roles in rehearsal. This method of creating physical expressions of textual meaning at a micro level results from exacting interpretive work with the dramatic text. This kind of interpretive work stems from Stein's conviction that the most conflict-laden, and therefore most dramatic, parts of a play appear between the lines and must be elucidated before an actor can develop an appropriate physical and vocal expression of the text. This dramaturgical work relies on the kinds of literary analysis that are taught at German universities.

Thus, in contrast to the majority of German theatre professionals, Stein did not come out of any institutional programme for developing theatrical artists. He developed his criteria for performative standards and creativity by exposing himself to theatrical practices as an audience member and as an amateur participant, but above all he used academic methods of literary interpretation as the basis for imagining how dramatic ideas and conflicts could be communicated physically. Stein has even gone so far as to say that 'my most fundamental conviction is that European theater is a literary theater ... that theatricality is even subordinate to a different kind of signification', by which he means a primacy of the literary text.[6] And yet there is no doubt that in transforming literary signification into the medium of theatre, Stein concentrates on the body and voice of the actor to achieve the effects he desires.

For someone without formal training in the mechanics of acting and stage work, Stein's directorial method of bridging the gap between text and actor becomes an original, or at least signature, feature of his theatre. Rehearsals for *Saved* ran two months, which became a typical minimum span for Stein's rehearsals. He spends weeks reading through the script with the actors before they even move to the stage. This is the period in which Stein works within the group with each actor line by line to connect the character with an expression of the text that communicates its importance for the themes of the play. Based on research and background readings, the group's perspectives, Stein's conception and the actor's interpretation, decisions are made during this work about intonation, expression and interaction. These microcosmic articulations then lead to ideas and practices about the physical expressions of the characters in the subsequent phases of rehearsals.

Fritz Kortner modelled exactly this kind of work between director and actors at the Kammerspiele. Kortner himself was one of the most famous actors working in Berlin in the 1920s, playing leading roles in some of the most influential productions of the period and working with legendary directors like Max Reinhardt, Erich Engel and Leopold Jessner. He is often identified as the paradigmatic actor of expressionism in theatre and film with an acting style characterized by an emphasis on exaggerated facial expression and emotive use of the body. As a director, Kortner invested a tremendous amount of time working with the actors on declamation and gesture, work that was based on detailed and nuanced readings of the play to be performed. Kortner was so insistent that the actors achieve their highest level of performance that he would even delay his premieres at the Kammerspiele past their advertised date. Although Stein worked directly with Kortner only after Stein had already directed his first plays, he still credits Kortner with having the greatest influence on his own approaches to directing.[7] Stein's second play at the Kammerspiele, Brecht's *Im Dickicht der Städte* (In the Jungle of the Cities, 1968), can easily be seen as a nod to Kortner, who played Shlink in the 1924 Berlin premiere of the play.

The other significant model for Stein at the Kammerspiele was Therese Giehse, an actress who had worked in Brecht's theatre productions both before and after the Nazi period. Giehse was directing at the Kammerspiele and was one of the first directors with whom Stein worked directly as assistant director. In her memoirs, Giehse was struck primarily by Stein's work with the text: 'He analyses a play exactly, pulls it apart, dissects it with incredible curiosity. ... He clarifies the piece, peels off its different layers with all his curiosity and imagination, but he does not change it.' She assesses his directorial style as 'gentle' and 'easy-going' in the manner of Brecht, which is to say, demanding without being authoritarian.[8] Giehse's comments derive from several different projects with Stein and corroborate their shared belief in the cooperative work of actors and director. Stein poignantly reflected his admiration for her in a eulogy that he contributed to West Germany's leading weekly news magazine, *Der Stern*, in which he praises above all her talents of expressiveness.[9]

Stein had thus already developed an actor- and text-centric working method when he was given the opportunity to stage his first production in the Werkraumtheater, or 'workshop' theatre, of the Kammerspiele early in 1967. Edward Bond's *Saved* treats contemporary coming-of-age problems in working-class South London: conflicts with parents and boyfriends/girlfriends, premarital pregnancy, violence born of idleness and resentment. A shocking and controversial scene shows a group of male friends tormenting the baby in its stroller in a park and ultimately stoning it to death.

Although *Saved* had been previously translated into standard German, the translator of the script for the Kammerspiele performance chose to translate the Cockney dialect of the English original into Bavarian dialect. Dialect in Germany is typically associated with less-educated populations, but Bavarian is more commonly spoken than most other dialects because of regional cultural values; it nevertheless retains an association with lower-class populations. In terms of the theatrical work on the piece, the rendition in dialect benefitted Stein: the actors, even those who were comfortable with

Bavarian, were forced to work diligently on enunciation and emphasis in order to make themselves as understandable as possible for the audience. In the process, the deliberate textual work afforded Stein the opportunity to develop the actors' performances with similar attention to detail. However, the dialogue remained difficult to decipher for many theatregoers who were less adept at Bavarian (including, of course, many critics from the national press), and this increased the alienation of those audience members who associated the dialect with regional patriotism.

The selection of actors also played into Stein's favour. Few of the regularly featured actors at the Kammerspiele were young enough to portray the characters in Bond's play, and so Stein was able to draw in young, less experienced actors who were less inculcated in the practices of the established theatres and more open to new working methods. Some of these actors would continue to work with Stein for many years and at several venues.

The stage design by Jürgen Rose also featured a number of elements that would characterize Stein's stages. The centre of the stage was left broadly open, with simple sets depicting partial interior rooms extending from the left and right sides. A series of panels, two rows and over 4 metres high, were simply coloured and variously lit to invoke a muted, run-down intimation of modernity; a lit-up juke box stood rear centre and played contemporary pop music during scene changes. The cast moved the plain furniture and other set pieces themselves during changes and remained visible at the wings of the stage throughout the performance. The props marked the space of the action, whether in a park, a living room or a bar. The removal of the curtain, scene changes provided by the actors and simplicity of the stage became hallmarks of Stein's productions.

Finally, the programme for the show deviated markedly from expectations of plot summary and background information. In addition to a translation of Bond's forward to the print edition of his play, Stein and the German translator for their rendition, Martin Sperr, presented a list of twenty-three questions that provoked the audience members to work out their own answers in response to the performance. Some prompted the audience to infer attributes of the characters beyond what was immediately shown – 'Is Liz good in bed?' – while others pushed viewers to think about larger social questions – 'Is television a viable opportunity as an alternative education?'[10] The play itself is open-ended, and the programme intentionally mirrored the shifted responsibility for constructing meaning from the stage to the audience.

In the rather brief justification that *Theater Heute* made for naming *Saved* the 'performance of the year', the authors predominantly cite the production's formal features; the article in fact consists mostly of photographs with citations.[11] Certainly in retrospect, these features do mark the production as a sharp contrast to what was happening in the theatres of West Germany at the time. But the thematic connections to the social changes occurring outside the theatre should not be overlooked. The younger generation in Bond's play feels abandoned by their parents and elders and lacks role models in general. These topics resonated for the first post-war generation of West Germans who were then entering the work force, starting careers or working on university degrees. Stein's contemporaries were increasingly strident about calling social norms and assumptions into question, faced as they were with an older generation that wanted to hide their complicity or passivity during the Nazi period or who simply wanted to forget the uncomfortable past.

A few months later, for his third production at the Werkraumtheater of the Kammerspiele, Stein staged Peter Weiss's *Viet Nam-Diskurs* (Vietnam Discourse, 1968). This is a documentary play, made up almost exclusively of textual excerpts from official governmental materials as well as published artefacts by media and anti-war groups. Documentary theatre was critically popular in West Germany of the 1960s, and Weiss was perhaps the most prominent dramatist of the movement. Staging the work in Munich made sense sociologically – Munich has one of the largest universities, and as the theatre and film centre of West Germany (second only to West Berlin), was home to student and other alternative theatre groups.[12]

Vietnam Discourse condemns the US involvement with its criticism of colonialist and imperialist practices of the Western states; there are clear connections drawn to the militarism of Nazi Germany, and implications that denazification in West Germany remained unfinished, particularly with regard to many of those who held political power. Stein added a group of intellectual observers at a cafe table onto his stage – which again was open with a simple backdrop and props used to mark settings – in order to extend the focus of criticism uncomfortably onto the audience as well. In spite of this extension of criticism to the viewing audience, Stein and his co-director, Wolfgang Schwiedrzik, also took sides with Weiss, and decided, with the unanimous agreement of the cast, to take up collections for the Viet Cong from the audience after the performances. The management of the Kammerspiele condemned this action and cancelled the play after three performances.

While *Saved* had made connections to a German social reality, the performance and actions surrounding *Vietnam Discourse* demonstrated Stein's shared convictions with the political student movements of the late 1960s that advocated egalitarian democratic structures across social institutions, and transparency in decision-making by persons in power. Stein and his collaborators believed that both of these reform ideas could be applied not only to political institutions, but to the theatre as well – hence, in part, the cafe table in the staging of *Vietnam Discourse*. Stein and Schwiedrzik took the play to West Berlin, where the student movement was most radical at the time, and despite even more lively audience response and participation, met with the same fate – three performances and then cancellation because of the collections for the North Vietnamese.

Producing the *Vietnam Discourse* allowed Stein to connect the work of the theatre with the political reforms of society that were happening across West Germany. The staging was thus important as an anchor for his conviction that a democratic form of theatre can best serve democratizing processes in general. In the concluding section of the article titled 'Democracy Is Also Action' ('Demokratie is auch Aktion', August 1968) that they published in *Theater Heute*, Stein and Schwiedrzik state:

> From the very beginning we understood the staging of the 'Vietnam Discourse' as a model of democracy in practice. We applied methods of production that largely eliminated the traditional and unproductive division of labor between actors and directors. ... And, of course, the question of creating democratic conditions is one of the central topics of the play. Only by using our work methods was it possible to critically evaluate the claims of the play, use the theater to mediate these claims, and formulate our own position on genocide.[13]

A play like *Vietnam Discourse* makes explicit the connection between a play about democracy and using democratic processes to create that play. One of Stein's most important contributions to contemporary theatre is his insistence on using those practices for plays in which such themes are not so evident, in the conviction that the mediation of ideas in the theatre mirrors the way that the cast brings about that performance in rehearsal.

Text and tradition: Goethe's *Torquato Tasso*

The *Vietnam Discourse* performances in Berlin were also significant for being Stein's first at the Schaubühne am Hallischen Ufer. The group was invited to perform there by Dieter Sturm, who would later fulfil the role of intendant in Stein's ensemble at the Schaubühne. Making such connections was important, for although Stein was creating productions in Zürich and Bremen, he was not securely hired on at any theatre – one result of the *Vietnam Discourse* furore in Munich was his dismissal from the Kammerspiele. Stein's next performance at the Schaubühne was as part of the Berliner Festspiele, also known as the *Theatertreffen*, an invitational festival of the best productions from the country's stages. Stein was invited to bring his production of Goethe's *Torquato Tasso*, which he had created in Bremen.

   Torquato Tasso may be Goethe's most accomplished transformation of autobiographical material into literature. Goethe dramatically traces the Renaissance Italian poet Torquato Tasso's completion of his epic poem *Jerusalem Liberated* (1581) and shows his doubts about whether a work of art can ever be finished. This theme is one of three in the play that shows Tasso's conflicts with his benefactor, the Duke: Tasso is in love with the

Duke's sister, a princess who is above his station; and he is in competition with Antonio, who pursues the Duke's worldly, political interests, as opposed to Tasso's restriction to the field of the literary arts. Each of these plots reflects very similar situations in Goethe's position at the Weimar court in the 1780s. The completed version of the play in 1789 ushered in Goethe's classical period of production; it is written primarily in blank verse using iambic pentameter.

Torquato Tasso presents a challenge for a staging that is intended to draw connections between its performance and contemporary reality. In addition to its own historical distance from the late twentieth century, Goethe's play itself draws on historical material even further removed in time. The verse form and its importance for helping to mark out the new classical period in Goethe's production make it difficult to disconnect the play from the period of its creation. Stein had recently been invited to direct a play written in roughly the same period, Friedrich Schiller's *Kabale und Liebe* (Intrigue and Love) at Bremen in 1967. *Intrigue and Love* was Stein's second career production, between *Saved* and *In the Jungle of Cities*, and Stein took it on as a guest director in a new city with unfamiliar actors. His treatment reflected again his careful work with the text and with the actors in bringing the text to performance. He focused on the love story in the play rather than on its political aspects; indeed, the staging was explicitly lauded for not trying to make the play's political content contemporarily relevant.[14]

Stein and the company chose to use *Torquato Tasso* to analyse the role of the artist in society. Tasso is beholden to his benefactor not only because of his Renaissance-era relationship to the Duke, to whom he owes allegiance in a feudalistic conception, but also because the Duke affords him the conditions under which he can produce art – food and shelter, a reprieve from other work requirements, etc. For his part of this exchange, Tasso must fulfil his role as artist, meaning that it is not his place to meddle in worldly affairs. He is a functionary with a specific role to play, and he is restricted from transgressing the historical and cultural codes of this role in any way. Stein's production sought to question whether this is a good, or even viable, position for the artist to assume. The staging also promoted a contemporary reading of the problem – has this position changed in the almost two centuries since Goethe's play appeared, or even since the sixteenth century, when the historical Tasso lived?

One of the remarkable features of Stein's treatment of the play was the careful selection of verses to excise and the rearrangement of the verses retained.[15] The vast majority of the lines kept for the performance were unchanged from Goethe's original version. And for the most part, even though Stein changed the five-act structure into a series of thematically titled stations (e.g. 'Crowning with laurels', 'Leonore's plan', 'Antonio's opinion'), the sequence of the lines was largely maintained. Stein and his collaborators did create a prologue and two intermezzos for which they drew lines from several parts of the play; but even here, the lines were original to the play;

only their arrangement was altered.[16] This treatment corroborated Stein's claims that he tries to bring out aspects of the text that are 'between the lines' yet inherent in the text for the perceptive interpreter.

Stein also added a pantomime at the beginning of the play for the actor playing Tasso. Volker Canaris described this part of the performance in his review:

> Arching his back, fingertips pressed against his desk, his head thrown back, he strains for a kiss from the Muses; with delicate grace he reaches for a page of paper, examines his poem, quill held ready, with furrowed brow; stages himself as 'the poet', one foot crossed preciously over the other; drapes himself, with ceremonious pantomime, in the robes of the High Priest of Poetry; solemnly goes to take his place on the Throne of the Poet King, drawing his robes around him, gazing with dignity into the distance – and lands on the floor; finally, elbow resting on his knee, head bowed forward in deep thought, holding an imaginary lyre in his right arm, he bursts forth in verse.[17]

This introduction immediately removes Tasso from the pedestal on which, for most interpreters of the play, Goethe has installed him. Canaris's description of the pantomime obviously adds his own interpretation of the figure's poses and gestures, but his reading coincides with that of the majority of theatre critics who described the opening in their reviews. This opening also marks the production's critical shift from Tasso's/Goethe's personal conflicts as artists to a critique of the artist as such through a textual rearrangement. Goethe's play actually opens with a scene between the two princesses, and Tasso joins them only after their expository dialogue. By beginning with Tasso instead, Stein immediately informed the audience, who were by and large very familiar with the original text, that this production would not be a straightforward, traditional staging.

The printed programme also effected an unsettling recontextualization of the play. A trifold A3 page with text on both sides, so that there were twelve panels (although the panel format was not strictly observed), it provided excerpts from essays by Marx and Engels on the role of the artist and the arts in capitalist society. The only exception was a panel with a lithograph of a Mediterranean-esque garden with a quote from a West Berlin senator on the responsibility of the Senate to be fiscally responsible in managing the public arts. There was no information on Goethe, the creation of the play, its content or themes, or established interpretations. As was typical throughout Stein's career, the programme provided a wealth of information, but in defiance of the conventions for the contemporary theatregoer.

The stage was also characteristically simple. The only significant prop was Tasso's desk, covered with papers, and a chair; to the side of the stage, a white plaster bust of Goethe stood on the floor. The background was gold-coloured cloth, connoting the royal environs, and the costumes were luxuriant period pieces. But surrounding the entire playing area, the stage designer, Wilfried Minks, had erected a Plexiglas wall. The wall obviously trapped the characters into the court milieu in which the play is set – the élite milieu of the artist and benefactor are closed off to commoners, but so too are the elites trapped away from the everyday reality outside of the court. For the viewers, the set implied a fish bowl for the star-struck to watch the tribulations of the rich and famous, but only from a distance and without the hope of ever being on the other side of the wall.

Stein and the actors tried to break through this wall, however, and through the fourth wall that it represented in theatrical terms. During the intermission, they announced that whoever would like to stay in the room could take part in a discussion led by the actors. The discussion began with the actors describing the ways in which the rehearsals led them to the ultimate incarnations of the roles they were playing, and they shared their perspectives on what the play meant in the hope that the audience members would add their own perspectives. Bruno Ganz, for example, who played Tasso, said:

> The topic of this play doesn't just apply to us here on stage as artists, but also directly to you, the audience. Because the dependencies that we as artists are subject to in our work and lives are not significantly different from the dependencies that you are subject to in your work. Like you, we work in an organization; like you, we create a product; like you, we produce under pressure. Like you, our possibilities to determine the conditions of our work are limited – we have to turn in our work to our superiors and, like most of you, we cannot influence how our products will be used or what effects they will have on others.[18]

We can reproduce exactly what Ganz and the others said because the theatre management in Bremen, after the premiere at which the cast tried this, insisted that the speeches be written rather than impromptu. Management also insisted on the right to edit these speeches and deleted the criticisms of management's decision that the cast had put into their speeches.[19]

Because of this intervention and censorship, Stein afterwards considered the intermission discussions to have been eviscerated, since the audiences never participated as fully after the first time, when the cast had interacted with the audience casually rather than reading from pages. The cast also later reflected on how effective the (theatrical) arts were or could be for promoting democratic principles. As Werner Rehm, who played Antonio, pointed out in an interview:

> The question is, can we communicate via art with the audience about issues that impact us [as artists]? And if so, with which means? On the one hand, we have artistic practices that, through long-standing traditions, have become empty of meaning; and on the other hand, we

have 'modern means' [such as greater latitude of body expression, etc.]. But I must admit that we found none of the means at our disposal to be convincing, and so we took recourse to a direct conversation with the audience during the intermission. For those of us who want to create theater, that is not a sufficient solution.[20]

While these initial responses may seem resigned to the inefficiency of theatre as a means of promoting egalitarian democracy, they also suggest that while *Torquato Tasso* may not have been the most effective play for these intentions, there remains the possibility that other plays might prove more successful.

Stein's *Torquato Tasso* was undoubtedly effective at provoking sharp-worded reviews. The controversial reinterpretation elicited responses from dozens of West German theatre critics. That impact was amplified by the group taking the production on tour throughout the country in the summer of 1969. Many critics reacted negatively to an interpretation of the play that drew attention away from the beauty of poetic language that the play is famous for; others did not like the Marxist contextualization of the critique of the artist in society, or even that the play could be interpreted to offer a criticism of the artist at all. But even critics who panned the approach quite often lauded the technical performances of the actors, a confirmation of the techniques Stein and the cast were using to prepare the roles.[21] And, of course, there were many who responded positively to a production of a drama from Germany's classical period, by Germany's most respected author, that offered a new interpretation in relation to contemporary, political issues.

Brechtian *praxis*: *The Mother*

Stein's next production after *Torquato Tasso* moved back into the twentieth century and to a political context that related more directly to the troupe's principle interests. Although Stein had already staged Bertolt Brecht's *In the Jungle of the Cities* in Munich, his production of *The Mother* (1970), with which he made his formal debut at the Schaubühne as a regular director, demonstrates the ways in which he adapted Brecht's theatrical practices more effectively than he did in *In the Jungle of Cities*. The very fact that Stein chose a Brecht play for his West Berlin debut, just a couple of kilometres from Brecht's Berliner Ensemble in East Berlin, marks the staging as a statement of principles – both homage and innovation. Both of these aspects come to the fore above all in the choices made about 'epic' acting and staging practices.

Brecht and his theories of epic theatre (which Brecht later termed 'dialectic theatre') dominated post-war German stages on both sides of the division between East and West. In addition to having been an important playwright and director in the 'golden era' of modern theatre in Germany in the 1920s, Brecht was also an innovator who was able to articulate the evolution of his dramatic structures in terms of a coherent theoretical model. Perhaps most importantly, he had linked his theories to Communist criticisms of capitalism. As a result, he became an immediate target for persecution when the Nazis came to power in 1933. Having spent the pre-war and war years in exile, Brecht accepted the invitation of the East German government to return to Berlin in 1948 with the promise of heading his own theatre, the Theater am Schiffbauerdamm, where he continued to refine his theories with his Berliner Ensemble until his death in 1956. For West German theatre professionals, Brecht's theories retained importance despite the anti-Communism of the period because of Brecht's unquestionable status as a critic of Nazism and because of cultural discomfort with the Western occupying forces which, in the context of the Cold War, often seemed to mandate anti-Communism. For Stein's and subsequent generations, Brecht's ensemble model of the theatre also presented itself as an egalitarian model, even if the reality of the Berliner Ensemble – which most had not, of course, experienced directly – was less consistently democratic than it appeared.

Brecht wrote *The Mother* in the early 1930s as an adaptation of Maxim Gorky's novel about the revolutionary movement in Russia at the beginning of the twentieth century. The story thus already had the form of an 'epic', since the novel moves through several disparate settings and across a time span of decades; Brecht was able to condense the story into scenic 'stations' to give it dramatic form. The period around 1930 was also when Brecht was focused on creating *Lehrstücke*, or 'teaching plays', and he considered *The Mother* to be one such play. The *Lehrstücke* were intended above all as internally relevant plays for the ensemble to develop an 'alienated' acting style that Brecht believed would not only show the character in the play but also expose the perspective of the actor playing the role. The actor could thereby demonstrate agreement or disagreement with the attitudes and actions of the character. The parable in the *Lehrstücke* also had meaning for an outside audience, and these plays were typically prepared for public performance, not just for the training of the ensemble. Most were one-act or short plays, but a few were full-length plays, including *The Mother*.

The choice of Brecht's *The Mother* as the play to continue the group's exploration of meaningful theatre seems logical, given the responses of the actors to the experiences of *Torquato Tasso*. At a press conference in May 1970, Stein explained, 'First, the subject of the play is of interest – the prehistory of the October Revolution in Russia.'[22] The ensemble's interest in the prehistory of the Russian revolution continued the tactic of critiquing capitalism that was already evident in the programme of *Torquato Tasso*; that is, they assumed the same approaches as the student/protest movement for criticizing political structures that obscure power and impede democratic decision-making by connecting capitalism to the inability of the West German state to eliminate repression and censorship. Unsurprisingly, the programme for *The Mother* cited not only Lenin and Clara Zetkin but also Mao and the Chinese Communist Party, as well as Brecht and members of the Schaubühne directorial group, regarding connections between capitalism and repression of the underprivileged.

Stein continued his comments at the press conference: 'Secondly, it is of interest because Brecht wrote it as a *Lehrstück; Lehrstück* represents a learning process for those who take part in it.'[23] The mother in the play, Pelagea Wlassowa, initially responds fearfully to her son's agitational work, as he spreads flyers advocating revolution in his factory. The act of disseminating information and dissenting viewpoints thus stands at the centre of the play, and Wlassowa becomes convinced that this is the right thing to do, even when her son is arrested and then executed. Her changing perspectives on her son's illegal, democratizing activities also present the fundamental process of the *Lehrstück* – each character, and each actor, responds to her model of evaluating the consequences of inactivity in the face of repression and violence and chooses instead to actively counter oppression by spreading information.

Given the appropriateness of the play's structure and themes, Stein and his collaborators needed to make only minimal changes to the original text: they deleted one scene and shifted one action to a later point in the play. However, they did make substantial changes to Brecht's stage directions. These had mostly to do with the banners, projections and textual insertions that characterized the epic staging in the theatre, as developed by Brecht and Erwin Piscator in the late 1920s. For the original staging of *The Mother* in 1932, these techniques were still radically new for contemporary audiences, and according to Stein, were inserted primarily for their formal, structural impact. The audiences of 1970, however, actually required information in order to understand the events and justifications of the action in the play, contextualizations that Brecht could assume were known to his audiences. Stein's group also inserted *Lesetexte* or 'readings' that characters would speak as text-in-hand speeches. These included excerpts from Gorky's novel that helped maintain the continuity of the story (again, audiences in the early 1930s were much more likely to have read the fairly recently published and more immediately relevant novel than were audience members in 1970), but also included insertions that provided historical knowledge about political events in Russia that led to the revolutions of 1905 and 1917. These insertions thus served the dissemination of information; they mirrored, in a consequential way, the actions of Wlassowa in the play.

Not only did the ensemble continue Stein's method of close textual reading in the development of stage action and character exposition, but it also profited from a guest performance by Therese Giehse. Most of the actors who made up the ensemble at the beginning of Stein's time at the Schaubühne had joined him from his work in Zürich and Bremen; as a connection back to his time at the Kammerspiele, Giehse attested to a consistency of method that Stein had been using since before he met most of his actors. Giehse had also worked directly with Brecht both before and during their years of exile and as recently as 1949–52 with the Berliner Ensemble. As such, she represented the politically untainted Germans of the exile from Nazism as well as the direct connection to the methods and performances of Brecht. Stein wanted her to provide a paradigm of Brechtian acting, which, at least according to the critic Volker Canaris, she did: 'This Mother remains from first to last a proletarian, but her behaviour changes (and the production demonstrates this growth of consciousness as a practical, not as a psychological, process).'[24] As Canaris also attests, Giehse did not simply play the role as it had been performed in the Berliner Ensemble; she participated in the methodical rehearsal process along with the entire cast and developed the role for this particular staging.

The stage design also continued the same practices as in Stein's earlier productions. Here the audience was seated on three sides of the stage, which was bare except for the minimal props needed for each scene. The actors sat in chairs at the back of the stage throughout the performance and made the scene changes themselves. The inserted descriptions and contexts of the scenes were projected onto a blank banner hanging above the rear of the stage, and a black curtain formed the back wall.

The critical response to the performance almost unanimously confirmed the success of the technical-theatrical ambitions of the ensemble. Wolfgang Rainer proclaimed, 'one could almost give in to the fantasy of having experienced the birth of a "West-Berliner-Ensemble" that transported the tradition of revolutionary theater from the Schiffbauerdamm to the Hallisches Ufer with a single performance'.[25] Ingeborg Keller attested to 'an unusually clear and intense production that drew its effects from its concentration on the text'.[26] By this time, of course, Stein and his troupe were known to the professional critics, and the ensemble's working methods and theatrical intentions were documented by these same critics. Their evaluations read as a recognition that the group had achieved its main goals, particularly in those criticisms that summarize the performance history of the group up to this point, as for example Hellmuth Karasek did.[27]

Still, enough of the corps of theatre critics opined on the irrelevance or inappropriateness of *The Mother* for contemporary West Germany that Yaak Karsunke, a member of the Schaubühne's directorial staff, published a response to clarify the ensemble's choice of the play. Ironically, this was addressed to a group of seventeen critics who had undersigned a letter in support of continued subventions for the Schaubühne in the face of accusations by conservative members of the West Berlin Senate that the theatre was subversively advocating the overthrow of the government. The apologetic or dismissive stance of these and other critics regarding the choice and contextualization of *The Mother* provoked the ensemble to point out that working-class West Germans continued to be underprivileged and disenfranchised in capitalist society: '*The Mother* has been seen by about 3,000 apprentices and young workers so far – and in the post-performance discussions organized in the theater, *this* audience never had a problem drawing and identifying connections between the play and their own personal experiences.'[28] This moment can be seen in hindsight as a determining point in the direction of Stein's theatre group: they had made clear connections with working-class viewers regarding the obstacles that still impeded a further, egalitarian development of democracy in their society. However, considering that the theatregoing population tended not to be working class meant that the question of the theatre's efficacy for promoting democratization remained open.

Stein's 'bourgeois' theatre: *Peer Gynt*

One of the goals Stein and the ensemble challenged themselves to achieve was a greater knowledge of their own role in social inequality, both personally and historically, as members of the bourgeoisie. Their next production, Henrik Ibsen's *Peer Gynt*, was chosen in part to address that background.[29] This decision represented a turn away from an idealistically oriented theatre that sought out an activist role in changing social realities towards a better democracy. Significantly, the printed programme stated, 'A division of labor would have to be adopted to tackle preparations for the production. ... The knowledge acquired by some people would have to be "exploited".' The rhetoric of this admission, and the still-voluble but less-agitational character of the texts in the programme, broadcast the significance of this introspective turn.

But this is not to say that the Schaubühne ensemble was abandoning a political agenda. Instead, it was a turning inward of the group to find out what they could create using the theatre, given their own backgrounds and that of their typical audiences. Their intentions, and the production of *Peer Gynt* that arose from them, aimed at a criticism of the bourgeois stylization of culture as the product of creative individuals. The working methods were still collective and perhaps even more communal in their staging than hitherto – six actors played the titular role. These, and other elements of the production, were designed to contest any presumption by West Germans that a good education and an interest in (literary) culture suffice to make a good person.

Choosing *Peer Gynt* to explore these issues was significant in aesthetic terms. Ibsen's work had a more profound effect on the German theatre than perhaps any other national dramatic literature, and *Peer Gynt* stood out prominently among his plays on German stages – in Berlin alone, in a three-and-a-half-year period around the turn of the century, the play was performed 250 times.[30] Its connections to *Faust*, a play that fascinates Stein and is often thought to reflect a peculiarly German individual, are readily apparent. Their similarities, both in characterization and in epic, untheatrical structures, led to a common, if problematic, designation of *Peer Gynt* as the

'Nordic *Faust*'. Ibsen also began writing his plays at a time when Europe generally, and Germany specifically, produced much greater achievements in prose works than in drama, and Ibsen is credited with helping to regenerate drama for German modernity in ways that would lead to Naturalism, and via Strindberg to Expressionism. To undertake an investigation into how *Peer Gynt* relates to bourgeois self-understanding and its theatrical mediation in Germany hits a nail on the head.

Two themes particularly stand out in the production. First, the idea that the character Peer Gynt represents individuality in its most unfettered qualities provokes the most coherent critical position that the staging articulates. Peer Gynt does what he wants, regardless of the wishes of others or the harm he causes to them; when he himself is stymied or under attack, he rushes off to a new part of the world and a new adventure. Nineteenth-century viewers could identify with these traits, steeped in societies that considered social Darwinism to be a truism and European colonialism to be the 'natural' order of things. In a country still recovering from the racism and imperialism of the Nazi regime, these cultural assumptions as antecedents of their contemporary society made clear, critical connections between dramatic idealizations of individuality and social realities. The critical stance of the Schaubühne staging becomes most clear in the final moments of the play when Peer Gynt finally returns to Solveig. While this return was connoted as redemptive in its time, Stein connotes all of the highlights of Peer's travels as kitsch by having the chair in which Solveig sat with Peer in her lap brought downstage to a photographer who transforms the Romantic *mise en scène* into just another souvenir.

Second, the performance brought out the intertextuality of Ibsen's play, a characteristic that legitimates a primarily aesthetic approach for working with the text. Peer Gynt escapes from trolls, survives shipwrecks and visits the Sphinx; the stations of his adventures alone conjure up a tension between prose and drama that is formally reminiscent of fairy tales, a connection that the events of the story underscore. The text of the play cites or alludes to numerous other texts, another connection to *Faust*, although Ibsen does this with much less sophistication than Goethe. Critics even frequently referred to the circus-like qualities of the Schaubühne performance, a feature that was certainly reinforced in the staging but which is rooted in the text. The production suggested that the justification for Peer's irresponsible individualism lay in a Quixotic constitution of identity; only the source material is far more diverse than courtly epics, and far less noble – hence the centrality for many critics of the scene in which Peer Gynt compared himself to an onion.

Critics were again impressed by the carefulness with which Stein and his dramaturge for the project, Botho Strauß, created a new translation of the work, and by the inclusiveness of the staging that left almost nothing out of the original play. For a director whose forte is developing nuanced characterizations of the dramatic figures based on a meticulously prepared text, this kind of commentary was about to disappear from criticism as Stein's practice became expected. But an exploration of a text that is drawn to its aesthetic contexts requires such attention to the inclusiveness and exactness of its source. Ibsen's text is in fact so completely absorbed in aesthetic culture that it ignores fundamental elements of material cultural of importance for an evaluation of nineteenth-century sources of contemporary bourgeois culture. It is telling that Stein and Strauß manipulated the text most significantly in their re-characterization of the Buttonmoulder, whom they transformed to represent industrial production methods; in other words, the sphere of economic production, in spite of its importance in the late nineteenth century, was entirely absent from the original and had to be added in.

Inclusiveness and textual accuracy had consequences. A play as long as *Peer Gynt* that depicts travels around the world compels an extraordinary staging in order to present the entire text. Thus, the performance lasted, according to various accounts, anywhere from six-and-a-half to almost eight hours and was played over two nights. The stage stretched the entire length of the theatre so that spectators sat on either side, and seating capacity was reduced to make space. The stage sloped from one end to the other, with the machinery for the Sphinx on the higher end, and the lower end equipped to contain water for the ship travels (see Figure 6.1). Most of the action, though, took place on a roughly flat area in the middle. It is easy to see how many critics could reminisce about the circus, given the spectacular dimensions of the staging.

Peer Gynt enjoyed virtually unanimous admiration from reviewers, even hyperbolic in some instances:

> The theater collective [has] now surprised us with a production that, without doubt, belongs to the most sensational and tremendous [performances] that have been seen on any international stage in the last several years; this reviewer must admit that he cannot recall a comparable event of this scope to have been directed on stage in the last few decades. The decision to perform Henrik Ibsen's sprawling 'Peer Gynt' already speaks to the solid self-awareness and self-confidence of the director Peter Stein and of the young theater ensemble, that without doubt must be seen, more than ever, as the most important center of German theater today.[31]

Such a review would seem over the top if it did not reflect the similar opinions of so many of the professional theatre critics who saw a performance. However, the opinions of two of Stein's most consistently supportive critics, Ivan Nagel and Peter Iden, provide more ambivalent and insightful commentary on the production. Nagel's review in the *Süddeutsche Zeitung* (Southern German News) appeared under the title 'Geburt einer Truppe' (Birth of a Troupe), indicating his view that, with this performance, Stein's

FIGURE 6.1 *Peter Stein staged Henrik Ibsen's* Peer Gynt *in 1971 at the Schaubühne in West Berlin. Egypt is one of the places visited by the title character on his long quest to find himself. Photo by Binder/ullstein bild via Getty Images (Getty #545957947).*

ensemble had made a quantum transformation into a more cohesive unit than they had been before. And yet he concluded his review with a series of rhetorical questions that problematize whether this troupe could accomplish its self-assigned task of ideologically debunking capitalism and exploitation. He then answers his questions, in a way: 'I don't feel competent to continue on to an answer, but rather to a preliminary admission: The performance yielded many insights for me, rather than one – its incomparable fun sprang from thousandfold perceptions, its sense of reason, and not, it seems to me, from a single, true insight.'[32] For Nagel, moving beyond the prescription of political critique to a more open, diverse and aesthetic exploration of themes had brought the ensemble to a new level of self-constitution. For Peter Iden, the turn to aesthetic contexts similarly opened a new way for the Schaubühne group to investigate West German social conflicts. 'The performance is also a part of the working through of our history. It shows where the models for the society in which we live have their origins. It questions, how important the value really is of fantasy, [of] imagination, and that means: the value of art. ... Peter Stein has defined anew – we can say that quite summarily – what it means when we say "critical theater"'.[33]

Peer Gynt represents a turning point in the preoccupations of Stein's theatre group; to this day, some would say that this production represents their highest achievement. In any case, the development of practices from *Saved* up through *Peer Gynt* culminates from this point on in an orientation towards specific kinds of theatrical problems and issues that would guide the decisions of the ensemble into the 1980s. The departure from a specifically anti-capitalist, pro-democracy theatre of advocacy coincided with a departure from practices that, up until *Peer Gynt*, had informed the identity of the group as a particularly principled ensemble organization.

The organization of the Schaubühne

By the production of *Peer Gynt* in May 1971, the ensemble organization of the Schaubühne was widely known and equally widely considered to be the basis for the success of the company. Ensembles have several positive features for producing consistent performances. There is greater knowledge about the other actors in the ensemble, their tendencies and strengths, and therefore often greater trust among the actors. The same is true for the relationship with the director, both individually and as a group. If the ensemble is supported by the theatre in which they play, then there is less pressure on the individual members to take guest roles with other companies, which involves absences during rehearsals or organizational meetings. And although many theatres prefer to use guest actors because they believe that well-known stars will increase box office revenues, there is an argument to be made for audience familiarity with the ensemble actors.

A group of actors began to cohere around Stein by the time of his second directorial engagement at the Bremer Theater in 1967. Several actors from there accompanied him to his engagement at the Schauspielhaus in Zürich, and several more followed from Zürich to the Schaubühne in Berlin. In Zürich, the group was already working informally, in addition to the rehearsals for the Schauspielhaus performances, on material that would become later productions. It was also in Zürich that the group set out in print some of the principles of their ensemble organization, which included benefits of such an organization for staging quality productions.[34] Several of these principles noted the correspondence between ensemble organization and egalitarian democratic decision-making, and these were codified into a set of rules at the Schaubühne. The idea of an ensemble was extended to the directors and directorial staff, so that technically all of the directors employed at the Schaubühne were listed as the directors of a staging; one of the accusations that Karsunke levelled at critics who did not understand the choice of *The Mother* as the first play for the ensemble at the Schaubühne is that they ignored the collective directorship of the play and ascribed its production to Stein alone.[35] But the ensemble organization was in fact extended to everyone who worked at the Schaubühne, including stage hands, carpenters, mechanics and electricians. As members of the ensemble, all of these persons were obligated to take part in all organizational meetings, which were held at least once a week, and typically more often. Moreover, everyone had a vote in all decisions made, which ranged from what plays to stage for the coming season to technical decisions about particular aspects regarding the production of a given play (see Figure 6.2).

Stein's intensive work with the text of the play entailed a substantial amount of research, which he often undertook himself along with the dramaturge and in some instances with other members of the directorial staff as well. From their initial research, they collected and distributed particularly important texts for everyone to read and discuss in preparation for their roles and the stagings. Although the actors and technical staff did not participate in the first phase of the research, the second phase was obligatory; not only were many of the texts rather challenging (e.g. Marx and Engels, Lenin, etc.), but for some productions there was a fairly large number of background readings, some of which were quite long, and

FIGURE 6.2 *Peter Stein works with his ensemble in 1974. Photo by Kneidl/ullstein bild via Getty Images (Getty #537136605).*

many of which were difficult; this was especially true for *Peer Gynt* and again later for the investigations in the drama of antiquity and Elizabethan England.

While these practices were in line with the ideals of egalitarian democracy that undergirded the ensemble organization, in practice they led to conflicts and required an enormous amount of work time. Thus, the requirements and qualifications for participation in the decisions of the ensemble began to erode rather quickly. The actual practice of sharing directorial authority and responsibilities never really appeared to have caught on, so that to a great extent, the directorial practices at the Schaubühne did not differ significantly from those of other theatres. The mechanical staff members were unionized and barred from working the kinds of hours that the directorial staff and actors typically put in at the theatre, which caused problems especially with Stein. By the time they were staging *Peer Gynt*, roughly a year after beginning at the Schaubühne, the most rigid of requirements for participation had dissipated, and only the actors and the directorial staff of a particular production conducted their work along more relaxed assumptions of democratic standards.[36]

The coincidence of the ensemble's increasing focus on aesthetic contexts of the role of theatre in society and the movement away from their efforts to raise consciousness about democratic principles, both in their productions and in their work organization, have not been a significant topic in the critical literature about the Schaubühne. It is quite possible that they were unrelated. The turn towards aesthetic concerns did, however, lead the ensemble down a path in which they became preoccupied with the heritage of the theatre. This appears most prominently in the creation of two original works, the *Antikenprojekt* (Antiquity Project, 1974) and *Shakespeare's Memory* (1976). Both were created on the same basic premises as Brecht's *Lehrstücke* – they were intended primarily as works through which the actors could explore the historical assumptions and conditions of theatre at particularly significant moments in the history of the Western stage. Although they were written for the actors, audiences were invited to the stagings and were even encouraged to watch the process of make-up, costuming and warm-up exercises. In this way, both actors and audiences were supposed to become more aware of the past developments and requirements of theatrical transmission and would be better prepared for productive experiences in the theatre, particularly for the productions that followed from these historical contextualizations – a single, unified performance of the *Oresteia* trilogy (1980), and *As You Like It* (1977), respectively.

These initiations into the origins and mechanics of theatre did not necessarily develop into performances that met expectations, however. These expectations became inflated to some extent by the grandeur of the stagings. For both the *Antiquity Project* and the Shakespeare projects, the company rented large industrial spaces and constructed enormous sets along the model of *Peer Gynt*. Some performances even extended beyond a single room, and audiences wandered through the spaces, watching the preparations, until ushered in to the staging area proper. Andrzej Wirth assessed the Schaubühne performance of the *Oresteia* in terms of this use of space and in the context of earlier ideals of democratization, suspicious of the necessity for the audience to ultimately sit on the floor in front of the stage:

> The trend toward theater of space, which characterizes postmodern aesthetics and is an expression of the emancipation of the viewer to become a sovereign co-participant in the theatrical event, articulates itself here in a perverse way as a reinforcement of the theater's authoritarian structure. ... Theater goers have seldom been treated so paternalistically as in this anniversary project of the *Schaubühne*, a theater that once so explicitly sought to emancipate the audience. [37]

Wirth adds that the performance itself also failed to advocate democracy until a half-hearted appeal at the closing of the seven-hour performance.

Lost in the majority of reviews from the late 1970s and early 1980s are the previously typical accolades for the actors. By now it had become an assumption that the ensemble would bring forth nuanced performances based on detailed readings of the dramatic texts, which they continued to do. Actors now began to feel constrained by the ensemble agreement that stipulated that they perform only at the Schaubühne. Exceptions began to be made for actors to appear on other stages, in television or film, and this caused some rancour. The original members were getting older as well, and as new actors were recruited to the theatre, more dissent developed over the distribution of roles.

In 1981, the theatre moved from the Hallisches Ufer to a newly renovated theatre at Lehniner Platz, a former movie theatre that had been redesigned for stage theatre according to plans on which Stein significantly contributed. The new theatre had moveable stage and seating features so that different kinds of space, and even multiple stages, could be created within the building. Stein was able to convince his co-directors to include the newest technology so that to this day, the Schaubühne am Lehniner Platz remains quite up to date. The move to the new theatre did not, however, alleviate any of the internal pressures on the group, nor did it significantly change the attitudes of critics. Barely three years later, Stein himself admitted that in his opinion, 'none of the productions in the new theater of the Schaubühne am Lehniner Platz has come close to the aesthetic constructs of the 1970s and their impact on contemporary consciousness'.[38]

This admission came in the immediate wake of Stein's announcement of his resignation from the Schaubühne. He justified his resignation in part because of self-criticism of his own creativity: 'I'm aware that I increasingly tend to fall into purely conventional practices.'[39] Personal and professional ruptures between himself and some of the actors played a significant role in his decision as well.[40] The new business model of the Schaubühne am Lehniner Platz, under which his two business partners also had a say in theatrical decisions, created further frustration that contributed to his decision. Upon leaving, he had not secured any contracts to continue his career elsewhere; it was unknown what his next steps would be.

After the Schaubühne: Salzburg, opera

Stein never stopped working in the theatre, even after his resignation. He was immediately contacted to direct at various theatres as guest director, and ultimately he even directed several productions in such a role at the Schaubühne am Lehniner Platz. But his first contracted position was as director of theatre at the Salzburger Festspiele.

This annual summer festival for classical music and the performing arts had been extremely influential during several periods since its inception in 1920. By the time Stein took over as director in 1992, though, the theatrical performances had become the least important part of the festival. Under Stein's directorship, the status of the theatrical arts was revived, as he lured prominent directors to create exclusive productions for the festival and directed plays himself for particular stages in Salzburg. Here the managerial experiences of the Schaubühne am Lehniner Platz, which had soured so completely, served him well to increase viewership and the prestige of the plays at the festival.

Stein's other main new professional work was as a director of opera. He had already directed an opera, Wagner's *Das Rheingold*, in Paris in 1976. After resigning from the Schaubühne, he increasingly accepted offers from around the world to direct operas, even though he informally commented to fellow theatre directors in 1998 that stage directors who moved to opera were 'cowardly' – this because the principle singers took the critical heat rather than the director. Interestingly, he also pointed out that ensemble organization is almost impossible in opera.[41] In terms of the trajectory of his career, it is rather easy to see the appeal of opera as an invitation to stage spectacular shows. His comment on ensemble and opera is striking, coming as it does in the late 1990s, since the ensemble model did not entirely work out for him. And yet he would return to this model in order to accomplish his longest-standing career goal: staging the entirety of Goethe's *Faust*.

Conclusion: *Faust*

Goethe's *Faust* remains one of the most challenging texts of world literature. Its dramatic composition does not presume any suitability for the theatre. Even Part One, which Goethe originally conceived at an early period when he was focused on drama and the theatre, so transgressed the theatrical norms and technical attributes of the late eighteenth century that Goethe himself only staged it a decade after its completion and only in a severely altered form. The structure and settings of Part Two, which Goethe finished over thirty years after Part One, reflect Goethe's diminished interest in the theatre in the last quarter of his life. By this time he developed modern epic forms of prose writing, as in his Wilhelm Meister novels, and further explored poetic modes of expression. These interests influence Part Two of *Faust* in more fundamental ways than any concerns with the theatre and performance.

The entire *Faust* was something of a grail for Stein. He had wanted to stage it at the Schaubühne but could not convince the ensemble of its feasibility.[42] In order to garner support for the undertaking – from potential players, audiences and sponsors alike – Stein embarked on an international tour on which he would read *Faust II* for anyone who wanted to come, a tour which turned out to be reasonably successful. He was ultimately able to gather an ensemble of some thirty actors together, including one of his former long-standing leading men, Bruno Ganz, to create the staging.

Stein's decision to stage both parts of the play in a textually accurate performance – that is, without a single edit or elision – was so peculiar and so huge (with its twenty hours of performance time over the initial weekend at the Hanover EXPO 2000) that it was billed specifically as *Steins Faust*, not just *Faust*. Audiences at the initial and subsequent performances were broadly enthusiastic, but not the professional critics, who expressed disdain particularly over the multi-media spectacle that, because of its textual inclusiveness, lacked directorial interpretation of the text. The critics also scorned the pleasure of lay audiences for being duped by the spectacular framing into believing that they were seeing a performance for the ages. As Hajo Kreuzenberger has written, 'Stein's "focus on the text" ran for many years against the development and trends of contemporary theater. Today it [this focus] stands in diametrical opposition.'[43] Kreuzenberger traces Stein's contrariness to theatrical trends back to his final production at the Schaubühne in 1984, Chekhov's *Three Sisters*; this was the production in which his approach to textual accuracy achieved almost universal disdain among critics in spite of positive popular responses. What had originally been Stein's strength was now seen as old hat, inadequately compensated for with overwrought spectacle of performance.

Steins Faust serves as a fitting summary of his career. The reviewers who panned the spectacle of any of his post-Schaubühne productions rarely have critical commentary about the acting. By again using an ensemble structure and working in detail with actors on transforming text into action in *Steins Faust*, Stein achieved great performances from them. What had changed from his early career was a new-found pleasure in spectacle as a central element of theatre. What had not changed was his focus on the text and his work in transmitting the text via the actors to the audience. He has continuously displayed his acumen for making actors fully aware of the meanings within dramatic texts and for getting actors to mediate those meanings to audiences from the stage. By remaining within an aesthetic realm for his productions, though, Stein moved away from the impact that he and his ensemble organization achieved in their early years.

CHRONOLOGIES OF MAJOR PRODUCTIONS STAGED BY EACH DIRECTOR

The lists are not exhaustive. Productions listed are ones mentioned in the text, usually the most representative of the style and range of each director.

Jean-Louis Barrault (1910–94)

Barrault also acted in most of the productions he directed.

1935   *Autour d'une mère* adapted by Barrault from William Faulkner's novel *As I Lay Dying*. Théâtre de l'Atelier.

1937   *Numance* adapted by Barrault from Miguel de Cervantes's tragedy *El cerco de Numancia*. Sets/costumes by André Masson. Théâtre Antoine.

1939   *La Faim (Hunger)* adapted by Barrault from Knut Hamsun's novel *Hunger*. Théâtre de l'Atelier.

1942   *Phèdre (Phaedra)* by Jean Racine. Sets/costumes by Jean Hugo. Comédie-Française.

1943   *Le Soulier de satin (The Satin Slipper)* by Paul Claudel. Sets/costumes by Lucien Coutard. Music by Arthur Honegger. Comédie-Française.

1945   *Antoine et Cléopâtre (Antony and Cleopatra)* by William Shakespeare, translated by André Gide. Comédie-Française.

1946   *Hamlet* by William Shakespeare, translated by André Gide. Sets/costumes by André Masson. Music by Arthur Honegger. Théâtre Marigny.

1946   *Les Fausses confidences (False Confidences)* by Marivaux. Théâtre
         Marigny.
         Baptiste by Jacques Prévert and Joseph Kosma. Théâtre Marigny.

1947   *Le Procès (The Trial)* adapted by André Gide and Barrault from
         the novel by Franz Kafka. Sets/costumes by Félix Labisse. Théâtre
         Marigny.
         Amphitryon by Molière. Sets/costumes by Christian Bérard. Music
         by François Poulenc. Théâtre Marigny.

1948   *Etat de siège (State of Siege)* by Albert Camus. Set by Balthus.
         Music by Arthur Honegger. Théâtre Marigny.
         Partage de midi (Break of Noon) by Paul Claudel. Sets by Félix
         Labisse. Costumes by Christian Bérard. Théâtre Marigny.
         Occupe-toi d'Amélie (Keep an Eye on Amelia) by Georges
         Feydeau. Sets by Félix Labisse. Costumes by Jean-Denis Maclès.
         Théâtre Marigny.

1950   *La Répétition, ou l'amour puni (The Rehearsal)* by Jean Anouilh.
         Sets/costumes by Jean-Denis Maclès. Théâtre Marigny.

1951   *L'Echange (The Exchange)* by Paul Claudel. Sets/costumes by
         Georges Wakhévitch. Théâtre Marigny.

1953   *Christophe Colomb (Christopher Columbus)*. Sets/costumes
         by Max Ingrand, with Marie-Hélène Dasté. Music by Darius
         Milhaud. Théâtre Marigny.
         Pour Lucrèce by Jean Giraudoux. Sets by A.M. Cassandre.
         Costumes by Christian Dior and A.M. Cassandre. Théâtre
         Marigny.

1954   *La Cerisaie (The Cherry Orchard)* by Anton Pavlovich Chekhov.
         Sets/costumes by Georges Wakhévitch. Théâtre Marigny.

1955   *L'Orestie (The Oresteia)* by Aeschylus. Sets by Félix Labisse.
         Costumes by Marie-Hélène Dasté. Théâtre Marigny.

1956   *Le Personnage combatant (The Character against Himself)* by Jean
         Vauthier. Set by Félix Labisse. Théâtre Marigny.
         Histoire de Vasco (Story of Vasco) by Georges Schéhadé, adapted
         by Georges Neveux. Sets by Jack Youngerman with Petrus Bride.
         Costumes by Marie-Hélène Dasté. Music by Joseph Kosma.
         Premiere in Zurich, then Théâtre Sarah-Bernhardt.

1957   *Le Château (The Castle)* adapted by Pol Quentin from the novel
         by Franz Kafka. Sets by Félix Labisse with Petrus Bride. Costumes
         by Marie-Hélène Dasté. Music by Maurice Leroux. Théâtre Sarah-
         Bernhardt.

1958 *La Vie parisienne (Parisian Life)* by Jacques Offenbach, Henri Meilhac and Ludovic Halévy. Sets/costumes by Jean-Denis Maclès. Théâtre du Palais-Royal.

1959 *Tête d'or* by Paul Claudel. Sets/costumes by André Masson. Music by Arthur Honegger. Odéon-Théâtre de France.

1960 *Rhinocéros* by Eugène Ionesco. Sets/costumes by Jacques Noël. Music by Michel Philippot. Odéon-Théâtre de France.

1968 *Rabelais* adapted by Barrault from the five books of François Rabelais. Costumes and scenic elements by Matias. Music by Michel Polnareff. Elysée Montmartre.

1974 *Ainsi parlait Zarathoustra (Thus Spake Zarathustra)* adapted by Barrault from writing by Friedrich Nietzsche. Sets/costumes by Matias. Music by Pierre Boulez. Elysée Montmartre.

1985 *Le Langage du corps (Language of the Body)* by Jean-Louis Barrault. Théâtre du Rond-Point.
Les Oiseaux (The Birds) adapted by Pierre Bourgeade from the comedy by Aristophanes. Setting by d'Agostino Pace. Costumes by Jacques Schmidt and Emmanuel Peduzzi. Music by Georges Auric. Théâtre du Rond-Point.

Ariane Mnouchkine (b. 1939)

1964 *Les Petits Bourgeois (Common People)* adapted by Arthur Adamov from the play by Maxim Gorky. Sets/costumes by Roberto Moscoso. Porte de Montreuil, then Théâtre Mouffetard.

1967 *La Cuisine (The Kitchen)* by Arnold Wesker. Set by Roberto Moscoso. Cirque de Montmartre.

1968 *Le Songe d'une nuit d'été (A Midsummer Night's Dream)* by William Shakespeare. Set by Roberto Moscoso. Costumes by Françoise Tournafond. Music by Jacques Lasry. Cirque de Montmartre.

1969 *Les Clowns*, a collective creation by the Théâtre du Soleil. Théâtre de la Commune d'Aubervilliers.

1970 *1789*, a collective creation by the Théâtre du Soleil. Set by Roberto Moscoso.Costumes by Françoise Tournafond. Piccolo Teatro de Milano, then La Cartoucherie de Vincennes.

1972 *1793*, a collective creation by the Théâtre du Soleil. Set by Roberto Moscoso. Costumes by Françoise Tournafond. Cartoucherie de Vincennes.

1979   *Méphisto, le roman d'une carrière,* adapted by Mnouchkine
            from the novel by Klaus Mann. Set by Guy-Claude François.
            Costumes by Nani Noël and Daniel Ogier. Music by Jean-
            Jacques Lemêtre. Masks by Erhard Stiefel. Cartoucherie de
            Vincennes.

1981–4   *Les Shakespeare.* Sets by Guy-Claude François. Costumes
            by Jean-Claude Barriera and Nathalie Thomas. Masks by
            Erhard Stiefel. Music by Jean-Jacques Lemêtre. Cartoucherie
            and on tour.

            1981   *Richard II* by William Shakespeare.

            1982   *La Nuit des rois (Twelfth Night)* by William
            Shakespeare.

            1984   *Henry IV, Part I.*

1985   *L'Histoire terrible mais inachevée de Norodom Sihanouk,
            roi de Cambodge (The Terrible but Unfinished Story of
            Norodom Sihanouk, King of Cambodia)* by Hélène Cixous
            (ten hours). Cartoucherie de Vincennes.

1987   *L'Indiade ou l'Inde de nos rêves (Epic of India or the India
            of Our Dreams)* by Hélène Cixous. Set by Guy-Claude
            François. Costumes by Jean-Claude Barriera and Nathalie
            Thomas. Masks by Erhard Stiefel. Music by Jean-Jacques
            Lemêtre. Cartoucherie and on tour.

1990–2   *Les Atrides (House of Atreus).* Four productions: Set by Guy-
            Claude François with sculptures by Erhard Stiefel. Costumes
            by Nathalie Thomas and Marie-Hélène Bouvet. Music by
            Jean-Jacques Lemêtre. Cartoucherie and on tour.

            1990   *Iphigénie à Aulis (Iphigenia at Aulis)* by Euripides.

            1990   *Agamemnon* by Aeschylus.

            1991   *Les Choéphores (The Libation Bearers)* by Aeschylus.

            1992   *Les Euménides (The Furies)* by Aeschylus.

1994   *La Ville perjure ou le Réveil des Erinyes* by Hélène Cixous.
            Set by Guy-Claude François. Costumes by Jean-Claude
            Barriera and Nathalie Thomas. Music by Jean-Jacques
            Lemêtre. Cartoucherie and on tour.

1995   *Le Tartuffe* by Molière. Set by Guy-Claude François. Costumes
            by Jean-Claude Barriera and Nathalie Thomas. Music by Jean-
            Jacques Lemêtre. Festival d'Avignon, Cartoucherie and on tour.

1997   *Et Soudain des nuits d'éveil (And Suddenly, Nights of Awakening),*
       a collective creation in collaboration with Hélène Cixous (four
       hours). Set by Guy-Claude François. Costumes by Nathalie
       Thomas and Marie-Hélène Bouvet. Cartoucherie and on tour to
       Moscow.

1999   *Tambours sur la digue, sous forme de pièce ancienne pour
       marionettes jouée par des acteurs (The Flood Drummers, in
       the form of an old play for puppets played by actors)* by Hélène
       Cixous. Set by Guy-Claude François, Ysabel de Maisonneuve and
       Didier Martin. Costumes by Nathalie Thomas and Marie-Hélène
       Bouvet. Music by Jean-Jacques Lemêtre. Cartoucherie and on tour.

2003   *Le Dernier Caravansérail (Odyssées) (The Last Inn for the
       Caravan, Odysseys),* a collective creation (seven hours). Set by Guy-
       Claude François. Costumes by Nathalie Thomas and Marie-Hélène
       Bouvet. Music by Jean-Jacques Lemêtre. Cartoucherie and on tour.

2006   *Les Ephémères (The Ephemerals),* a collective creation. Set by
       Ariane Mnouchkine. Costumes by Nathalie Thomas and Marie-
       Hélène Bouvet. Music by Jean-Jacques Lemêtre. Tour.

2010   *Les Naufragés du Fol Espoir (Aurores) (The Castaways of the Fol
       Espoir, Sunrises)* by Hélène Cixous with some collective creation.
       Costumes by Nathalie Thomas and Marie-Hélène Bouvet.
       Cartoucherie and on tour.

2016   *Une Chambre en Inde (A Room in India)* by Hélène Cixous.
       Music by Jean-Jacques Lemêtre. Cartoucherie and on tour.

Peter Stein (b. 1937)

1967   *Gerettet (Saved)* by Edward Bond, translation adapted by Martin
       Sperr. Sets/costumes by Jürgen Rose. Werkraumtheater der
       Kammerspiele, Munich.
       Kabale und Liebe (Intrigue and Love) by Friedrich Schiller. Sets/
       costumes by Jürgen Rose. Bremer Theater.

1968   *Im Dickicht der Städte (In the Jungle of Cities)* by Bertolt Brecht.
       Sets/costumes by Karl-Ernst Herrmann. Music by Peter Fischer.
       Werkraumtheater der Kammerspiele, Munich.
       Viet Nam Diskurs (Vietnam-Discourse) by Peter Weiss. Sets/
       costumes by F. Lechenperg-Recker. Music by Peter Fischer.
       Werkraumtheater der Kammerspiele, Munich.

1969   *Torquato Tasso* by Johann Wolfgang von Goethe. Sets/costumes by
       Wilfried Minks. Bremer Theater.

Kikeriki (Cock-a-Doodle Dandy) by Sean O'Casey. Sets/costumes by Karl Kneidl. Zurich Schauspielhaus.

1970   *Die Mutter (The Mother)* by Bertolt Brecht, based on the novel by Maxim Gorky. Sets by Klaus Weiffenbach. Costumes by Susanne Raschig. Music by Hanns Eisler. Schaubühne am Halleschen Ufer, West Berlin.

1971   *Peer Gynt* by Henrik Ibsen. Sets by Karl-Ernst Herrmann. Costumes by Moidele Bickel, Susanne Raschig and Joachim Herzog. Masks by Ricarda Poppy and Ulrich Hilbert. Schaubühne am Halleschen Ufer, West Berlin.

1972   *Optimistische Tragödie (Optimistic Tragedy)* by Vsevolod Vishnevsky. Sets by Klaus Weiffenbach. Costumes by Susanne Raschig. Music by Peter Fischer. Schaubühne am Halleschen Ufer, West Berlin.
        Kleists Traum vom Prinzen Homburg (Kleist's Dream of the Prince of Homburg) by Heinrich von Kleist. Sets by Karl-Ernst Herrmann. Costumes by Moidele Bickel. Schaubühne am Halleschen Ufer, West Berlin.

1973   *Das Sparschwein (La Cagnotte, The Piggy Bank)* by Eugène Labiche. Sets by Karl-Ernst Herrmann. Costumes by Susanne Raschig. Schaubühne am Halleschen Ufer, West Berlin.

1974   *Antikenprojekt I (Antiquity Project I)*, acting exercises. Set by Karl-Ernst Herrmann. Costumes and masks by Moidele Bickel. Music by Peter Fischer. Schaubühne am Halleschen Ufer, West Berlin.
        Sommergäste (Summerfolk) by Maxim Gorky. Sets by Karl-Ernst Herrmann. Costumes by Susanne Raschig. Music by Peter Fischer. Schaubühne am Halleschen Ufer, West Berlin; and on tour to London.

1976   *Shakespeare's Memory*, a collective creation. Set by Karl-Ernst Herrmann. Costumes by Moidele Bickel, Susanne Raschig and Joachim Herzog. CCC Film Studios, Berlin.

1977   *Wie es euch gefallt (As You Like It)* by William Shakespeare. Sets by Karl-Ernst Herrmann. Costumes by Moidele Bickel. CCC Film Studios, Berlin.

1978   *Gross und klein (Great and Small)* by Botho Strauss. Set by Karl-Ernst Herrmann. Costumes by Moidele Bickel. Schaubühne am Halleschen Ufer, West Berlin.

1980   *The Oresteia* by Aeschylus (seven hours). Set by Karl-Ernst Herrmann. Costumes by Moidele Bickel. Schaubühne am Lehniner Platz. Restaged in Russian with Moscow Art Theatre actors (nine hours) in 1994.

1983   *Die Neger (The Blacks)* by Jean Genet. Schaubühne am Lehniner Platz, West Berlin.

1984   *Drei Schwestern (Three Sisters)* by Anton Pavlovich Chekhov. Sets by Karl-Ernst Herrmann. Schaubühne am Lehniner Platz, West Berlin. Revived and modified in 1988 at the Schaubühne and on tour to France.

1986   *The Hairy Ape* by Eugene O'Neill. Schaubühne am Lehniner Platz (Stein as freelance director there).

1989   *Der Kirschgarten (The Cherry Orchard)* by Anton Pavlovich Chekhov. Schaubühne am Lehniner Platz (Stein as freelance director there).

1992   *Julius Caesar* by William Shakespeare. Set by Dionissis Fotopoulos. Costumes by Moidele Bickel. Salzburg Festival. *Pelléas et Mélisande,* opera by Claude Debussy. Conducted by Pierre Boulez. Sets by Karl-Ernst Herrmann. Costumes by Moidele Bickel. Welsh National Opera, Cardiff.

1995   *Moïse et Aaron (Moses and Aaron)*, opera by Arnold Schoenberg. Conducted by Pierre Boulez. De Nederlandse Opera, Amsterdam.

2000   *Faust I and II* (21 hours) by Johann Wolfgang von Goethe. EXPO 2000, Hanover; also Berlin and Vienna.

2003   *The Seagull* by Anton Pavlovich Chekhov (Stein's first production directed in English). King's Theatre, Edinburgh.

2006   *Troilus and Cressida* by William Shakespeare. Set by Ferdinand Wörgerbauer. Costumes by Anna Maria Heinrich. King's Theatre, Edinburgh; then Stratford-upon-Avon.

2007   *Wallenstein* by Friedrich Schiller (ten hours). Berliner Ensemble at a former beer warehouse in the Neukölln district of Berlin.

2009   *I Demoni (Demons)*, adapted from the novel by Fyodor Dostoevsky (twelve hours). Teatro Stabile di Torino and on tour to Lincoln Center, New York.

2010   *Boris Godunov* by Modest Mussorgsky. Metropolitan Opera, New York City.

2012   *Simon Boccanegra* by Giuseppe Verdi. Wiener Staatsoper.

2013   *King Lear* by William Shakespeare. Burgtheater, Vienna.

2016   *La Damnation de Faust* by Hector Berlioz. Bolshoi Theatre, Moscow. *Die Zauberflöte (The Magic Flute)* by Wolfgang Amadeus Mozart. Teatro alla Scala, Milan.

NOTES

Introduction to the Series

1 Simon Shepherd, *Direction* (Basingstoke: Palgrave Macmillan, 2012).

2 P.P. Howe, *The Repertory Theatre: A Record & a Criticism* (London: Martin Secker, 1910).

3 Alexander Dean, *Little Theatre Organization and Management: For Community, University and School* (New York: Appleton, 1926), 297–8.

4 Constance D'Arcy Mackay, *The Little Theatre in the United States* (New York: H. Holt, 1917).

5 William Lyon Phelps, *The Twentieth Century Theatre: Observations on the Contemporary English and American Stage* (New York: Macmillan, 1920); Hiram Kelly Moderwell, *Theatre of Today* (New York: Dodd, Mead & Co., 1914, 1923); Dean, *Little Theatre Organization and Management*.

Introduction to Volume 7

1 Peter Lichtenfels, 'Peter Stein', in *In Contact with the Gods? Directors Talk Theatre*, ed. Maria M. Delgado and Paul Heritage (Manchester: Manchester University Press, 1996), 151–2.

2 Catherine Steinegger, *Pierre Boulez et le théâtre: De la Compagnie Renaud-Barrault à Patrice Chéreau* (Wavre, Belgique: Mardaga, 2012), 24–6.

3 Ibid., 37–8.

4 Bettina Knapp, 'Jean-Louis Barrault', in *Off-Stage Voices: Interviews with Modern French Dramatists*, ed. Alba Amoia (Troy, NY: Whitston, 1975), 42.

5 David Williams, 'Introduction: A Grain of Sand in the Works: Continuity and Change at the Théâtre du Soleil', in *Collaborative Theatre: The Théâtre du Soleil Sourcebook*, comp. and ed. David Williams (London: Routledge, 1999), xi.

6 Maria M. Delgado, 'Ariane Mnouchkine', in *In Contact with the Gods? Directors Talk Theatre*, ed. Maria M. Delgado and Paul Heritage (Manchester: Manchester University Press, 1996), 184.

7 Williams, 'Introduction', xiii.

8 Josette Féral, *Trajectoires du Soleil: autour d'Ariane Mnouchkine* (Paris: Editions Théâtrales, 1998) is a collection of Féral's interviews with seven

actors and seven other collaborators as a means of tracing the Soleil's trajectory over many years (Préface, 9).

9   Ariane Mnouchkine, *L'Art du présent: Entretiens avec Fabienne Pascaud* (Paris: Plon, 2005), 162–3.

10   Féral, *Trajectoires du Soleil*, 103.

11   Ibid., 104.

12   Ariane Mnouchkine interviewed by the editors of *Théâtre/Public*, 'The Individual and the Collective', in *Collaborative Theatre: The Théâtre du Soleil Sourcebook*, comp. and ed. David Williams (London: Routledge, 1999), 60.

13   Quoted in David Whitton, *Stage Directors in Modern France* (Manchester: Manchester University Press, 1987), 255.

14   Shomit Mitter, 'Peter Stein', in *Fifty Key Theatre Directors*, ed. Shomit Mitter and Maria Shevtsova (London: Routledge, 2005), 149.

15   Klaus van den Berg, 'Karl-Ernst Herrmann: Unfolding Shakespeare's Space', in *Designers' Shakespeare*, ed. John Russell Brown and Stephen Di Benedetto (London: Routledge, 2016), 55.

16   Ibid., 71.

17   Steinegger, *Pierre Boulez et le théâtre*, 315.

18   Knapp, 'Jean-Louis Barrault', 42–3.

19   David Bradby, 'Blacking Up – Three Productions by Peter Stein', in *A Radical Stage: Theatre in Germany in the 1970s and 1980s*, ed. W.G. Sebold (Oxford: Berg, 1988), 19.

20   Jack Zipes, 'Utopia as the Past Conserved: An Interview with Peter Stein and Dieter Sturm of the Schaubühne am Halleschen Ufer', *Theater* 9, no. 1 (1977): 53.

21   Lichtenfels, 'Peter Stein', 254.

22   Béatrice Picon-Vallin, 'Leaving Room for the Others', from an Interview with Members of the Théâtre du Soleil', in *Collaborative Theatre: The Théâtre du Soleil Sourcebook*, comp. and ed. David Williams (London: Routledge, 1999), 219.

23   Ariane Mnouchkine, 'Les acteurs sont des poètes', interview with Raymonde Temkine, *Europe, revue littéraire mensuelle* 61e année, no. 648 (April 1983): 57.

24   Delgado, 'Ariane Mnouchkine', 187.

25   Bradby, 'Blacking Up', 20.

26   Ibid.

27   Maria Shevtsova, 'Ariane Mnouchkine', in *Fifty Key Theatre Directors*, ed. Shomit Mitter and Maria Shevtsova (London: Routledge, 2005), 160.

28   Michael Patterson, 'Peter Stein', in *The Routledge Companion to Directors' Shakespeare*, ed. John Russell Brown (London: Routledge, 2008), 427.

29   Catherine Levasseur, *Dans l'intimité des Renaud Barrault*, souvenirs recueillis par Martine Desèvre (Paris: Pygmalion, 2003), 134–6.

30   David Bradby and David Williams, *Directors' Theater* (New York: St. Martin's Press, 1988), 218.

31 Mnouchkine, *L'art du présent*, 203.

32 John O'Mahony, 'Master of the Rebels', *The Guardian*, 9 August 2003.

33 Van den Berg, 'Karl-Ernst Herrmann', 60.

34 Jean-Louis Barrault, *A Propos de Shakespeare et du théâtre* (Massy: La Parade, 1949), 10–11.

35 The term 'collective creation' gained widespread usage along with the international renown of the Théâtre du Soleil's *1789*, although the practice of creating a production from scratch by the ensemble certainly did not originate with Mnouchkine. Later, as the company turned to text-based productions, she insisted that the work was still 'collective creation' in that all company members contributed to the realization of the text as an intrinsically new work of art for the stage. In recent years, the term 'devised theatre' has been used for work generated in rehearsal without a preexisting text.

36 Delgado, 'Ariane Mnouchkine', 181.

37 Ibid., 180.

38 Barrault, *A Propos de Shakespeare et du théâtre*, 20.

39 Ibid., 21.

40 Jonathan Kalb, 'The Thirty Years' War, All 10 Hours of It', *New York Times*, 1 July 2007.

41 Mnouchkine, *L'Art du présent*, 157–8.

42 Ibid., 159.

43 Ibid., 163–4.

44 Jean-Louis Barrault, *Une vie sur scène: Entretiens inédits avec Guy Dumur* (Paris: Flammarion, 2010), 155–6.

45 Jean-Louis Barrault, *Memories for Tomorrow*, trans. Jonathan Griffin (New York: E.P. Dutton, 1974), 207.

46 Pierre Boulez, 'Musique et Théâtre', in *Jean-Louis Barrault: une vie pour le théâtre*, ed. Noelle Giret (Paris: Gallimard, 2010), 90–4.

47 Sue-Ellen Case, 'Peter Stein Directs *The Oresteia*', *Theater* 11, no. 3 (Summer 1980): 23–4.

48 Charles Isherwood, 'A Daughter's Revenge Is on the Menu, So Expect a Meal Served Bitter Cold', *New York Times*, 12 October 2007.

Chapter 1

1 Paul-Louis Mignon, *Renaud Barrault: Paris: notre siècle* (Paris: Editions de Messine/Collection Pierre Bergé, 1984), quoting Georges Sadoul, *Les Lettres françaises* (17 March 1945), 120.

2 Marie-Françoise Christout, 'Chronologie Jean-Louis Barrault: Repères biographiques', *Revue de la Société d'Histoire du Théâtre*, 48th year, I-II, no. 189–190 (Paris: Ministère de la Culture, CNRS, and SACD, 1996), 12.

3   Jean-Louis Barrault, *Memories for Tomorrow*, trans. Jonathan Griffin (New York: E.P. Dutton, 1974), 151; see also Jean-Louis Barrault, *Souvenirs pour demain* (Paris: Editions du Seuil, 1972), 168–9.

4   Jean-Louis Barrault, *Je suis homme de théâtre* (Paris: Editions du Conquistador, 1955), 13.

5   Jean-Louis Barrault and Guy Dumur, *Une vie sur scène: Entretiens inédits*, ed. Denis Guénoun and Karine Le Bail (Paris: Flammarion, 2010), 97.

6   Paul Claudel and Jean-Louis Barrault, *Correspondance 1939–1954*, Preface by Jean-Louis Barrault, ed. Michel Lioure (Paris: Editions Gallimard, 2010), 6–7.

7   Catherine Steinegger, *Pierre Boulez et le théâtre: De la Compagnie Renaud-Barrault à Patrice Chéreau* (Wavre: Editions Mardaga, 2012), 24.

8   Claude Brovelli, *Ils ont réussi* (Paris: Editions France-Empire, 1984), 22. Note that Barrault used very similar language on the subject of influences in his *Memories*, 49; *Souvenirs*, 62–3.

9   Barrault and Dumur, *Une vie sur scène*, 73. See also Brovelli, *Ils ont réussi*, 21.

10 Denis Podalydès, 'Notes sur Jean-Louis Barrault', in *Jean-Louis Barrault: une vie pour le théâtre*, ed. Colline Faure-Poirée and Philippe Demanet (Paris: Editions Gallimard, 2010), 135–6.

11 Catherine Levasseur, *Dans l'intimité des Renaud Barrault*, souvenirs recueillis par Martine Desèvre, présenté par Jean Desailly et Simone Valère (Paris: Pygmalion, 2003), 84–5, 180.

12 Brovelli, *Ils ont réussi*, 27.

13 Barrault, *Memories*, 33.

14 Barrault, *Souvenirs*, 59.

15 Barrault, *Memories*, 56; see also Barrault, *Souvenirs*, 72.

16 Barrault, *Memories*, 57; see also Barrault, *Souvenirs*, 72.

17 Barrault, *Memories*, 70; see also Barrault, *Souvenirs*, 89.

18 Barrault, *Memories*, 71; see also Barrault, *Souvenirs*, 90.

19 Mignon, *Renaud Barrault: Paris, notre siècle*, 69.

20 Paul-Louis Mignon, *Jean-Louis Barrault: Le théâtre total* (Paris: Editions du Rocher, 2000), 60.

21 Ibid., 62, 88–93.

22 Levasseur, *Dans l'intimité des Renaud Barrault*, 50, 68.

23 Colette Godard, 'Madeleine Renaud: elle a traversé le siècle', *Le Monde*, 9 May 2008.

24 Christout, 'Chronologie Jean-Louis Barrault', 14.

25 Jean-Louis Barrault, 'Numance-65', *Cahiers Renaud Barrault* 51 (Paris: Gallimard, November 1965), 81.

26 Mignon, *Jean-Louis Barrault: Le théâtre total*, 64–6.

27 Mignon, *Renaud Barrault: Paris, notre siècle*, 69; see also Claudel and Barrault, *Correspondance 1939–1954*, 20–1; Jean-Louis Barrault, *Nouvelles réflexions sur le théâtre* (Paris: Flammarion, 1959), 204.

28 Mignon, *Jean-Louis Barrault: Le théâtre total*, 75.

29 Ibid., 79.

30 Barrault, *Memories*, 119; see also Barrault, *Souvenirs*, 149.

31 The author of this essay was lucky enough to see the 52-year-old Barrault's ever youthful Hamlet at the Odéon-Théâtre de France on 5 October 1962. That same week, she saw him and Edwige Feuillère in *Break of Noon*.

32 Barrault, *Memories*, 119; see also Barrault, *Souvenirs*, 149.

33 Barrault, *Memories*, 120; see also Barrault, *Souvenirs*, 151.

34 Barrault, *Memories*, 124–5; see also Barrault, *Souvenirs*, 155–6.

35 Barrault, *Memories*, 125; see also Barrault, *Souvenirs*, 157.

36 Barrault, *Memories*, 125; see also Barrault, *Souvenirs*, 156.

37 Christout, 'Chronologie Jean-Louis Barrault', 18; see also Claudel and Barrault, *Correspondance 1939–1954*, 22.

38 Christout, 'Chronologie Jean-Louis Barrault', 18.

39 Mignon, *Jean-Louis Barrault: Le théâtre totale*, 125–6.

40 Barrault, *Souvenirs*, 161; see also Barrault, *Memories*, 145.

41 Barrault, *Nouvelles réflexions*, 220.

42 Christout, 'Chronologie Jean-Louis Barrault', 20. In *Memories for Tomorrow* (148), Barrault puts the opening on 23 November 1943. Michel Lioure's Introduction to the Claudel/Barrault, *Correspondance 1939–1954* (27), specifies 25 November for the matinée *répétition générale*, with evening performances on 27 and 29 November.

43 Barrault, *Memories*, 146; see also Barrault, *Souvenirs*, 162.

44 Barrault, *Memories*, 147, and Barrault, *Souvenirs*, 163.

45 Barrault, *Nouvelles réflexions*, 215.

46 Claudel and Barrault, *Correspondance 1939–1954*, 28.

47 Barrault, *Nouvelles réflexions*, 221.

48 Mignon, *Jean-Louis Barrault: Le théâtre total*, 142.

49 Jacques Lorcey, *La Comédie Française* (Paris: Editions Fernand Nathan, 1980), 93–4.

50 Barrault, *Memories*, 158; see also Barrault, *Souvenirs*, 179.

51 Mignon, *Jean-Louis Barrault: Le théâtre total*, 150.

52 Barrault and Dumur, *Une vie sur scène*, 128.

53 Ibid., 126.

54 Barrault, *Memories*, 163; see also Barrault, *Souvenirs*, 185.

55 Barrault and Dumur, *Une vie sur scène*, 129–30.

56 Barrault, *Memories*, 172; see also Barrault, *Souvenirs*, 196.

57 Barrault, *Memories*, 173; see also Barrault, *Souvenirs*, 197.

58 Barrault, *Memories*, 173; see also Barrault, *Souvenirs*, 197.

59 Mignon, *Jean-Louis Barrault: Le théâtre total*, 175.

60 Ibid., 176–9.

61 Ibid., 183–5.

62 Michel Bertay, 'Jean-Louis Barrault, metteur en scène. Comment travaillait-il?', in *Revue de la Société d'Histoire du Théâtre*, 48th year I-II, no. 189–90 (Paris: Ministère de la Culture, CNRS, and SACD, 1996), 207.

63 Ibid., 208.

64 Barrault, *Memories*, 169; see also Barrault, *Souvenirs*, 192.

65 Bertay, 'Jean-Louis Barrault, metteur en scène', 209–10.

66 Ibid., 210.

67 Ibid., 211.

68 Ibid., 212.

69 Barrault, *Je suis homme de théâtre*, 23.

70 Bertay, 'Jean-Louis Barrault, metteur en scène', 213–14.

71 Barrault, *Je suis home de théâtre*, 40.

72 Ibid., 43–4.

73 Ibid., 44.

74 Bertay, 'Jean-Louis Barrault, metteur en scène', 215.

75 Ibid.

76 Barrault, *Je suis homme de théâtre*, 68–9.

77 Ibid., 86–7.

78 Ibid., 89–90.

79 Bertay, 'Jean-Louis Barrault, metteur en scène', 209.

80 André Bataille, *Lexique de la machinerie théâtrale* (Paris: Librairie Théâtrale, 1989), 34.

81 Bertay, 'Jean-Louis Barrault, metteur en scène', 219–20.

82 Ibid., 220–2.

83 Barrault and Dumur, *Une vie sur scène*, 136–7.

84 Barrault, *Souvenirs*, 245.

85 Ibid., 246.

86 Tom Bishop, 'La vie errante; les tournées de la compagnie Renaud-Barrault', in *Renaud Barrault*, ed. Noelle Giret (Paris: Bibliothèque nationale de France, 1999), 118.

87 Barrault, *Memories*, 212–14 and Barrault, *Souvenirs*, 248–9.

88 Barrault, *Memories*, 221; see also Barrault, *Souvenirs*, 258.

89 Barrault, *Memories*, 239; Barrault, *Souvenirs*, 281.

90 Barrault, *Souvenirs*, 283; see also Barrault, *Memories*, 241.

91 Barrault, *Memories*, 243; see also Barrault, *Souvenirs*, 286.

92 Barrault, *Memories*, 258; see also Barrault, *Souvenirs*, 304.

93 Barrault and Dumur, *Une vie sur scène*, 141–3.

94 Levasseur, *Dans l'intimité des Renaud Barrault*, 128.

202 NOTES

95   Mignon, *Jean-Louis Barrault: Le Théâtre total*, 243–5.

96   Barrault, *Memories*, 269; see also Barrault, *Souvenirs*, 319.

97   Barrault, *Memories*, 271; see also Barrault, *Souvenirs*, 321.

98   Barrault, *Souvenirs*, 328; see also Barrault, *Memories*, 293.

99   Barrault, *Memories*, 295; Barrault, *Souvenirs*, 329–30.

100 Jean-Louis Barrault, *Saisir le présent* (Paris: Robert Laffont, 1984), 81–2.

101 Lenora Champagne, *French Theatre Experiment since 1968* (Ann Arbor: UMI Research Press, 1984), 3 (quoting Alfred Williner, *The Action Image of Society: On Cultural Politicization*).

102 Barrault, *Memories*, 320; see also Barrault, *Souvenirs*, 362. Additional sources for the story of May 1968 and the aftermath include: Barrault, *Saisir le présent*, 84–93; Mignon, *Jean-Louis Barrault: Le théâtre total*, 284–91.

103 Mignon, *Jean-Louis Barrault: Le théâtre total*, 295.

104 Barrault, *Memories*, 328; see also Barrault, *Souvenirs*, 372.

105 Barrault, *Memories*, 329; see also Barrault, *Souvenirs*, 374.

106 Rosette C. Lamont, 'Jean Louis Barrault's *Rabelais*', *Yale French Studies* 46: From Stage to Street, special ed. Jacques Guicharnaud (New Haven, CT: Yale University, 1971), 125–38.

107 Barrault, *Saisir le présent*, 114.

108 Barrault, *Memories*, 331–2; Barrault, *Souvenirs*, 377; ibid., 112–13; Barrault and Dumur, *Une vie sur scène*, 190–2.

109 Barrault, *Saisir le présent*, 119–20.

110 Ibid., 121–2.

111 Ibid., 128–32; Barrault and Dumur, *Une vie sur scène*, 193–8.

112 Barrault and Dumur, *Une vie sur scène*, 197.

113 Barrault, *Saisir le présent*, 134–5.

114 Ibid., 151. Catherine Naugrette-Christophe claims that Barrault's plans were drawn up in 1948: 'Les théâtres de Jean-Louis Barrault,' *Revue de la Société d'Histoire du Théâtre*, 48th year I-II, no. 189–90 (Paris: Ministère de la Culture, CNRS, and SACD, 1996), 244.

115 Barrault and Dumur, *Une vie sur scène*, 207.

116 Christout, 'Chronologie Jean-Louis Barrault', 64.

117 Barrault and Dumur, *Une vie sur scène*, 202.

118 Mignon, *Jean-Louis Barrault: Le théâtre total*, 347.

Chapter 2

1   Mildah Polia, 'Le Rabelais de Barrault', *France-Amerique*, 28 May 1970 (clipping from the files of La Compagnie Madeleine Renaud—Jean-Louis Barrault).

2   Unable to obtain authorization to use *Tandis que j'agonise*, the published
     French translation of the title of Faulkner's novel *As I Lay Dying* as the title
     for his production, Barrault titled it *Autour d'une mère*, which would translate
     literally as *Around a Mother* or *In a Mother's Close Circle*. However, in the
     English translation of Barrault's memoir *Souvenirs pour demain* (Memories for
     Tomorrow), the production is referred to by the novel's title *As I Lay Dying*,
     which will thus will be used here.

3   Antonin Artaud, '*Autour d'une mère*: A Dramatic Action by Jean-Louis
     Barrault', in *The Theatre and Its Double*, trans. Mary Caroline Richards (New
     York: Grove Press, 1958), 145.

4   Lucien Descaves, 'A l'Atelier: *La Faim*', 20 April 1939 (unidentified
     publication, clipping from the archives of the Bibliothèque de l'Arsenal, Paris).

5   Robert Kemp, 'Sur une édition de *Phèdre*', *Une Semaine dans le Monde*, 15
     June 1946 (clipping, Bibliothèque de l'Arsenal).

6   Harold Hobson, *The French Theatre of Today: An English View* (London:
     George G. Harrap, 1953), 47.

7   [Béatrix] Dussane, *Notes de théâtre: 1940–1950* (Paris: Lardanchet, 1951), 99.

8   Jacques Copeau, *Appels*, Registres, vol. 1 (Paris: Gallimard, 1974), 300.

9   Eric Bentley, *In Search of Theatre* (New York: Alfred A. Knopf, 1953), 213–14.

10   Ibid., 403.

11   Barrault, *Souvenirs*, 343. Note that in the case of books for which published
     translations exist, I often quote from that edition; sometimes, however, I
     translate myself in order to capture relevant nuances.

12   Bentley, *In Search of Theatre*, 382.

13   Barrault, *Nouvelles réflexions*, 13.

14   André Galas, 'Théâtre de France: Le Mystique Barrault veut en faire un
     temple', *Lectures pour Tous*, March 1967, 31.

15   Jean-Louis Barrault, 'Il n'y a que le sang qui compte', *Arts*, 26 June 1952
     (clipping, Bibliothèque de l'Arsenal, Paris).

16   Jean-Louis Barrault, *The Memoirs of Jean-Louis Barrault: Memories for
     Tomorrow*, trans. Jonathan Griffin (New York: E.P. Dutton, 1974), 224.

17   Barrault, *Nouvelles réflexions*, 14–16.

18   Barrault, *Souvenirs*, 95.

19   Barrault, *Nouvelles réflexions*, 161.

20   Jean-Louis Barrault, *Le Phénomène théâtrale* (Oxford: Clarendon Press,
     1961), 8–9.

21   Barrault, *Souvenirs*, 95.

22   Barrault, *Le Phénomène théâtrale*, 16–17, 21. Barrault seems to have been
     influenced by Copeau's spiritual vision of the theatre and description of the
     audience experience of performance as communion, ideas which were carried
     on by some members of the Cartel. See, for instance, Jacques Copeau, *Notes
     sur le métier de comédien* (Paris: Michel Brient), 38–9; Louis Jouvet, *Le
     Comédien désincarné* (Paris: Flammarion, 1954), 19; Charles Dullin, *Ce sont
     les dieux qu'il nous faut* (Paris: Gallimard, 1969), 35.

23 Barrault, *Nouvelles réflexions*, 81. Barrault seems to have derived this concept from his readings in Eastern religious works, readings suggested by Artaud. See Barrault, *Souvenirs*, 105.

24 Barrault, *Nouvelles réflexions*, 81.

25 Barrault, *Le Phénomène théâtrale*, 21.

26 Ibid., 14.

27 Jean-Louis Barrault, 'A French Reaction', *World Theatre* 4 (Spring 1954): 32.

28 Barrault, *Nouvelles réflexions*, 12. My Barrault occasionally refers to 'the double' in a quasi-mystical sense, but without much explanation.

29 Barbara Gordon has suggested that Barrault 'was especially attracted by the oneiric, metaphysical aspects of the Surrealist experience. He was fascinated most by that element of the movement which was the least committed to political and social issues, and the most compatible with the mystical aura of the Atelier'. Barbara Gordon, '"Le Théâtre Total" as envisioned by Jean-Louis Barrault' (PhD diss., Ann Arbor, MI: University Microfilms, 73–29-830, 1975), 84–5.

30 Barrault, *Souvenirs*, 39.

31 Jean-Louis Barrault, 'Conviction et malaise dans le théâtre contemporain', *Cahiers de la Compagnie Madeleine Renaud—Jean-Louis Barrault*, no. 71 (1970): 75.

32 Barrault, *Nouvelles réflexions*, 12.

33 Barrault, *Souvenirs*, 30.

34 Ibid., 34.

35 Jacques Copeau, *Critiques d'un autre temps: Études d'art dramatiques*, 7th edition (Paris: Éditions de la nouvelle revue française, 1923), 249.

36 Barrault, *Nouvelles réflexions*, 266.

37 Ibid.

38 Ibid., 270.

39 Charles R. Lyons, 'La Compagnie Madeleine Renaud—Jean-Louis Barrault: The Idea and the Aesthetic', *Educational Theatre Journal* 9 (December 1967): 419.

40 Jean-Louis Barrault, *Réflexions sur le théâtre* (Paris: Éditions Jacques Vautrain, 1949), 60.

41 Antonin Artaud, *The Theatre and Its Double*, trans. Mary Caroline Richards (New York: Grove Press, 1958), 7.

42 Ibid., 38.

43 Ibid., 57.

44 Ibid., 140.

45 Ibid., 28.

46 Ibid., 74.

47 Ibid., 41.

48 Ibid., 48.

49   Ibid., 103–4.

50   Ibid., 145–6.

51   Ibid., 146.

52   Ibid., 13.

53   Bentley, *In Search of Theatre*, 203.

54   Léon Chancerel, *Jean-Louis Barrault ou 'l'Ange Noir du théâtre'* (Paris: Presses Littéraires de France, 1953), 69.

55   Ibid., 70; Maurice Kurtz, *Jacques Copeau: Biographie d'un théâtre*, trans. Claude Cézan (Paris: Éditions Nagel, 1950), 135.

56   Marie-Hélène Dasté, personal interview, Paris, 28 December 1972. Recorded on tape; this technique was also employed by Copeau; see Kurtz, *Jacques Copeau*, 135.

57   Dasté, personal interview.

58   Barrault, *Je suis homme de théâtre*, 44.

59   Jacques Guicharnaud in collaboration with June Guicharnaud, *Modern French Theatre from Giraudoux to Genet* (New Haven, CT: Yale University Press, 1967), 306.

60   Barrault, *Réflexions*, 26.

61   Helen Krich Chinoy, 'The Emergence of the Director', in *Directors on Directing; A Source Book of the Modern Theatre*, rev. edition, ed. Toby Cole and Helen Krich Chinoy (New York: Bobbs-Merrill, 1963), 69.

62   Max Favalelli, 'Après dix ans d'existence, la Compagnie Renaud – Barrault va parcourir le monde en attendant que Paris lui offre un théâtre', *Paris-Presse l'Intransigeant*, 15 March 1956 (clipping, Bibliothèque de l'Arsenal, Paris).

63   Jean-Louis Barrault, public interview, Théâtre d'Orsay, Paris, 11 December 1972; recorded in note form.

64   See Suzanne Burgoyne Dieckman, 'Theory and Practice in the Total Theatre of Jean-Louis Barrault' (PhD diss., University of Michigan, Ann Arbor, 1975), 287, 313–14.

65   Jean-Louis Barrault, 'Une répétition du *Château*', *Cahiers de la Compagnie Madeleine-Renaud—Jean-Louis Barrault*, no. 50 (1965): 107.

66   Ibid.

67   Ibid., 108.

68   Barrault, *Nouvelles réflexions*, 134.

69   Marcelle Capron, '*La Cerisaie* au théâtre Marigny', *Combat*, 11 October 1995 (clipping, Bibliothèque de l'Arsenal).

70   Barrault, *Nouvelles réflexions*, 134.

71   Barrault, *Memories*, 67.

72   Barrault, *Souvenirs*, 85.

73   Barrault, *Memories*, 67.

74   Bill Wallis, 'Production Casebook No. 3: Jean-Louis Barrault's *Rabelais*', *Theatre Quarterly* 1 (July–September 1971): 90.

75 André Frank and G.-A. Astre, Introduction to 'Mise en scène de *Autour d'une mère*', by Jean-Louis Barrault, *Cahiers de la Compagnie Madeleine-Renaud—Jean-Louis Barrault*, no. 71 (1970): 27.

76 Ibid., 26.

77 Barrault, 'Mise en scène de *Autour d'une mère*', 31–2.

78 Barrault, *Réflexions*, 49.

79 Barrault, 'Mise en scène de *Autour d'une mère*', 36–7.

80 Bentley, *In Search of Theatre*, 201.

81 J. Decogy, '"Je ne trahirai pas Kafka en faisant rire le public", nous dit Jean-Louis Barrault qui donne vendredi *Le Procès* au théâtre Marigny', *Franc-Tireur*, 4 October 1947 (clipping, Bibliothèque de l'Arsenal).

82 Dieckman, 'Theory and Practice', 329.

83 Jean-Louis Barrault and Simone Benmussa, 'Travail de scène pour *Le Procès*', *Cahiers de la Compagnie Madeleine Renaud—Jean-Louis Barrault*, no. 50 (1965): 99.

84 Ibid., 96.

85 Barrault, *Memories*, 174. Translation modified.

86 Claude Roy, 'Le *Procès*.' *Action*, 5 November 1947 (clipping, Bibliothèque de l'Arsenal).

87 Ibid.

88 Benjamin Crémieux, '*Hamlet* et *La Faim* au théâtre de l'Atelier', *La Lumière*, 5 May 1939 (clipping, Bibliothèque de l'Arsenal); Wallis, 'Barrault's *Rabelais*', 95.

89 Barrault, 'Une répétition du *Château*'.

90 Barrault, *Nouvelles réflexions*, 90.

91 Jean-Louis Barrault, *Mise en scène de Phèdre de Racine* (Paris: Éditions du Seuil, 1946), 117.

92 Barrault, 'Mise en scène de *Autour d'une mère*', 47–9.

93 Jean-Louis Barrault, 'Fragments de *La Faim*, adaptation de Jean-Louis Barrault, d'après Knut Hamsun', *Cahiers de la Compagnie Madeleine Renaud—Jean-Louis Barrault*, no. 51 (1965): 55–62.

94 Jean-Louis Barrault, '*Rhinocéros*: Notes de mise en *scène*', in *Eugène Ionesco*, by Simone Benmussa, Théâtre de tous les temps, no. 1 (Paris: Éditions Seghers, 1966), 121.

95 René Farabet, 'J.-L. Barrault répète *Le Rhinocéros*', *Combat*, 4 January 1960 (clipping, Bibliothèque de l'Arsenal).

96 Barrault, *Nouvelles réflexions*, 97.

97 Ibid.

98 Copeau, *Notes sur le métier de comédien*, 59.

99 Jean-Louis Barrault and Paul Claudel, '*Le Soulier de satin* à la Comédie-Française', *Revue des Beaux-Arts de France*, December 1943–January 1944, 87.

100 Ibid.

101 Barrault, *Mise en scène de Phèdre*, 28.

102 Ibid., 167.

103 Barrault, *Réflexions*, 92.

104 Barrault, *Souvenirs*, 125.

105 Barrault and Benmussa, 'Travail de scène pour *Le Procès*', 101.

106 Wallis, 'Barrault's Rabelais', 86. This description refers to the London production directed by Barrault; I assume that in the Paris production, the actors found caricature voices more familiar to the French audience.

107 Barrault, *Souvenirs*, 108–9.

108 Barrault and Benmussa, 'Travail de scène pour *Le Procès*', 105.

109 Robert Kemp, 'L'État de siège au théâtre Marigny', *Le Monde*, 29 October 1948 (clipping, Bibliothèque de l'Arsenal).

110 Barrault, 'Mise en scène de *Autour d'une mère*', 35.

111 Ibid.

112 Ibid.

113 Barrault, *Memories*, 67.

114 Ibid., 190.

115 Darius Milhaud, 'Mes deux partitions pour *Christophe Colomb*', *Cahiers de la Compagnie Madeleine Renaud—Jean-Louis Barrault*, no. 1 (1953): 43.

116 Barrault, *Nouvelles réflexions*, 102.

117 Guy Verdot, '*L'Orestie* d'Eschyle', *Franc-Tireur*, 28 and 29 May 1955 (clipping, Bibliothèque de l'Arsenal).

118 Wallis, 'Barrault's *Rabelais*', 97.

119 Ibid.

120 Barrault, *Memories*, 99.

121 Pierre Quemeneur, '*Hamlet* au théâtre Marigny', *Réforme*, 16 November 1946 (clipping, Bibliothèque de l'Arsenal).

122 Robert Kemp, 'Jean-Louis Barrault joue *l'Orestie*', *Le Soir* (Brussels), 13 October 1955 (clipping, Bibliothèque de l'Arsenal).

123 Barrault and Benmussa, 'Travail de scène pour *Le Procès*', 101.

124 Barrault, *Nouvelles réflexions*, 269.

125 Ibid.

126 Pierre Lagarde, 'Reprise à la Comédie-Française: *Le Soulier de satin* de Paul Claudel', *Libération*, 15 April 1949 (clipping, Bibliothèque de l'Arsenal).

127 See Barrault, 'Mise en scène de *Autour d'une mère*', 41; Barrault, *Réflexions*, 155; Barrault, *Nouvelles réflexions*, 269; Jean-Jacques Gautier, *Théâtre d'auiourd'hui* (Paris: Gallimard, 1972), 293.

128 Barrault, *Réflexions*, 155.

129 Barrault, *Nouvelles réflexions*, 269.

130 Ibid.

131 Barrault, 'Mise en scène de *Autour d'une mère*', 46.

132 Barrault, *Nouvelles réflexions*, 270.

133 Wallis, 'Barrault's *Rabelais*', 92.

134 See Barrault, *Nouvelles réflexions*, 275.

135 Barrault, *Mise en scène de Phèdre*, 32.

136 See photographs from the production in Eugène Ionesco, *Rhinocéros*, ed. Reuben Y. Ellison and Stowell C. Goding (New York: Holt, Rinehart and Winston, 1961), 174–5.

137 Farabet, 'J.-L. Barrault répète *Le Rhinocéros*'.

138 Renée Saurel, '*Le Rhinocéros*', *Information*, 27 January 1960 (clipping, Bibliothèque de l'Arsenal).

139 See photograph in Ionesco, *Rhinocéros*, 192.

140 Barrault and Benmussa, 'Travail de scène pour *Le Procès*', 86–106.

141 Bentley, *In Search of Theatre*, 197.

142 Ibid.

143 Barrault, *Memories*, 190.

144 Ibid., 289. Translation modified.

145 Barrault, *Réflexions*, 147.

146 Barrault, *Nouvelles réflexions*, 100.

147 '*L'Orestie*', *Combat*, 4 October 1955 (clipping, Bibliothèque de l'Arsenal).

148 Barrault, *Réflexions*, 47.

149 Wallis, 'Barrault's *Rabelais*', 94.

150 Ibid., 88.

151 Ibid., 95.

152 Ibid., 89.

153 Ibid., 95.

154 See Barrault, *Mise en scène de Phèdre*, 31, 67, 81, 99, 169, 181.

155 Jean-Louis Barrault, 'Bulletin de la dernière minute: à propos de *Christophe Colomb*', *Cahiers de la Compagnie Madeleine Renaud—Jean-Louis Barrault*, no. 2 (1953): 126.

156 Wallis, 'Barrault's *Rabelais*', 91.

157 Thierry Maulnier, 'Mise en scène et interprétation', *Spectateur*, 22 October 1946 (clipping, Bibliothèque de l'Arsenal).

158 Barrault and Benmussa, 'Travail de scène pour *Le Procès*', 103.

159 Gautier, *Théâtre d'aujourd'hui*, 293.

160 '*L'Orestie*', *Combat*, 4 October 1955 (clipping, Bibliothèque de l'Arsenal).

161 Rosette C. Lamont, 'Interview with Jean-Louis Barrault', *Drama and Theatre* 9 (Fall 1970): 3.

162 Gautier, *Théâtre d'aujourd'hui*, 293.

163 Barrault, 'Fragments de *La Faim*', 46.

164 Ibid., 50.

165 Crémieux, '*Hamlet* et *La Faim* au théâtre de l'Atelier'.

166 See Barrault, 'Fragments de *La Faim*', 48–52.

167 Ibid., 53.

168 Ibid., 53–4.

169 Barrault, *Mise en scène de Phèdre*, 165.

170 Ibid.

171 Ibid., 167.

172 Max Favalelli, '*L'État de siège* au théâtre Marigny expose (allégoriquement) notre "mal du siècle"', *Paris- Presse L'intransigeant*, 29 October 1948 (clipping, Bibliothèque de l'Arsenal).

173 Descaves, 'A l'Atelier: *La Faim*' (clipping, Bibliothèque de l'Arsenal).

174 Poirot-Delpech, 'Reprise du *Procès* de Kafka par la Compagnie Renaud-Barrault', *Le Monde*, 21 October 1961 (clipping, Bibliothèque de l'Arsenal).

175 Michel Mohrt, 'Three Plays of the Current Paris Season', *Yale French Studies*, no. 5 (1950): 100.

176 Jean-Jacques Gautier, 'Au théâtre Marigny: *L'État de siège* d'Albert Camus', *Le Figaro*, 29 October 1948 (clipping, Bibliothèque de l'Arsenal).

177 Hobson, *The French Theatre of Today*, 51.

178 André Ransan, 'Au théâtre Marigny: *Le Procès*', *Paris-Matin*, 12 and 13 October 1947 (clipping, Bibliothèque de l'Arsenal).

179 Hobson, *The French Theatre of Today*, 51.

180 Louis Cheronnet, 'A la Comédie-Française: *Le Soulier de satin*', *Revue des Beaux-Arts de France*, 24 December 1943 (clipping, Bibliothèque de l'Arsenal).

181 Jacques Lemarchand, personal interview, Paris, 13 December 1972; recorded in note form.

182 Barrault, *Memories*, 176.

183 Jean-Louis Barrault, *Reflections on the Theatre* (London: Salisbury Square, 1951), 169.

Chapter 3

1 Ariane Mnouchkine interviewed by Andrew Dickson, 'Ariane Mnouchkine and the Théâtre du Soleil: A Life in Theatre', *The Guardian*, 10 August 2012, https://www.theguardian.com/culture/2012/aug/10/ariane-mnouchkine-life-in-theatre.

2 Claire Linda, 'Ariane Mnouchkine: 40 ans de Théâtre du Soleil', TouteLaCulture.com, 8 March 2010, http://toutelaculture.com/spectacles/theatre/ariane-mnouchkine-son-theatre-du-soleil-a-40-ans/.

3 Josette Féral and Anne Husemoller, 'Building up the Muscle', interview with Ariane Mnouchkine, *TDR* 33, no. 4 (1989): 95.

4 Gilles Costaz, 'La Reine Soleil', interview with Ariane Mnouchkine, *Le Matin*, 17 January 1984, 23.

5 Artaud, *The Theatre and Its Double*, 13.

6 John T. Scott, 'Rousseau and the Melodious Language of Freedom', *The Journal of Politics* 59, no. 3 (1993): 803–29.

7 Angela C. Pao, *The Orient of the Boulevards: Exoticism, Empire, and Nineteenth-Century French Theater* (Philadelphia: University of Pennsylvania Press, 1998), 33.

8 Béatrice Picon-Vallin, 'A la recherche du théâtre – le Soleil, de *Et soudain des nuits d'éveil* à *Tambours sur la digue* – Les longs cheminements de la troupe du Soleil', *Théâtre/Public* 152 (2000): 5–13, http://www.theatre-du-soleil. fr/thsol/nos-spectacles-et-nos-films/nos-spectacles/et-soudain-des-nuits-d-eveil-1997/les-longs-cheminements-de-la#nb14.

9 Peter Brooks, *The Melodramatic Imagination: Balzac, Henry James, Melodrama, and the Mode of Excess* (New Haven, CT and London: Yale University Press, 1995), 21.

10 Ibid.

11 Ibid., 22.

12 Paul Louis Mignon, 'Ariane Mnouchkine', *L'Avant-Scène* 526–527 (October 1973): 17.

13 Marie-Louise Bablet and Denis Bablet, *Le Théâtre du Soleil, ou La quète du Bonheur. Diapolivre I* (Paris: Centre National de la Recherche Scientifique, 1979), 8.

14 Ibid.

15 Short video clip of *Genghis Khan*: http://www.ina.fr/video/CPF08006068/ genghis-khan-a-lutece-video.html.

16 Jacques Copeau, *Régistres I: Appels*, textes recueillis et établis par Marie-Hélène Dasté et Suzanne Maistre Saint-Denis (Paris: Gallimard, 1974), 187.

17 David Bradby, *Modern French Drama 1940–1980* (Cambridge: Cambridge University Press, 1984), 2.

18 Ibid., 2.

19 Bradby, *Modern French Drama 1940–1980*, 192.

20 Ariane Mnouchkine and Jean-Claude Penchenat, 'L'aventure du Théâtre du Soleil', *Preuves* 7, no. 3 (1971): 120.

21 Bablet and Bablet, *Diapolivre I*, 13.

22 Ibid.

23 R. Hilbert, '*Les Petits Bourgeois* de Gorky remarquablement interpretés par le Théâtre du Soleil', *Le Berry Républicain*, November 1966.

24 *Les Petits Bourgeois* video clip, http//:www.ina.fr/video/CAF88047334.

25 Quoted in Bablet and Bablet, *Diapolivre I*, 16–17.

26 Quoted in ibid., 20.

27 Bablet and Bablet, *Diapolivre I*, 23.

28 Ibid., 24.

29 Pierre Marcabru, 'Spectacle La Cuisine', *Paris-Presse*, 26 July 1967.

30 For further consideration of Lecoq's influence on Mnouchkine, see Helen Richardson, 'Jacques Lecoq, Ariane Mnouchkine, and the Théâtre du Soleil', in *The Routledge Companion to Jacques Lecoq*, ed. Mark Evan and Rick Kemp (London: Routledge, 2016), 307–15.

31 The following two videos of *La Cuisine* and The Living Theatre's *The Brig* provide insight into the comparison: http://www.ina.fr/video/I05318458/ theatre-du-soleil-la-cuisine-video.html and https://www.youtube.com/ watch?v=qYVvf50CUig.

32 Théâtre du Soleil programme notes for *A Midsummer Night's Dream*: http:// www.theatre-du-soleil.fr/thsol/nos-spectacles-et-nos-films/nos-spectacles/le-songe-d-une-nuit-d-ete-1968/programme-1055.

33 Jan Kott, *Shakespeare Our Contemporary*, trans. Boleslaw Taborski (New York: W.W. Norton, 1974), 218.

34 Théâtre du Soleil programme notes for *A Midsummer Night's Dream*.

35 Video clip of Mnouchkine coaching an actor in *commedia dell'arte* mask-work: https://www.youtube.com/watch?v=PSH6Ct4Knmo.

36 Video clips on the Théâtre du Soleil's *A Midsummer Night's Dream*: http:// www.ina.fr/video/CPF10005481/shakespeare-a-montmartre-video.html and http://www.ina.fr/video/CAF89031267/les-spectacles-de-la-semaine-video. html.

37 Gilles Sandier, 'Ariane Mnouchkine sacrifie 300 chèvres à Shakespeare', *Elle*, 4 April 1968, http://www.theatre-du-soleil.fr/thsol/nos-spectacles-et-nos-films/ nos-spectacles/le-songe-d-une-nuit-d-ete-1968/la-part-du-reve-2-le-songe-d-une#nb16.

38 Sophie Lemasson, *1789, Création collective du Théâtre du Soleil. Etude de mise en scène*. Notes of the assistant director, unpublished typescript (1970–1), 8.

39 Philippe Madral, 'Héritiers ou bâtisseurs?' Interview with Ariane Mnouchkine. *L'Humanité* (May 1969).

40 Bablet and Bablet, *Diapolivre I*, 39.

41 Video clips and interviews on *Les Clowns*: http://www.ina.fr/video/I05294028/ ariane-mnouchkine-et-les-clowns-video.html and http://www.ina.fr/video/ RAF03032538/les-clowns-d-ariane-mnouchkine-au-festival-d-avignon-video.html.

42 Alfred Simon, 'Des Clowns et des Hommes', *Esprit*, June 1969, 1093.

43 Jean-Claude Penchenat, 'La Vida de una compañia', *El Público*, September 1986, 49.

44 Mnouchkine and Penchenat, 'L'aventure du Théâtre du Soleil', 121.

45 Sophie Lemasson, 'From Production to Collective Creation', *Gambit 5*, no. 2 (1971), 59.

46 Video on the company's move to the Cartoucherie de Vincennes: http://www. ina.fr/video/I11125845/amenagement-de-la-cartoucherie-en-salle-de-spectacle-video.html.

47 Video clips on *1789* include a documentary on the production: https://www.youtube.com/watch?v=2N7A7JUHODM and one on rehearsals at the Cartoucherie: http://www.ina.fr./video/I05294047/a-la-cartoucherie-repetitions-de-1789-video.html and the scene of the taking of the Bastille: https://www.youtube.com/watch?v=9ms9xAQxFSI.

48 'Théâtre a vu à Paris *1789*', *Plaisir de la Maison*, March 1971.

49 Nicole Herbert, 'Une Réussite Collective Orchestrée par Ariane Mnouchkine', *Paris Normandie*, 15 February 1971.

50 '*1789* au Théâtre du Soleil', *France Nouvelle,* 17 February 1971.

51 Georges Conchon, 'Théâtre: Hérésie et Révolution', *La Galerie des Arts*, 15 February 1971.

52 Marc-Antoine Muret, *Le Figaro Littéraire*, Paris, 3 November 1970.

53 Alfred Simon, 'Le Théâtre du Soleil et le Théâtre de la Révolution', *Esprit*, February 1971, 422.

54 Ariane Mnouchkine, 'Le Théâtre du Soleil: *1789, La Révolution doit s'arrêter à la perfection du Bonheur',* interview and public discussion with Michael Kustow, Jonathan Miller, Kenneth Tynan and Arnold Wesker, *Performance Magazine*, October 1971, 137.

55 Ibid., 139.

56 Ibid., 140.

57 Ariane Mnouchkine, 'Une prise de conscience', *Le Théâtre 1968–1*, Cahiers dirigés par Arrabal (Paris: Christian Bourgois, 1968), 122.

58 Video clip of opening scene of *L'Age d'or*: http://www.ina.fr/video/I11138926/le-theatre-du-soleil-l-age-d-or-video.html.

59 Video interview with Ariane Mnouchkine on making *Molière*: http://www.ina.fr/video/I00019659/ariane-mnouchkine-a-propos-de-son-film-moliere-video.html. Video clips of *Molière*: https://www.youtube.com/watch?v=KgStsJ34F4A and https://www.youtube.com/watch?v=jnbvfl1c6c0.

60 Video clips of the Shakespeares: http://www.ina.fr/video/CAA8201172001 and http://www.ina.fr/video/CAB8401267401/los-angeles-video.html.

61 Video clip on *L'Indiade*, including an interview with Hélène Cixous: http://www.ina.fr/video/CAB87033998/ariane-mnouchkine-l-indiade-ou-l-inde-de-leurs-reves-video.html.

62 *Les Atrides* rehearsal: https://www.youtube.com/watch?v=fjPiUNbyVsM.

63 John Rockwell, 'Critic's Notebook: New Project from Director of *Les Atrides*', *New York Times*, 8 June 1994, http://www.nytimes.com/1994/06/08/theater/critic-s-notebook-new-project-from-director-of-les-atrides.html.

64 Loren Ringer, '*Et soudain des nuits d'éveil* (And Suddenly, Nights of Awakening), a collective work in harmony with Hélène Cixous, le Théâtre du Soleil, Paris, 25 January 1998', Theatre Review, *Theatre Journal 509*, no. 4 (December 1998): 529–31.

65 Ron Jenkins, 'As if they are puppets at the mercy of tragic fate', *New York Times*, 27 May 2001.

66 Video clips of *Tambours sur la digue*: http://www.ina.fr/video/CAB99041934 and https://www.youtube.com/watch?v=N5RXsjTU34M&list=RDN5RXsjTU 34M&index=1. On the making of the film of *Tambours*: https://www.youtube. com/watch?v=uwG7jukHEHM.

67 On the making of the film version of *Le Dernier Caravansérail*: https://www. youtube.com/watch/v=Giib9w0JITY and a press conference on the film: https://www.theatre-video.net/video/Avignon-2006-conference-de-presse-du-10-juillet.

68 Putting together the set for *Les Ephémères*: https://www.youtube.com/ watch?v=kiIN0qPzLJg. A scene from the show: http:///boutique.arte.tv/ f4866-ephemeres_serie. Press interview: https://www.theatre-video.net/video/ Conference-de-presse-du-13-juillet-2007?autostart.

69 Video clips of *Les Naufragés du Fol Espoir*: https://www.youtube. com/watch?v=mg0Q-qTNMqo and https://www.youtube.com/ watch?v=YsRw8DUwgCw. Interview with Mnouchkine on the production: https://www.youtube.com/watch?v=oUrBWETg4x0.

70 Announcement of 2016 production: http://www.theatre-du-soleil.fr/thsol/nos-actualites/une-chambre-en-inde/article/premiere-le-26-octobre-2016.

Chapter 4

1   Train station near Sangatte, where trains connect France to England.

2   Such as *Gilgamesh*, trans. Andrew Georges; Spôjmaï Zariâb, *La Plaine de Caïn*; Jacques Derrida, *Of Hospitality*, trans. Rachel Bowlby. For a comprehensive list of the books used during the creation of *The Last Caravanserai*, please contact the author of this article.

3   Voltaire, 'Equality', *Philosophical Dictionary* (1764).

4   Extract of a poem by Attar, a mystic Persian poet who lived between the twelfth and thirteenth centuries and who was persecuted for criticizing the clergy's hypocrisy and sectarianism. During rehearsal, Ariane replaced 'to love' with 'to act'.

5   Dated 6 September 2001, originally in Kurdish.

6   Dated 9 October 2001.

7   Dated 8 September 1999, signed Majnoun, extract from a poem by Nalî, a Kurdish polymath from the nineteenth century.

8   Dated 17 November 2002. 'Callas' should probably be 'Calais'.

9   Dated 8 September 1997, signed Azad.

10 Marked 'Sangatte, 2002'.

11 Amnesty International report, 2002.

12 Dante Alighieri, *The Divine Comedy*, in 'The Paradise', Chant XVII.

13 By Salah al-Hamdani, an Iraqi poet who left Iraq in 1974 and lives in France now.

14 Examples of two 'Landays', poems in (two) free verses, of twenty-two syllables in total, each made of either nine or thirteen syllables. Pashto women improvise and transmit 'Landays' as a way to defy the conditions to which men reduced them.

15 By Forough Farrockhzad, an Iranian poet born in 1934 in Teheran.

16 By Achough Djivani, a nineteenth-century Armenian poet.

17 Hélène Cixous, in the programme of *The Last Caravanserai*.

Chapter 5

1 Herbert Mainusch and Achim Benning, *Regie und Interpretation* (Munich: Fink, 1985), 112.

2 In 2005, the Berlin newspaper *Die Welt* listed Peter Stein 28th in its rankings among Germany's contemporary intellectuals.

3 Dieter Kranz, *Positionen: Strehler, Planchon, Koun, Dario Fo, Långbacka, Stein: Gespräche mit Regisseuren des europäischen Theaters* (Berlin: Henschel, 1981), 170.

4 Roswitha Schieb, *Peter Stein: ein Portrait* (Berlin: Berlin Verlag, 2005), 34.

5 Fritz Kortner, *Aller Tage Abend* (Munich: Kindler, 1969), 314.

6 Ibid., 305–6.

7 August Wilhelm Schlegel (1767–1845) had insisted that Shakespeare's dramatic idiom was 'compressed' and therefore language in the plays had more functions than did normal speech in everyday life. Since verse 'is more concentrated in meaning than is prose', German verse was a natural language for Shakespearean performance. Schlegel's comprehensive knowledge of Shakespeare was due to his verse translations of the tragedies, and his influential essays established Shakespeare as a national figure in Germany.

8 Karlheinz Braun and Klaus Völker, eds, *Spielplatz. 1, Jahrbuch für Theater 71–72* (Berlin: Wagenbach, 1972), 53.

9 Jutta Lampe, *Neue Zürcher Zeitung*, 3 December 2005.

10 Kortner, *Aller Tage Abend*, 304.

11 Production programme for *Gerettet*. Werkraumtheater der Münchner Kammerspiele, 15 April 1967. The scene in which young East London punks stone a baby to death had created a scandal in London, but a more difficult scene to design and stage involved a rowboat on a small lake. Designer Jürgen Rose used a real boat cut at the bottom to make it appear sunk into the floor; actors Michael König and Jutta Schwarz rolled it out onto the bare stage with their feet while sitting in it because Rose had installed two sets of concealed wheels. The effect was stunning but unspectacular.

12 Sperr was a distinctly minor playwright, but Stein had enjoyed his 1966 *Hunting Scenes from Lower Bavaria* when it premiered that year in Bremen. He found Sperr's dialogue 'authentic', much as Bond's original in *Saved* had captured the brutish nonchalance of the play's thugs and their girlfriends. To make sure the actors got their accents right, Stein kept Sperr in the cast as one of the young thugs in the infamous 'baby stoning' scene.

13 Interview in *Münchner Merkur,* 15 April 1967.

14 *Bayerische Staatszeitung,* 21 April 1967.

15 Michael Patterson, *Peter Stein, Germany's Leading Theatre Director* (Cambridge: Cambridge University Press, 1981), 7.

16 Carl Weber, 'Brecht as Director', *TDR* 12, no. 1 (1967): 101–2.

17 Botho Strauss, *Theater heute* 12 (1967): 32.

18 Ibid., 33.

19 John O'Mahony, 'Master of the Rebels', *The Guardian,* 9 August 2003.

20 Bruno Ganz, 'Auffassungen zur Theaterarbeit', in Braun and Völker, *Spielplatz. 1,* 53.

21 Hans-Thies Lehmann, *Postdramatisches Theater* (Frankfurt am Main: Verlag der Autoren, 1999), 175.

22 *Theater heute, Jahrbuch* 13 (1969), 23.

23 'Der Schauspieler lasse kein Schnupftuch auf dem Theater sehen, noch weniger schnaube er die Nase, noch weniger spucke er aus. Es ist schrecklich, innerhalb eines Kunstprodukts an diese Natürlichkeiten erinnert zu werden'. *Goethes Werke: Vollstandige Ausgabe letzter Hand,* Volume 44 (Stuttgart: Cotta, 1833), 310.

24 Botho Strauss, 'Das schöne Umsonst', *Theater heute* 10 (1969): 30.

25 Reinhard Baumgart, 'Seidenwürmern und Schmetterlingen', *Süddeutsche Zeitung,* 30 May 1970.

26 Schieb, *Peter Stein,* 76.

27 Kranz, *Positionen,* 185.

28 Patterson, *Peter Stein,* 20.

29 Braun and Völker, *Spielplatz. 1,* 53.

30 'Die kollektive Bühne', *Christ und Welt,* 4 September 1970.

31 Christine Nippe, *Kunst der Verbindung* (Berlin: LiT, 2006), 34.

32 They included the Freie Volksbühne, the Hebbel-Theater, the Komödie (private), the Renaissance (private), the Hansa, the Theater am Kurfürstentendamm (private), the Schiller (three theatre spaces), and the Theater des Westens, a private theatre specializing in musicals. Not all of these theatres received similar amounts of government support; in years when tickets sales were considerable at private theatres, the Berlin Senate's subsidy was considerably less.

33 Peter Iden, *Die Schaubühne* (Munich: Hanser, 1979), 34.

34 Patterson, *Peter Stein,* 43.

35 Therese Giehse, *Ich hab' nichts zu sagen,* ed. Monika Sperr (Gütersloh: Bertelsmann, 1972), 11–12.

36 The term *agitprop* in German evolved from the Soviet Department for Agitation and Propaganda, which was part of Bolshevik plan to agitate the masses with propaganda glorifying the workers' struggle. Brecht, Piscator and other German communists who sympathized with the Bolshevik cause attempted to emulate their practices, but *agitprop* came to mean almost any kind of politicized performance. Stein spelled out his updated conception of *agitprop* when he said, 'For us, agitation means simply attempting to have an impact on the audience's consciousness, so that anyone who comes [to see *The Mother*] can at least acknowledge *agitprop* as a topic for discussion' (*Berliner Zeitung*, 18 January 1971).

37 'Was erklären Verklärungen?' *Die Zeit*, 28 April 1972.

38 The term *dacha* originated with the seventeenth-century czars, who awarded their favourites small estates intended for part-time habitation, usually in summer. By the nineteenth century, wealthy bourgeois families began to build summer houses in the country to escape urban congestion. Occupants of these summer houses thus became *dachniki*, individuals affluent enough to enjoy entire months during summers in bucolic surroundings. See Stephen Lovell, *Summerfolk: A History of the Dacha* (Ithaca, NY: Cornell University Press, 2003), 90–5.

39 Quoted in Patterson, *Peter Stein*, 115.

40 Bradby and Williams, *Directors' Theater*, 207.

41 *Protocol* of 21 October 1970.

42 Schaubühne production programme, 13 May 1971.

43 Ivan Nagel, *Süddeutsche Zeitung*, 19–20 May 1971.

44 Volker Canaris, 'Eine Rolle, sechs Schauspieler–wozu?' *Theater heute* 13 (1971): 32.

45 Patterson, *Peter Stein*, 75.

46 Hellmuth Karasek, *Die Zeit*, 7 September 1973.

47 Benjamin Hinrichs, *Süddeutsche Zeitung*, 3 September 1973.

48 Schaubühne programme for *Das Sparschwein*, 1 September 1973.

49 Quoted in *Kleists Erzählungen und Dramen: neue Studien*, ed. Paul Michael Lützeler and David Pan (Würzburg: Königshausen und Neumann, 2001), 163.

50 Interview with Barbara Lehmann, *Die Zeit*, 15 July 2004.

51 Interview with Jack Zipes in *Theatre* 9, no. 1 (1977), 53.

52 For an account of the curious and often problematic production history of *As You Like It* in German, see Adolf Winds, '*Wie es euch gefällt*', *Shakespeare-Jahrbuch* 53, 181–4.

53 Beatrice Schlag, 'Peter Stein', in *Kreativität und Dialog*, ed. Joachim Fiebach and Helmar Schramm (Berlin: Henschel, 1983), 264–5.

54 Ivan Nagel, *Kortner Zadek Stein* (Munich: Hanser, 1989), 78.

55 *Darmstädter Echo*, 18 October 1980.

56 Joachim Kaiser, 'Wie Peter Stein dem Aischylos dient', *Süddeutsche Zeitung*, 20 October 1980.

57 Mainusch and Benning, *Regie und Interpretation*, 114.

58 Georges Banu, *Avec Brecht, Peter Stein et d'autres* (Paris: Conservatoire national supérieur d'art dramatique, 1999), 39–40.

59 Vladimir Nabokov, *Lectures on Russian Literature*, ed. Fredson Bowers (New York: Harcourt Brace Jovanovich, 1981), 253.

60 Ibid., 158.

61 Stein had most successfully premiered three Strauss plays at the Schaubühne: *Trilogie des Wiedersehens* (Trilogy of Remembrance) and *Gross und Klein* (Great and Small) in 1978, and *Der Park* (The Park) in 1984, all of which received *Theatreffen* invitations.

62 One of the cast members extraordinarily well trained was standard poodle, whose appearance in the first act reminded audiences that Goethe hated dogs onstage; this production was one of the few in German theatre history that permitted the breed called for in the text to make its appearance – which many critics fulsomely praised.

63 Peter Stein, '"Das wird eine ganz fürchterlich strenge Übung:" ein Gespräch mit Peter Stein über sein *Faust I* und *II* Projekt', *Theater heute* 4 (1998): 2.

64 'Der Selbsthass des Theater-Tyrannosaurus', *Die Welt*, 11 September 2007.

Chapter 6

1   Stein's production of Berlioz' opera *Le damnation de Faust* ceremoniously concluded the 240th season of Moscow's Bolshoi Theater in July 2016.

2   Cf. Schieb, *Peter Stein*, 35 ff.

3   Patterson, *Peter Stein*, 2 ff.

4   Schieb, *Peter Stein*, 40–8.

5   Ibid., 39. Ivan Nagel, *Kortner – Zadek – Stein* (Munich: Hanser, 1989), 69 ff., among other authors, draws on Stein's early biography to connect this attention to detail in the service of a whole with his upbringing as the son of a mechanical engineer.

6   'Das ist in der Tat meine Grundüberzeugung, daß das europäische Theater literarisches Theater ist ... daß das theatralische Element also durch ein anderes Zeichensystem zurückgedrängt wird.' Herbert Mainusch, 'Das Theater ist eine Art Museum: Gespräch mit Peter Stein', in Mainusch and Achim Benning, *Regie und Interpretation* (Munich: Fink, 1989), 116.

7   Schieb, *Peter Stein*, 55–9; Botho Strauss, 'Das Mass der Wörtlichkeit: Über Peter Stein', in *Der Gebärdensammler* (Frankfurt am Main: Verlag der Autoren, 1999), 68–70.

8   Quoted in Patterson, *Peter Stein*, 8.

9   Peter Stein, 'Wenn ihr wüsstet, was da gestorben ist' (If you only knew what has now passed away), *Der Stern*, 10 March 1975, 78–9.

10 Martin Sperr, Peter Stein and Ivan Nagel, 'Wie wir Bonds Stück inszenierten' (How we staged Bond's play), *Theater Heute* 8 (1967), Jahressonderheft (Year-end edition): 76.

11 'Aufführung des Jahres' (Production of the Year), *Theater Heute* 8 (1967), Jahressonderheft (Year-end edition), 56–73.

12 Perhaps most prominently, and largely contemporaneously, the Action-Theater group that Rainer Werner Fassbinder became involved with, as well as other street theatre and alternative performance art groups and movements.

13 'Die Inszenierung des "Vietnam-Diskurses" hat sich von Anfang an als Modell für demokratische Praxis verstanden. Es wurden Arbeitsmethoden angewandt, die die traditionelle, unproduktive Arbeitsteilung zwischen Schauspielern und Regie weitgehend aufgehoben…. Dazu kommt der Umstand, daß im Stück die Frage der Durchsetzung demokratischer Verhältnisse zum Thema wird. Nur durch die genannten Arbeitsmethoden war es möglich, die Thesen des Stückes zu überprüfen, theatralisch zu vermitteln und unsere Haltung zum Völkermord zu formulieren.' Wolfgang Schwiedrzik and Peter Stein, 'Demokratie ist auch Aktion', *Theater Heute* 8 (August 1968): 3.

14 'Die Kritik lobte einhellig Steins Verzicht auf ein grobe, anbiedernde Aktualisierung des Dramas' (Critics unanimously praised Stein for refraining from any crude, pandering modernization of the play). Schieb, *Peter Stein*, 48–54, here 49.

15 The verse numbers that are retained and their arrangement are listed in Goethe et al., *Torquato Tasso: Regiebuch der Bremer Inszenierung* (Torquato Tasso: Stage Script of the Bremen Production) (Frankfurt am Main: Suhrkamp, 1970), 129–31.

16 For example, for the first intermezzo: Verses 760–6, 943 f., 947–50, 788, 790–800, 83–8, 138–41, 147–60, 163 f., 167–70, 173–8, 182–206, 212–23, 3035–40, 2948–51, 116 f., 123–33, 750–3, 2956–61, 2964 f., 2846–9, 2942 f., 2850 f. Goethe et al., *Torquato Tasso*, 129.

17 'Den Körper zum Bogen spannend, die Fingerspitzen auf den Tisch gedrückt, den Kopf in den Nacken geworfen, streckt er sich dem Kuss der Muse entgegen; mit delikatem Schwung greift er nach dem Papier, mustert, die Feder in der Hand, stirnrunzelnd sein Poem; stellt sich, einen Fuss preziös über den andern setzend, als "der Dichter" vor; hüllt mit weihevoller Gestik den weiten Mantel des Hohen Priesters aller Poesie um sich; nimmt, den Umhang zusammenraffend, feierlich Platz auf dem Thron des Dichterfürsten und setzt sich, würdevoll ins Weite blickend – daneben; endlich, den Ellenbogen auf das Knie gestützt, den gedankenschweren Kopf nach vorn geneigt, mit der Rechten eine imaginäre Leier haltend, entlässt er den Gesang aus sich.' Goethe et al., *Torquato Tasso*, 171.

18 'Das Thema des Stücks [betrifft] nicht nur uns auf der Bühne als Künstler, sondern auch Sie im Publikum direkt. Denn die Abhängigkeiten, unter denen wir als Künstler leben und arbeiten, sind nicht wesentlich verschieden von den Abhängigkeiten, unter denen Sie arbeiten. Wie Sie arbeiten wir in einem Betrieb, wie Sie arbeiten wir an einem Produkt, wie Sie produzieren wir unter Zwängen. Wie Sie sind wir in unseren Mitbestimmungsmöglichkeiten eingeengt – müssen wir abliefern und können wie die meisten von Ihnen nicht über die Verwendung und die Auswirkung unserer Arbeit bestimmen.' Goethe et al., *Torquato Tasso*, 124.

19 Goethe et al., *Torquato Tasso*, 118.

20 'Die Frage ist, kann man dem Publikum überhaupt noch Inhalte, die uns betreffen, mit den Mitteln der Kunst vermitteln? Und mit welchen Mitteln? Da haben wir auf der einen Seite Formen, die durch lange Tradition sinnentleert geworden sind, auf der anderen sogenannten "moderne Mittel" (wie z.B. die Körpersprache der *Mass-für-Mass*-Inszenierung von Peter Zadek o.ä.). Nun, ich muss zugeben, wir fanden keine überzeugenden, und wir griffen deshalb zu dem Mittel des direkten Gesprächs mit dem Publikum in der Pause. Das ist, wenn man Theater machen will, keine Lösung.' Goethe et al., *Torquato Tasso*, 143–4.

21 For example, 'In spite of all the conceptual reservations that we have to articulate here, every one of the acting performances was admirable.' (Im einzelnen sind die schauspielerischen Leistungen bei allen konzeptiven Vorbehalten, die wir vorbringen müssen, bewunderungswürdig.), Peter Schloßberg, 'Den Tasso abgewertet' ('Tasso debased'), *Die Wahrheit*, 15 May 1970.

22 Quoted in Patterson, *Peter Stein*, 46.

23 Ibid.

24 Ibid., 51. 'Dabei ist diese Mutter von Anfang bis Ende eine Proletarierin, aber sie ändert ihre Praxis (und über diesen Vorgang demonstriert die Aufführung den Bewußtseinsprozeß der Wlassowa, als praktischen, nicht als psychologischen).' Bertolt Brecht, *Die Mutter: Regiebuch der Schaubühnen-Inszenierung* (The Mother: Stage Script of the *Schaubühne* Production) (Frankfurt am Main: Suhrkamp, 1971), 117.

25 'Daß man sich fast der Illusion hingeben konnte, der Geburtsstunde eines West-"Berliner Ensembles" beigewohnt zu haben, das mit einem Schlag die Tradition des Theaterrevolutionärs vom Schiffbauerdamm ans Hallische Ufer herüberholte'. 'Schöner, grüner Klassenkampf: Genialische "Mutter" – Schiffbauerdamm am Halleschen Ufer' (Pretty, green class struggle: Brilliant 'Mother' – Schiffbauerdamm on the Hallisches Ufer), *Stuttgarter Zeitung*, 12 October 1970.

26 'Eine ungemein klare und intensive Inszenierung, die aus der Konzentration auf das Wort die Wirkung bezog'. 'Purer Brecht: "Die Mutter" in der Schaubühne' (Pure Brecht: 'The Mother' at the *Schaubühne*), *Telegraf*, Berlin-West, 10 October 1970.

27 Hellmuth Karasek, 'Zurück zur Mutter: Die neue Berliner Schaubühne beginnt mit Brecht' (Back to Mother: The new Berlin Schaubühne begins with Brecht), *Die Zeit*, Hamburg, 16 October 1970.

28 '"Die Mutter" ist inzwischen auch von ca. 3000 Lehrlingen und Jungarbeitern besucht worden – und in den anschließend im Theater veranstalteten Diskussionen hatte *dieses* Publikum nie Mühe, Beziehungen zwischen dem Stück und der eigenen Erfahrung herzustellen bzw. zu erkennen'. Brecht, *Die Mutter*, 126.

29 Cf. Patterson, *Peter Stein*, 66–89; Schieb, *Peter Stein*, 123–30; Zipes, 'The Irresistable Rise of the *Schaubühne am Hallischen Ufer*', *Theater* 9, no. 1 (1977): 24–7.

30 Hellmuth Karasek, 'Ein Höhepunkt deutschen Theaters' (A Highpoint of the German Theater), *Die Zeit*, Hamburg, 21 May 1971.

31 'Das Theaterkollektiv [hat[jetzt mit einer Aufführung überrascht, die zweifellos zum Sensationellsten und Tollsten gehört, was in den letzten Jahren auf internationalen Bühnen überhaupt geschehen ist; der Rezensent muß gestehen, daß ihm ein vergleichbares Ereignis dieses Ausmaßes in der Regiegeschichte der letzten Jahrzehnte gar nicht zur Verfügung steht. Der Entschluß, Henrik Ibsens ausladenden "Peer Gynt" auf den Spielplan zu setzen, spricht bereits für das fundierte Selbstverständnis und Selbstbewußtsein des Regisseurs Peter Stein und des jungen Theaterensembles, das heute zweifellos mehr denn je als wichtigstes Zentrum des deutschen Schauspiels angesehen werden muß.' Peter-Hans Göpfert, 'Die Bühnen-Sensation' (The Stage Sensation), *Nürnberger Zeitung*, 20 May 1971.

32 'Ich fühle mich nicht kompetent, mit der Antwort weiterzugehen als bis zum präliminaren Eingeständnis: Die Aufführung hat mir viele Erkenntnisse eher als eine Erkenntnis eingebracht – ihr unvergleichlicher Spaß entsprang tausendfacher Klarsicht, Vernunft und nicht, wie mir scheint, der einen, wahren Lehre.' Nagel, *Kortner – Zadek – Stein*, 62.

33 'Die Aufführung ist auch ein Stück Aufarbeitung unserer Geschichte. Sie zeigt, wo die Muster der Gesellschaft, in der wir leben, ihren Ursprung haben. Sie fragt, wie groß denn nun wirklich der Wert von Phantasie, Imagination und also: der Wert von Kunst ist.... Peter Stein hat neu definiert – man kann das so summarisch sagen – was das heißt, kritisches Theater.' Peter Iden, 'Ein schönes Stück Leben' (A Pretty Piece of Life), *Frankfurter Rundschau*, Frankfurt, 17 May 1971.

34 Reprinted in Schieb, *Peter Stein*, 93–5.

35 In fact, plays were assigned to a primary director, but the others did in fact participate in all the stagings, at least according to the constitution of the ensemble.

36 Patterson, *Peter Stein*, 40–5, summarizes the most significant details of this deterioration of principles.

37 'Der Drang zum Raumtheater, der die postmodernistische Ästhetik charakterisiert und Ausdruck der Emanzipation des Zuschauers zum souveränen Mitgestalter des Theaterereignisses ist, artikulierte sich hier auf eine pervertierte Weise als Verstärkung des autoritären Theateranspruchs.... Selten war der Zuschauer so paternalistisch behandelt wie in diesem Jubiläumsprojekt der Schaubühne, die sich einst so ausdrucklich für seine Emanzipation einsetzte.' *Theater Heute* 21 (1981): 47.

38 'Keine der Inszenierungen im neuen Haus der Schaubühne am Lehniner Platz hat die ästhetischen Entwürfe der siebziger Jahre und ihre Wirkungen aufs zeitgenössische Bewußtsein noch... annähernd erreicht.' *Theater Heute* 24, no. 1 (1984): 4.

39 'Ich bemerke, daß ich immer mehr dazu neige, dem rein Konventionellen anheimzufallen.' *Theater Heute* 24, no. 4 (1984), 3.

40 Ibid.

41 Scheib, *Peter Stein*, 432.

42 Hajo Kurzenberger, *Gegen den Strom* (Tübingen: Niemeyer, 2002), 205.

43 Ibid., 203.

BIBLIOGRAPHY

General

Barrault, Jean-Louis. *A propos de Shakespeare et du Théâtre*. Massy: La Parade, 1949.

Barrault, Jean-Louis. *Une vie sur scène: Entretiens inédits avec Guy Dumur*. Paris: Flammarion, 2010.

Boulez, Pierre. 'Musique et Théâtre'. In *Jean-Louis Barrault: une vie pour le théâtre*, edited by Noelle Giret, 89–97. Paris: Gallimard, 2010.

Bradby, David. 'Blacking Up – Three Productions by Peter Stein'. In *A Radical Stage: Theatre in Germany in the 1970s and 1980s*, edited by W.G. Sebold. Oxford: Berg, 1988, 18–30.

Bradby, David and David Williams. *Directors' Theater*. New York: St. Martin's Press, 1988.

Case, Sue-Ellen. 'Peter Stein Directs *The Oresteia*'. *Theater* 11, no. 3 (Summer 1980): 23–8.

Delgado, Maria M. 'Ariane Mnouchkine'. In *In Contact with the Gods? Directors Talk Theatre*, edited by Maria M. Delgado and Paul Heritage, 175–90. Manchester: Manchester University Press, 1996.

Isherwood, Charles. 'A Daughter's Revenge Is on the Menu, So Expect a Meal Served Bitter Cold'. *New York Times*, 12 October 2007.

Kalb, Jonathan. 'The Thirty Years' War, All 10 Hours of It'. *New York Times*, 1 July 2007.

Knapp, Bettina. 'Jean-Louis Barrault'. In *Off-Stage Voices: Interviews with Modern French Dramatists*, edited by Alba Amoia, 41–6. Troy, NY: Whitston, 1975.

Levasseur, Catherine. *Dans l'intimité des Renaud Barrault*, souvenirs recueillis par Martine Desèvre. Paris: Pygmalion, 2003.

Lichtenfels, Peter. 'Peter Stein'. In *In Contact with the Gods? Directors Talk Theatre*, edited by Maria M. Delgado and Paul Heritage, 239–59. Manchester: Manchester University Press, 1996.

Mitter, Shomit. 'Peter Stein'. In *Fifty Key Theatre Directors*, edited by Shomit Mitter and Maria Shevtsova, 148–54. London: Routledge, 2005.

Mnouchkine, Ariane. *L'Art du présent: Entretiens avec Fabienne Pascaud*. Paris: Plon, 2005.

Mnouchkine, Ariane. 'Les acteurs sont des poètes', interview with Raymonde Temkine. *Europe, revue littéraire mensuelle* 61e année, no. 648 (April 1983): 56–9.

Mnouchkine, Ariane. 'The Individual and the Collective'. In *Collaborative Theatre: The Théâtre du Soleil Sourcebook*, compiled and edited by David Williams, 59–64. London: Routledge, 1999.

Patterson, Michael. 'Peter Stein'. In *The Routledge Companion to Directors'*
    Shakespeare, edited by John Russell Brown, 425–39. London: Routledge, 2008.
Picon-Vallin, Béatrice. 'Leaving Room for the Others,' from an interview with
    members of the Théâtre du Soleil'. In *Collaborative Theatre: The Théâtre du*
    Soleil Sourcebook, compiled and edited by David Wiliams, 202–19. London:
    Routledge, 1999.
Shevtsova, Maria. 'Ariane Mnouchkine'. In *Fifty Key Theatre Directors*, edited by
    Shomit Mitter and Maria Shevtsova, 160–6. London: Routledge, 2005.
Steinegger, Catherine. *Pierre Boulez et le théâtre: De la Compagnie Renaud-*
    Barrault à Patrice Chéreau. Wavre: Mardaga, 2012.
Williams, David. 'Introduction: A Grain of Sand in the Works: Continuity and
    Change at the Théâtre du Soleil'. In *Collaborative Theatre: The Théâtre du*
    Soleil Sourcebook, compiled and edited by David Williams, x–xviii. London:
    Routledge, 1999.
Zipes, Jack. 'Utopia as the Past Conserved: An Interview with Peter Stein and
    Dieter Sturm of the Schaubühne am Halleschen Ufer'. *Theater* 9, no. 1 (1977):
    50–7.

Jean-Louis Barrault

Artaud, Antonin. *Lettres d'Antonin Artaud à Jean-Louis Barrault*. Préface by Paul
    Arnold. Note luminaire d'André Frank. France: Bordas, 1952.
Artaud, Antonin. *The Theatre and Its Double*. Translated Mary Caroline Richards.
    New York: Grove Press, 1958.
Barrault, Jean-Louis. 'A French Reaction'. *World Theatre* 4 (Spring 1954): 32.
Barrault, Jean-Louis. *A propos de Shakespeare et du théâtre*. Massy: La Parade,
    1949.
Barrault, Jean-Louis. 'Bulletin de la dernière minute: à propos de *Christophe*
    Colomb'. *Cahiers de la Compagnie Madeleine Renaud—Jean-Louis-Barrault*,
    no. 2 (1953): 125–7.
Barrault, Jean-Louis. *Comme je le pense*. Paris: Gallimard, 1983.
Barrault, Jean-Louis. 'Conviction et malaise dans le théâtre contemporain'. *Cahiers*
    de la Compagnie Madeleine Renaud—Jean-Louis Barrault, no. 71 (1970):
    52–91.
Barrault, Jean-Louis. 'Fragments de *La Faim*, adaptation de Jean-Louis Barrault,
    d'après Knut Hamsun'. *Cahiers de la Compagnie Madeleine Renaud–Jean-Louis*
    Barrault, no. 51 (1965): 46–62.
Barrault, Jean-Louis. 'Il n'y a que le sang qui compte'. *Arts*, 26 June 1952.
    Clipping, Bibliothèque de l'Arsenal, Paris.
Barrault, Jean-Louis. *Jarry sur la butte*, spectacle d'après les oeuvres completes
    d'Alfred Jarry. Paris: Gallimard, 1970.
Barrault, Jean-Louis. *Je suis homme de théâtre*. Paris: Editions du Conquistador,
    1955.
Barrault, Jean-Louis. *Le Phénomène théâtrale*. Oxford: Clarendon Press, 1961.
Barrault, Jean-Louis. *Memories for Tomorrow: The Memoirs of Jean-Louis*
    Barrault. Translated by Jonathan Griffin. New York: E.P. Dutton, 1974.
Barrault, Jean-Louis. 'Mise en scène de *Autour d'une mère*'. *Cahiers de la*
    Compagnie Madeleine-Renaud—Jean-Louis Barrault, no. 71 (1970): 22–51.

Barrault, Jean-Louis. *Mise en scène de Phèdre de Racine*. Paris: Editions du Seuil, 1946.

Barrault, Jean-Louis. *Nouvelles réflexions sur le théâtre*. Paris: Flammarion, 1959.

Barrault, Jean-Louis. *Rabelais, A Dramatic Game in Two Parts Taken from the Five Books of François Rabelais*. Translated by Robert Baldick. New York: Hill & Wang, 1971.

Barrault, Jean-Louis. *Reflections on the Theatre*. Translated by Barbara Wall. London: Rockliff Publishing, 1951.

Barrault, Jean-Louis. *Réflexions sur le théâtre*. Paris: Éditions Jacques Vautrain, 1949.

Barrault, Jean-Louis. *Souvenirs pour demain*. Paris: Éditions du Seuil, 1972.

Barrault, Jean-Louis. Théâtre d'Orsay, Paris. Public interview, 11 December 1972. Recorded in note form.

Barrault, Jean-Louis. 'Une répétition du *Château*'. *Cahiers de la Compagnie Madeleine-Renaud–Jean-Louis Barrault*, no. 50 (1965): 107–20.

Barrault, Jean-Louis. *Une troupe et ses auteurs*. Paris: Compagnie Madeleine Renaud—J.-L. Barrault and Jacques Vautrain Editeurs, 1950.

Barrault, Jean-Louis. *Une vie sur scène: Entretiens inédits avec Guy Dumur*. Entretiens radiophoniques diffusé du 16 au 27 février 1981 sur France Culture. Texte établi, présenté et annoté par Denis Guénoun and Karine Le Bail. Paris: Flammarion, 2010.

Barrault, Jean-Louis and Simone Benmussa. *Odéon Théâtre de France*. Paris: Les Editions du Temps, 1965.

Barrault, Jean-Louis and Simone Benmussa. 'Travail de scène pour *Le Procès*'. *Cahiers de la Compagnie Madeleine Renaud—Jean-Louis Barrault*, no. 50 (1965): 86–106.

Barrault, Jean-Louis and Paul Claudel. '*Le Soulier de satin* à la Comédie-Française.' *Revue des Beaux-Arts de France*, December 1943–January 1944, 81–8.

Benmussa, Simone. *Eugène Ionesco*. Théâtre de tous les temps, no. 1. Paris: Éditions Seghers, 1966.

Bentley, Eric. *In Search of Theatre*. New York: Alfred A. Knopf, 1953.

Bentley, Eric. 'Jean-Louis Barrault'. *The Kenyon Review* 12, no. 2 (Spring 1950): 224–42.

Bishop, Tom. 'La vie errante: les tournées de la compagnie Renaud-Barrault'. In *Renault Barrault*, edited by Noëlle Giret, 112–18. Paris: Bibliothèque nationale de France, 1999.

Brovelli, Claude. *Ils ont réussi*. Paris: Editions France-Empire, 1984, 19–28.

Brown, Frederick. 'A Thirties Harlequinade: Artaud and Jean-Louis Barrault'. *Theater* 5, no. 3 (1974): 60–5.

Cairnes, Nancy Lee. '*Hamlet*, Gide, and Barrault'. In *Perspectives on Hamlet*, edited by William G. Holzberger and Peter B. Waldeck, 207–46. Lewisburg: Bucknell University Press, 1975.

Calas, André. 'Théâtre de France: Le Mystique Barrault veut en faire un temple'. *Lectures pour Tous*, March 1967, 36–41.

Capron, Marcelle. '*La Cerisaie* au théâtre Marigny'. *Combat*, 11 October 1954. Clipping, Bibliothèque de l'Arsenal.

Carné, Marcel and Jacques Prévert. *Les Enfants du paradis*. Translated by Dinah Brooke. London: Faber and Faber, 1988.

Champagne, Lenora. *French Theatre Experiment since 1968*. Ann Arbor: UMI Research Press, 1984.

Chancerel, Léon. *Jean-Louis Barrault ou 'l'Ange Noir du théâtre*. Paris: Presses Littéraires de France, 1953.

Cheronnet, Louis. 'A la Comédie-Française: *Le Soulier de satin*', *Revue des Beaux-Arts de France*, 24 December 1943. Clipping, Bibliothèque de l'Arsenal.

Christout, Marie-Françoise. 'Chronologie Jean-Louis Barrault. Repères biographiques'. *Revue d'histoire du théâtre*, I-II, nos. 189–90 (1996): 1–64.

Claudel, Paul and Jean-Louis Barrault. *Correspondance 1939–1945*. Preface by Jean-Louis Barrault. Edited by Michel Lioure. Paris: Gallimard, 2010.

Cole, Toby and Helen Krich Chinoy, eds. *Directors on Directing; A Source Book of the Modern Theatre*, revised edition. New York: Bobbs-Merrill, 1963.

Collection Pierre Bergé. *Renaud Barrault: Paris, notre siècle*. Editions de Messine, 1982.

Copeau, Jacques. *Critiques d'un autre temps: Études d'art dramatiques*, 7th edition. Paris: Éditions de la Nouvelle Revue Française, 1923.

Copeau, Jacques. *Notes sur le métier de comédien*. Paris: Michel Brient, 1955.

Copeau, Jacques. *Régistres I: Appels*. Edited by Marie-Hélène Dasté and Suzanne Maistre Saint-Denis. Paris: Gallimard, 1974.

Crémieux, Benjamin. '*Hamlet* et *La Faim* au théâtre de l'Atelier,' *La Lumière*, 5 May 1939. Clipping, Bibliothèque de l'Arsenal.

Dasté, Marie-Hélène. Personal interview with Suzanne Burgoyne, 28 December 1972. Théâtre d'Orsay, Paris. Recorded on tape.

Deák, Frantisek. 'Antonin Artaud and Charles Dullin: Artaud's Apprenticeship in Theatre'. *Educational Theatre Journal* 29, no. 3 (October 1977): 345–53.

Decogy, J. '"Je ne trahirai pas Kafka en faisant rire le public," nous dit Jean-Louis Barrault qui donne vendredi *Le Procès* au théâtre Marigny'. *Franc-Tireur*, 4 October 1947. Clipping, Bibliothèque de l'Arsenal.

Descaves, Lucien. 'A l'Atelier: *La Faim*', 20 April 1939. Unidentified publication, clipping from the archives of the Bibliothèque de l'Arsenal, Paris.

Dieckman, Suzanne Burgoyne. 'Theory and Practice in the Total Theatre of Jean-Louis Barrault'. PhD diss. University of Michigan, Ann Arbor, 1975.

Dullin, Charles. *Ce sont les dieux qu'il nous faut*. Paris: Gallimard, 1969.

Dussane [Béatrix]. *Notes de théâtre: 1940–1950*. Paris: Lardanchet, 1951.

Farabet, René. 'J.-L. Barrault répète *Le Rhinocéros*'. *Combat*, 4 January 1960. Clipping, Bibliothèque de l'Arsenal.

Faure-Poirée, Colline and Philippe Demanet, eds. *Jean-Louis Barrault: une vie pour le théâtre*. Préface de Pierre Bergé. Ouvrage publiée à l'occasion du Centenaire de Jean-Louis Barrault. Gallimard, 2010.

Favalelli, Max. 'Après dix ans d'existence, la Compagnie Renaud–Barrault va parcourir le monde en attendant que Paris lui offre un théâtre'. *Paris-Presse l'Intransigeant*, 15 March 1956. Clipping, Bibliothèque de l'Arsenal, Paris.

Favalelli, Max. '*L'État de siège* au théâtre Marigny expose (allégoriquement) notre "mal du siècle"'. *Paris-Presse L'intransigeant*, 29 October 1948. Clipping, Bibliothèque de l'Arsenal.

Frank, André. *Jean-Louis Barrault*. Théâtre de tous les temps 15. Seghers, 1971.

Gautier, Jean-Jacques. 'Au théâtre Marigny: *L'État de siège* d'Albert Camus'. *Le Figaro*, 29 October 1948. Clipping, Bibliothèque de l'Arsenal.

Gautier, Jean-Jacques. *Théâtre d'aujourd'hui*. Paris: Gallimard, 1972.

Germain, Anne. *Renaud-Barrault: Les feux de la rampe et de l'amour*. Paris: Editions du Félin, 1992.

Gide, André and Jean-Louis Barrault. *The Trial: A Dramatization Based on Franz Kafka's Novel*. Translated by Leon Katz and Joseph Katz. New York: Schocken Books, 1974.

Gilles, Christian. 'Portraits-Entretiens de 19 Comédiens: Madeleine Renaud et Jean-Louis Barrault'. In *Théâtre: Passions*, 141–61. Paris: L'Harmattan, 2002.

Giret, Noëlle, ed. *Renault Barrault*. Paris: Bibliothèque nationale de France, 1999.

Godard, Colline. 'Madeleine Renaud: elle a traversé le siècle'. *Le Monde*, 9 May 2008.

Gordon, Barbara. '"Le Théâtre Total"' as envisioned by Jean-Louis Barrault'. PhD diss., Ann Arbor, University Microfilms, 73-29-830, 1975.

Guicharnaud, Jacques, in collaboration with June Guicharnaud. *Modern French Theatre from Giraudoux to Genet*. New Haven: Yale University Press, 1967.

Helm, Everett. 'Reports from Rome and Paris' [review of *La Vie Parisienne*], *The Musical Times* 101, no. 1405 (March 1960), 174.

Heylen, Romy. *Translation, Poetics, and the Stage: Six French Hamlets*. London: Routledge, 2014.

Hobson, Harold. *The French Theatre of Today: An English View*. London: George G. Harrap, 1953.

Hubert, Marie-Claude. 'Entretien avec Jean-Louis Barrault. A Marseille, le 5 juin 1984'. In *Langage et corps fantasmé dans le théâtre des années cinquante*, 273–89. Librairie José Corti, 1987.

Ionesco, Eugène. *Rhinocéros*. Edited by Reuben Y. Ellison and Stowell C. Goding. New York: Holt, Rinehart and Winston, 1961.

Jouvet, Louis. *Le Comédien désincarné*. Paris: Flammarion, 1954.

Kemp, Robert. 'Jean-Louis Barrault joue *l'Orestie*'. *Le Soir* (Brussels), 13 October 1955. Clipping, Bibliothèque de l'Arsenal.

Kemp, Robert. 'L'État de siège au théâtre Marigny'. *Le Monde*, 29 October 1948. Clipping, Bibliothèque de l'Arsenal.

Kemp, Robert. 'Sur une édition de *Phèdre*'. *Une Semaine dans le Monde*, 15 June 1946. Clipping, Bibliothèque de l'Arsenal, Paris.

Knapp, Bettina. 'Jean-Louis Barrault'. In *Off-Stage Voices: Interviews with Modern French Dramatists*, edited by Alba Amoia, 41–6. Troy, NY: Whitston, 1975.

Kurtz, Maurice. *Jacques Copeau: Biographie d'un théâtre*. Translated Claude Cézan. Paris: Éditions Nagel, 1950.

Lagarde, Pierre. 'Reprise à la Comédie-Française: *Le Soulier de satin* de Paul Claudel'. *Libération*, 15 April 1949. Clipping, Bibliothèque de l'Arsenal.

Lamont, Rosette C. 'Interview with Jean-Louis Barrault'. *Drama and Theatre* 9 (Autumn 1970): 2–4.

Lamont, Rosette C. 'Jean Louis Barrault's *Rabelais*'. *Yale French Studies* 46: *From Stage to Street*, special ed. Jacques Guicharnaud, 125–38. New Haven: Yale University, 1971.

Leiter, Samuel L. *From Stanislavsky to Barrault: Representative Directors of the European Stage*. Westport, CT: Greenwood Press, 1991.

Lemarchand, Jacques. Paris. Personal interview by Suzanne Burgoyne, 13 December 1972. Recorded in note form.

Levasseur, Catherine. *Dans l'intimité des Renaud Barrault: souvenirs recueillis par Martine Desèvre*. Présenté par Jean Desailly et Simone Valère. Paris: Pygmalion (Flammarion), 2003.

Lorcey, Jacques. *La Comédie Française*. Paris: Editions Fernand Nathan, 1980.

'*L'Orestie*'. *Combat*, 4 October 1955. Clipping, Bibliothèque de l'Arsenal.

Loriot, Noelle. *Madeleine Renaud*. Paris: Presses de la Renaissance, 1993.

Lyons, Charles R. 'La Compagnie Madeleine Renaud—Jean-Louis Barrault: The Idea and the Aesthetic'. *Educational Theatre Journal 9* (December 1967): 419.

Maulnier, Thierry. 'Mise en scène et interprétation'. *Spectateur*, 22 October 1946. Clipping, Bibliothèque de l'Arsenal.

Mignon, Paul-Louis. *Jean-Louis Barrault: Le théâtre total*. Monaco: Editions du Rocher, 2000.

Mignon, Paul-Louis. *Renaud Barrault: Paris: notre siècle*. Conception et réalization de Joel Le Bon, avec la collaboration de Thadée Klossowski. Paris: Editions de Messine/Collection Pierre Bergé, 1984.

Milhaud, Darius. 'Mes deux partitions pour *Christophe Colomb*'. *Cahiers de la Compagnie Madeleine Renaud—Jean-Louis Barrault*, no. 1 (1953): 42–4.

Mohrt, Michel. 'Three Plays of the Current Paris Season'. *Yale French Studies*, no. 5 (1950): 100–5.

Podalydès, Denis. 'Notes sur Jean-Louis Barrault'. In *Jean-Louis Barrault: une vie pour le théâtre*, edited by Colline Faure-Poirée and Philippe Demanet. Paris: Editions Gallimard, 2010.

Poirot-Delpech, Bertrand. 'Reprise du *Procès* de Kafka par la Compagnie Renaud Barrault'. *Le Monde*, 21 October 1961. Clipping, Bibliothèque de l'Arsenal.

Polia, Mildah. 'Le Rabelais de Barrault'. *France-Amérique*, 28 May 1970. Clipping from the files of La Compagnie Madeleine Renaud—Jean-Louis Barrault.

Prévert, Jacques. *Les Enfants du paradis: Le scénario original*. Paris: Gallimard/ Arte éditions, 2012.

Quemeneur, Pierre. '*Hamlet* au théâtre Marigny'. *Réforme*, 16 November 1946. Clipping, Bibliothèque de l'Arsenal.

Ransan, André. 'Au théâtre Marigny: *Le Procès*'. *Paris-Matin*, 12 and 13 October 1947. Clipping, Bibliothèque de l'Arsenal.

Revue d'histoire du théâtre, I-II, nos. 189–90: Jean-Louis Barrault (1910–1990), 1996.

Saurel, Renée. '*Le Rhinocéros*'. *Information*, 27 January 1960. Clipping, Bibliothèque de l'Arsenal.

Simon, Alfred. 'The theatre in May', trans. William F. Panici. *Yale French Studies 46: From Stage to Street*, special ed. Jacques Guicharnaud, 139–48. New Haven: Yale University, 1971.

Slaney, Helen. 'Seneca in '68'. In *The Senecan Aesthetic: A Performance History*, published to Oxford Scholarship Online: January 2016. DOI:1093/acprof: oso/9780198736769.003.0009.

Steinegger, Catherine. *Pierre Boulez et le théâtre: De la Compagnie Renaud-Barrault à Patrice Chéreau*. Preface by Joël Huthwohl. Wavre: Mardaga, 2012.

Verdot, Guy. '*L'Orestie* d'Eschyle'. *Franc-Tireur*, 28 and 29 May 1955. Clipping, Bibliothèque de l'Arsenal.

Wallis, Bill. 'Production Casebook No. 3: Jean-Louis Barrault's *Rabelais*'. *Theatre Quarterly* 1 (July–September 1971), 90.

Ariane Mnouchkine

Ariane Mnouchkine du théâtre au cinéma. Ville de Bobigny: Collection Magic Cinéma, 2006.

Bablet, Marie-Louise and Denis Bablet. *Le Théâtre du Soleil ou la quête du bonheur*. Paris: CNRS (Théâtre du XXe siècle, Collection de diapolivres, no. 1), 1979.

Bellugi-Vannuccini, Duccio. 'A Sun Rises in Afghanistan: An Actor's View'. *Theater* 36 (2006): 78–81.

Blumenthal, Eileen. 'Excavations of the Soul'. *American Theatre*, May 1992, 24–6.

Bradby, David. *Modern French Drama 1940–1980*. Cambridge: Cambridge University Press, 1984.

Bradby, David and Maria M. Delgado, eds. *The Paris Jigsaw: Internationalism and the City's Stages*. Manchester: Manchester University Press, 2002, 113–45.

Bradby, David and David Williams. *Directors' Theater*. New York: St. Martin's Press, 1988.

Brooks, Peter. *The Melodramatic Imagination: Balzac, Henry James, Melodrama, and the Mode of Excess*. New Haven and London: Yale University Press, 1995.

Champagne, Lena and Franise Kourilsky. 'Political Theatre in France since 1968'. *The Drama Review* 19, no. 2 (1975): 43–52.

Cixous, Hélène. *The Terrible but Unfinished Story of Norodom Sihanouk, King of Cambodia*. Translated by Juliet Flower MacCannell, Judith Pike and Lollie Groth. Lincoln: University of Nebraska Press, 1994.

Cohn, Ruby. 'Ariane Mnouchkine: Twenty-one Years of Théâtre du Soleil'. *Theater* XVII, no. 1 (Winter 1985): 78–84.

Delgado, Maria M. and Paul Heritage, eds. *In Contact with the Gods? Directors Talk Theatre*. Manchester: Manchester University Press, 1996.

Dickson, Andrew. 'Ariane Mnouchkine and the Théâtre du Soleil: A Life in Theatre'. *The Guardian*, 10 August 2012.

Féral, Josette. *Rencontres avec Ariane Mnouchkine: Dresser un Monument à l'Ephémère*. Montréal: XYZ Editeur (Collection Documents), 1995.

Féral, Josette. *Trajectoires du Soleil: autour d'Ariane Mnouchkine*. Paris: Editions théâtrales, 1998.

Féral, Josette and Anna Husemoller. 'Mnouchkine's Workshop at the Soleil: A Lesson in Theatre'. *The Drama Review* 33, no. 4 (1989): 77–87.

Franck, Martine and Claude Roy. '*Le Théâtre du Soleil: Shakespeare*'. *Double Page*, no. 21 (1982).

Freixe, Guy. *La Filiation: Copeau-Lecoq-Mnouchkine*. Lavérune: editions l'Entretemps, 2014.

Glynn, Dominic. 'Ariane Mnouchkine's *Les Atrides*: Uncovering a Classic'. In *Contemporary Adaptations of Greek Tragedy: Auteurship and Directorial Visions*, edited by George Rodosthenous. London: Bloomsbury, 2017.

Jeffery, David. 'Ariane Mnouchkine'. In *International Dictionary of Theatre 3: Actors, Directors and Designers*, edited by David Pickering, 526–7. Detroit: St. James Press, 1996.

Kiernander, Adrian. *Ariane Mnouchkine and the Théâtre du Soleil*. Cambridge: Cambridge University Press (Directors in Perspective), 1993.

Kirby, Victoria Nes. '1789'. *The Drama Review* 15, no. 4 (1971): 73–91.

Lamont, Rosette C. 'Ariane Mnouchkine's Theater of History'. *Theater Week*, 5–11 October 1992, 16–20.

'Le Théâtre du Soleil, notre théâtre'. *L'avant-scène théâtre*, no. 1284–1285 (July 2010).

Miller, Judith G. *Ariane Mnouchkine*. London: Routledge, 2007.

Mnouchkine, Ariane. *Ariane Mnouchkine*. Introduction, choix et presentation des textes par Béatrice Picon-Vallin. Actes Sud: Mettre en scène, série dirigée par Béatrice Picon-Vallin, 2009.

Mnouchkine, Ariane. *L'Art du présent: Entretiens avec Fabienne Pascaud*. Paris: Plon, 2005.

Mnouchkine, Ariane. 'Les acteurs sont des poètes', interview with Raymonde Temkine. *Europe, revue littéraire mensuelle* 61, no. 648 (April 1983): 56–9.

Mnouchkine, Ariane. 'Méphisto' (trans. Timberlake Wertenbaker). In *Theatre and Politics: An International Anthology*, 361–469. New York: Ubu Repertory Theatre Publications, 1990.

Pascaud, Fabienne. *L'Art du présent: Ariane Mnouchkine, Entretiens avec Fabienne Pascaud*. Paris: Editions Plon, 2005.

Richardson, Helen. 'Ariane Mnouchkine and the Théâtre du Soleil: Theatricalising History; The Theatre as Metaphor; The Actor as Signifier'. In *Actor Training*, edited by Alison Hodge, 250–67. London: Routledge, 2010.

Shevtsova, Maria. 'Ariane Mnouchkine'. In *Fifty Key Theatre Directors*, edited by Shomit Mittner and Maria Shevtsova, 160–6. London: Routledge, 2005.

Singleton, Brian. 'Ariane Mnouchkine: Activism, Formalism, Cosmopolitanism'. In *Contemporary European Theatre Directors*, edited by Maria M. Delgado and Dan Rebellato, 29–48. London: Routledge, 2010.

Whitton, David. *Stage Directors in Modern France*. Manchester: Manchester University Press, 1987.

Williams, David, comp. and ed. *Collaborative Theatre: The Théâtre du Soleil Sourcebook*. Translated by Eric Prenowitz and David Williams. London: Routledge, 1999.

Videos and filmography

Darmon, Eric and Catherine Vilpoux, with Ariane Mnouchkine. *Au Soleil même la nuit*. Paris: Agat Films/La Sept ARTE/Théâtre du Soleil, 1995.

Mnouchkine, Ariane. *1789*. Paris: les Films Ariane, 1974.

Mnouchkine, Ariane. *Le Dernier Caravansérail* (Odyssées). Paris: Bel Air Classiques/SCEREN-CNDP, 2006.

Mnouchkine, Ariane. *Les Ephémères*. Une coproduction Le Théâtre du Soleil, Bel Air Media, ARTE France, avec le soutien du Centre National de la Cinématographie. Paris: Bel Air Classiques, 2009.

Mnouchkine, Ariane. *Les Naufragés du Fol Espoir*. Paris: Bel Air Classiques, 2014.

Mnouchkine, Ariane. *Molière ou la vie d'un hônete homme*. Paris: Les Films du Soleil de la Nuit/Claude Lelouche; DVD, Paris: Bel Aire Classiques/SCEREN-CNDP, 1976–7.

Mnouchkine, Ariane. *Tambours sur la digue: Sous forme de pièce ancienne pour marionettes joué par des acteurs*. Paris: Le Théâtre du Soleil/ARTE France/Bel Air Media, 2002.

Mnouchkine, Ariane/Théâtre du Soleil. *La Nuit Miraculeuse* (dialogues by Hélène Cixous). Paris: France Telecom/La mission du Bicentenaire/et al, 1989.

Vannuccini, Bellugi, Duccio, Sergio Canto Sabido and Philippe Chevallier. *Un soleil à Kaboul ... ou plutôt deux*. Paris: Bel Air Media/Théâtre du Soleil/Bell-CantoLaï/Voltaire Production, 2006.

Vilpoux, Catherine. Film d'après *La Ville Parjure ou le réveil des Erinyes*. Vidéo de Poche/Le Théâtre du Soleil, 1999.

Websites

http://www.theatre-du-soleil.fr/.

Peter Stein

'Aufführung des Jahres' (Production of the Year). *Theater Heute* 8 (1967).

Banu, Georges. *Avec Brecht, Peter Stein et d'autres*. Paris: Conservatoire.

Bradby, David. 'Blacking Up – Three Productions by Peter Stein'. In *A Radical Stage: Theatre in Germany in the 1970s and 1980s*, edited by W.G. Sebold, 18–30. Oxford: Berg, 1988.

Bradby, David and David Williams. *Directors' Theater*. New York: St. Martin's Press, 1988, 186–223.

Brandt, George. 'German-language Theatre'. In *The Continuum Companion to Twentieth Century Theatre*, 310–16. London: Continuum, 2002.

Braun, Karlheinz and Klaus Völker, eds. *Spielplatz 1*, Jahrbuch für Theater 1971–72. Berlin: Wagenbach, 1972.

Brecht, Bertolt. *Die Mutter: Regiebuch der Schaubühnen-Inszenierung* (The MotherStage Script of the Schaubühne Production). Frankfurt am Main: Suhrkamp, 1971.

Carlson, Marvin. *Theatre Is More Beautiful Than War: German Stage Directing in the Late Twentieth Century*. Iowa City: University of Iowa Press, 2009.

Delgado, Maria M. and Paul Heritage, eds. *In Contact with the Gods? Directors Talk Theatre*. Manchester: Manchester University Press, 1996.

Fiebach, Joachim. *Manifeste europäischen Theaters: Grotowski bis Schleef* (Manifestoes of European Theater: Grotowski to Schleef). Recherchen 13. Berlin: Theater der Zeit, 2003.

Fiebach, Joachim and Helmar Schramm, eds. *Kreativität und Dialog*. Berlin: Henschel, 1983.

Giehse, Therese. *Ich hab' nichts zu sagen*. Edited by Monika Sperr. Gütersloh: Bertelsmann, 1972.

Goethe, Johann Wolfgang. *Werke: Vollstandige Ausgabe letzter Hand*, Volume 44. Stuttgart: Cotta, 1833.

Goethe, Johann Wolfgang et al. *Torquato Tasso: Regiebuch der Bremer Inszenierung*. Frankfurt am Main: Suhrkamp, 1970.

Hortmann, Wilhelm. *Shakespeare on the German Stage: The Twentieth Century*. Cambridge: Cambridge University Press, 1998.

Iden, Peter. *Die Schaubühne am Halleschen Ufer 1970-1979*. Munich: Hanser, 1979.

Iden, Peter. 'Ein schönes Stück Leben: Peter Steins Inszenierung von Ibsens "Peer Gynt" an der Berliner Schaubühne' (A Pretty Piece of Life: Peter Stein's Production of Ibsen's 'Peer Gynt' at the Berlin Schaubühne). *Frankfurter Rundschau*, 17 May 1971.

Iden, Peter. *Theater als Widerspruch: Plädoyer für die zeitgenössische Bühne* (Theater as Contradiction: An Entreaty for the Contemporary Stage). Munich: Kindler, 1984.

Karasek, Hellmuth. 'Zurück zur Mutter: Die neue Berliner Schaubühne beginnt mit Brecht' (Back to Mother: The New Berlin Schaubühne Begins with Brecht). *Die Zeit*, 16 October 1970.

Keller, Ingeborg. 'Purer Brecht: "Die Mutter" in der Schaubühne' (Pure Brecht: 'The Mother' at the Schaubühne). *Telegraf*, Berlin-West, 10 October 1970.

Kennedy, Dennis. 'Peter Stein'. In *International Dictionary of Theatre 3: Actors, Directors and Designers*, edited by David Pickering, 722–4. Detroit: St. James Press, 1996.

Kortner, Fritz. *Aller Tage Abend*. Munich: Kindler, 1969.

Kranz, Dieter. *Positionen: Strehler, Planchon, Koun, Dario Fo, Långbacka, Stein: Gespräche mit Regisseuren des europäischen Theaters*. Berlin: Henschel, 1981.

Kurzenberger, Hajo. '"Gegen den Strom": Ein Nachtrag zu "Steins Faust" auf der EXPO 2000' ('Against the Current': An Addendum to 'Steins Faust' at the EXPO 2000). In *Auftrieb: Grenzüberschreitungen mit Goethes 'Faust' in Inszenierungen der neunziger Jahre* (Stirred Up: Pushing Boundaries with Goethe's 'Faust' in Productions of the 1990s), edited by Hans-Peter Bayerdörfer, 201–20. Tübingen: Niemeyer, 2002.

Lackner, Peter. 'Peter Stein's Path to Shakespeare'. *The Drama Review* 74, 21, no. 2 (June 1977): 79–102.

Lehmann, Hans-Thies. *Postdramatisches Theater*. Frankfurt am Main: Verlag der Autoren, 1999.

Lovell, Stephen. *Summerfolk: A History of the Dacha*. Ithaca, NY: Cornell University Press, 2003.

Lützeler, Paul Michael and David Pan, eds. *Kleists Erzählungen und Dramen: neue Studien*. Würzburg: Königshausen und Neumann, 2001.

Mainusch, Herbert. 'Das Theater ist eine Art Museum: Gespräch mit Peter Stein.' In *Regie und Interpretation*, edited by Herbert Mainusch and Achim Benning, 111–18. Munich: Fink, 1989.

Mainusch, Herbert and Achim Benning. *Regie und Interpretation*. Munich: Fink, 1985.

Mitter, Shomit. 'Peter Stein'. In *Fifty Key Theatre Directors*, edited by Shomit Mitter and Maria Shevtsova, 148–54. London: Routledge, 2005.

Müller, Harald and Jürgen Schitthelm, eds. *40 Jahre Schaubühne 1962–2002*. Berlin: Theater der Zeit, 2002.

Nabokov, Vladimir. *Lectures on Russian Literature*, edited by Fredson Bowers. New York: Harcourt Brace Jovanovich, 1981.

Nagel, Ivan. *Kortner – Zadek – Stein*. Munich: Hanser, 1989.

Nagel, Ivan, Martin Sperr and Peter Stein. 'Wie wir Bonds Stück inszenierten' (How We Staged Bond's Play). *Theater Heute* 8 (1967), Jahressonderheft (Year-end edition), 74–6.

Nippe, Christine. *Kunst der Verbindung*. Berlin: LIT Verlag, 2006.

O'Mahony, John. 'Master of the Rebels'. *The Guardian*, 9 August 2003.

Ortolani, Olivier. 'Le père du théâtre du vingtième siècle: Tchékhov et *Les trois soeurs*, entretien avec Peter Stein'. *Théâtre/Public* 84 (November–December 1988): 66–75.

Patterson, Michael. 'Peter Stein'. In *The Routledge Companion to Directors' Shakespeare*, edited by John Russell Brown, 425–39. London: Routledge, 2008.

Patterson, Michael. *Peter Stein: Germany's Leading Theatre Director*. Cambridge: Cambridge University Press (Directors in Perspective), 1981.

Rainer, Wolfgang. 'Schöner, grüner Klassenkampf: Genialische "Mutter" – Schiffbauerdamm am Halleschen Ufer' (Pretty, Green Class Struggle: Brilliant 'Mother' – Schiffbauerdamm on the Hallisches Ufer). *Stuttgarter Zeitung*, Stuttgart, 12 October 1970.

Schieb, Roswitha. *Peter Stein: ein Portrait*. Berlin: Berlin Verlag, 2005.

Schloßberg, Peter. 'Den Tasso abgewertet: Kritische Anmerkung zu einer Goethe-Inszenierung von Peter Stein' (Tasso Debased: Critical Comments on a Goethe Production by Peter Stein). *Die Wahrheit*, Berlin, 15 May 1970.

Schwiedrzik, Wolfgang and Peter Stein. 'Demokratie ist auch Aktion' (Democracy Is Also Action). *Theater Heute* 8 (August 1968): 2–3.

Stein, Peter. 'Das wird eine ganz fürchterlich strenge Übung'. *Theater Heute* 4 (1998): 1–2.

Strauss, Botho. 'Das schöne Umsonst: Peter Stein inszeniert Tasso'. *Theater Heute* 5 (1969): 12–16.

Strauss, Botho. 'Die Kraft der Diskretion: Peter Stein inszeniert Kabale und Liebe'. *Theater Heute* 12 (1967): 32–4.

Strauß, Botho. 'Das Mass der Wörtlichkeit: Über Peter Stein' (The Standard of Literalness: Regarding Peter Stein). In *Der Gebärdensammler: Texte zum Theater* (The Gesture Collector: Writings on Theater), 68–78. Frankfurt am Main: Verlag der Autoren, 1999.

van Den Berg, Klaus. 'Karl-Ernst Herrmann: Unfolding Shakespeare's Space'. In *Designers' Shakespeare*, edited by John Russell Brown and Stephen Di Benedetto, 54–80. London: Routledge, 2016.

Weber, Carl. 'Brecht as Director'. *The Drama Review* 12, no. 1 (1967): 101–7.

Winds, Adolf. 'Wie es euch gefällt'. *Shakespeare-Jahrbuch* 53: 181–4.

Zipes, Jack. 'The Irresistible Rise of the Schaubühne am Halleschen Ufer: A Retrospective of the West Berlin Theater Collective'. *Theater* 9, no. 1 (1977): 7–49.

Zipes, Jack. 'Utopia as the Past Conserved: An Interview with Peter Stein and Dieter Sturm of the Schaubühne am Halleschen Ufer'. *Theater* 9, no. 1 (1977): 50–7.

INDEX

Ackermann, Konrad Ernst 132
acting/actor training 9, 10, 12, 14, 17,
    19, 30, 31, 41–2, 94, 96, 97,
    113–15, 120–4, 131, 135, 143,
    148, 151, 154, 166, 167
actors 10, 14, 41, 48, 64, 66, 68,
    69–70, 85, 90, 99, 102, 104,
    105, 106, 109, 134, 147, 156,
    168, 173, 185
Adamov, Arthur 95, 191
adapting/cutting play text 136–7, 149,
    150, 163
Adenauer, Konrad 131
Aeschylus 14, 16, 17, 62, 64, 81, 109,
    132, 152, 155, 190, 192, 194
Africa 14, 115, 152–3
Agamemnon (Aeschylus) 192
Age d'or, L' (Golden Age) 108
agitprop 143, 216 n.36
Ainsi parlait Zarathoustra (Thus Spake
    Zarathustra) 13, 191
Allégret, Marc 24
Amante anglaise, L' (The English
    Lover) (Duras) 51
Amphitryon (Molière) 16, 190
Andreas, Sabine 140
Andreone, Liliana 9
Annecchino, Arturo 159
Anouilh, Jean 190
Antikenprojekt and *Antikenprojekt*
    II (The Antiquity Project) 14,
    152–4, 184, 194
Antiquity Project. See Antikenprojekt
Antoine, André 99
Antony and Cleopatra (Shakespeare)
    15, 35, 189
Arbeiterwohlfahrt (Workers' Welfare
    Association). *See* AWO
Arènes Lutèce 93

Ariosto, Ludovico 136
Aristophanes 191
Artaud, Antonin 11, 23, 25, 28, 55, 56,
    57, 58, 59–61, 86, 87, 91, 94,
    101, 106
Arts et Spectacles 96
Asian theatre forms 9, 14, 16, 17, 81,
    85, 86, 90, 93, 94, 97, 108, 109,
    110–11
As I Lay Dying. See Autour d'une mere
Association des Spectateurs 99
As You Like It (Shakespeare) 11, 13,
    15, 151–2, 184, 194
L'Atelier (Dullin's school and theatre).
    See Théâtre de l'Atelier
ATEP (Association Théâtrale des
    Etudiants de Paris) 93, 94
Atrides, Les (House of Atreus)
    (Aeschylus) 17, 84, 109, 192
audience 13, 19, 48, 50, 54, 57–8, 75,
    83, 84, 85, 94, 106, 133, 152,
    153, 157, 159, 164, 168, 169,
    173, 177, 184–5, 187
Auric, Georges 191
Auschwitz 92
Autour d'une mere (As I Lay Dying)
    (Faulkner) 23, 27, 33, 55, 56,
    61, 63, 65, 66, 67, 69, 74, 189,
    203 n.2
avant garde 25, 30, 37, 81, 86
Avignon Festival (France) 47, 51, 87,
    94, 101, 192
AWO (*Arbeiterwohlfahrt*) 140

Baal (Brecht) 103
Bacchae, The (Euripides) 14, 153
Balthus 190
Baptiste 35, 45, 46, 190
Baquet, Maurice 28

Barba, Eugenio 84
Barrault, Jean-Louis 7, 8, 11, 12, 13,
    14, 15, 16, 17, 18, 19, 23–78,
    94, 100, 189–91
  composers and music 8, 17, 25,
    34–5, 68, 189–91
  designers 8, 17, 189–91
  directing 11, 30, 39–43
  films 23–4, 28–9, 30, 35
  influences 24, 25, 55–6
  tours 12, 17, 26, 44–7, 52–4
  writers 8, 25, 32, 38, 39
Barrault, Jules (Barrault's father) 26
Barrault, Marcelle (Barrault's mother)
    26, 31
Barrault, Max-Henry (Barrault's
    brother) 26
Barriera, Jean-Claude 192
Barthes, Roland 94
Bastille 13, 105
Bataille, Georges 28
Baty, Gaston 43
Bauchau, Henri 93
Bayrische Staatzeitung (journal) 133
Beckett, Samuel 52
Beheshti, Shaghayegh 116
Béjart ballet company 100
Bell, Marie 32, 34
Bentley, Eric 56
Bérard, Christian 47, 190
Berlin. See East Berlin; West Berlin
Berliner Ensemble 94, 130, 160, 174–5,
    177, 195
Berliner Festspiel. See Theatertreffen
Berlioz, Hector 195
Bertay, Michel 39, 43
Bertin, Pierre 35
Bibliothèque Nationale de France 9
Bickel, Moidele 11, 154, 194, 195
Blacks, The (Genet) 14, 195
Blin, Roger 28, 30, 50, 60, 94
Bochum (Germany) 131, 161
Bond, Edward 132–4, 163, 165, 167,
    169, 193
Boris Godunov (Mussorgsky) 195
Boulevard of Crime, Paris 23
Boulez, Pierre 8, 11, 17, 25, 35, 38, 46,
    68, 191, 195
Bourgeade, Pierre 191

Bourgeois Gentilhomme (Bourgeois
    Gentleman) (Molière) 63
Bouvet, Marie-Hélène 9, 192, 193
Bradby, David 11, 13, 145
Brandauer, Klaus Maria 159
Brandt, Willy 141
Brangues (Claudel's home) 31, 33
Brazil 17, 44–5, 64–5, 72
Break of Noon. See Partage de midi
Brecht, Bertolt/Brechtian theatre 9, 10,
    19, 85, 87, 91, 92, 93, 95, 103,
    106, 107, 109, 130, 131, 134,
    142, 143, 164, 167, 174–7, 184,
    193, 194
Bremen (Germany) 129, 136, 137, 140,
    161, 164, 173, 176, 182
Bremer Theater 193
Breton, André 58
Bride, Petrus 190
Brig, The 99
Brigadier de l'Association des
    Régisseurs 99
Broca, Philippe de 92
Brook, Peter 84, 91, 130, 137
Brooks, Peter 89
Brunot, André 35
Büchner, Georg 107
bunraku 82, 110

Cagnotte, La (Labiche). See Piggy
    Bank, The
Cahiers Renaud-Barrault (Renaud-
    Barrault Notebooks) 18
Cambodia 84, 89, 91, 93
Camus, Albert 8, 39, 67, 190
Canada 45
Canaris, Volker 148, 172, 177
Capitaine Fracasse, Le 96
Carné, Marcel 24, 92
Carneiro da Cunha, Juliana 17, 92
Cartel des Quatre (directors Dullin,
    Jouvet, Pitoëff, Baty) 27, 55, 56,
    59, 60, 62
Cartoucherie de Vincennes 8, 19, 82,
    83, 84, 85, 105, 191–3
Case, Sue-Ellen 18
Cassandre, A.M. 190
Castaways of the Fol Espoir, The. See
    Naufragés du Fol Espoir, Les

CCC Film Studios 151, 194
Centres Dramatiques Nationaux 94
Cerisaie, La. See The Cherry Orchard
Cervantes, Miguel 17, 28, 29, 189
Changeling, The (Middleton and
    Rowley) 140
Chaptal, Collège de 26
Château, Le (The Castle) 62, 190
Chekhov, Anton Pavlovich 14, 15, 145,
    147, 152, 156–8, 187, 190, 195
Cheronnet, Louis 77
Cherry Orchard (*La Cerisaie; Das
    Kirschgarten*) (Chekhov) 14, 47,
    62, 78, 156–8, 190, 195
*Children of Paradise. See Enfants du
    paradis, Les*
China 84, 93, 110
Choéphores, Les (Aeschylus) 192
chorus 17, 18, 65, 76, 109, 154, 157
Christoph Colombus (Claudel) 34, 47,
    67, 69, 74, 190
Cid, Le (Corneille) 31
cinema. *See* film
Cirque Médrano (Cirque de
    Montmartre) 99, 101, 191
Civil War (Spain) 30
Cixous, Hélène 9, 87, 89, 92, 108, 112,
    119, 192, 193
Claudel, Paul 8, 25, 30, 31, 32–4, 38,
    43, 47, 48, 49, 51, 52–3, 54, 55,
    66, 67–8, 72, 77, 189, 190, 191
Clever, Edith 10, 134, 135, 145, 146,
    152, 154
Clowns, Les (Théâtre du Soleil) 103,
    106, 191
Cock-a-Doodle-Dandy (O'Casey) 140,
    194
collaboration 8, 9, 10, 27, 81, 88
collective/collaborative creation 9, 10,
    12, 25, 58, 67, 16, 82, 93–7,
    101–3, 106, 107, 108–9, 115,
    140, 178, 191, 193, 198 n.35
Comédie-Française 15, 28, 31–5, 43,
    56, 72, 189
commedia dell'arte 27, 81, 86, 94,
    96–7, 101, 102, 104, 105, 108
*Common People. See Petits Bourgeois,
    Les*
Communism 142, 175, 176

Compagnie Madeleine Renaud–Jean-
    Louis Barrault 7, 14, 17, 26, 30,
    32, 34–9, 47, 48, 50, 56
company. *See* collective; ensemble
Conchon, Georges 107
Copeau, Jacques 8, 31, 35, 36, 43, 56,
    59, 60, 61, 65, 91, 94, 95
Corneille, Pierre 31
costumes 14, 26, 30, 42, 43, 44, 73–4,
    75, 87, 96, 105–6, 109, 114,
    136, 154
Coutard, Lucien 189
Craig, Edward Gordon 136
Cuisine, La (The Kitchen) (Wesker)
    97–9, 100, 106, 191
Cukor, George 95

Dalí, Salvador 64
Damnation de Faust, La (Berlioz) 195
dance 13, 14, 32, 63, 65, 75, 76, 100,
    109, 153
Dante 154
Daquemine, Jacques 35
Dasté, Marie-Hélène (Maïène) 35, 61,
    190
Daudet, Léon 12
Dauphin, Claude 28
death, as theme or motive 30, 57, 63,
    67, 102
Deburau, Jean-Baptiste 23–4, 27, 45–6
Debussy, Claude 11, 195
Decroux, Etienne 27, 56
Defoe, Daniel 39
De Gaulle, General Charles 48, 50
Demons (adapted from Dostoevsky)
    195
Derenne, Jacqueline 92
Dernier Caravanserail, Le (The Last
    Caravanserai) 90, 92, 111,
    115–25, 193
Der Stern (journal) 167
Desailly, Jean 35
Descaves, Lucien 55, 77
Desnos, Robert 28, 30, 32, 33
Dior, Christian 190
directing, philosophy of 10, 11–12, 24,
    43, 56, 61–2, 77
Dostoevsky, Fyodor 195
Domaine musical 47

Donzenac, Georges 95, 96
Donzenac, Myrrha 95
Drei Schwestern. See Three Sisters
drôle de guerre (phoney war) 31
Drums on the Dike. See Tambours sur la digue
Dullin, Charles 8, 15, 27, 28, 32, 43, 51, 56, 62, 91, 93, 94, 95
Dumur, Guy 24, 25, 44, 54
Duras, Marguerite 51
Dürrenmatt, Friedrich 131, 140
Dussane, Béatrix 56

Early Morning (Bond) 140
East Berlin 130, 174
L'Echange (The Exchange) (Claudel) 34, 190
Edinburgh Festival 15
Eisler, Hanns 194
Electra (Sophocles) 18
Elizabethan elements 87
Elle (journal) 101
Elysée-Montmartre 51–2, 191
Emigrés (Mrozek) 53
Enfants du paradis, Les (Children of Paradise) 23–4, 27, 33, 35, 45, 46
Engel, Erich 167, 183
ensemble 7, 10, 11, 25, 30, 92, 94, 99, 129, 141–2, 164, 177, 178, 182, 183, 184, 185
Ephémères, Les (The Ephemerals) 92, 193
Erhard, Ludwig 131
Etat de siege (State of Siege) (Camus) 67, 190
Et Soudain des nuits d'éveil (And Suddenly, Nights of Awakening) 193
Euménides, Les (Euripides) 192
Euripides 14, 17, 81, 109, 132, 153, 192
Everding, August 133
expressionism 167

Faim, La. See Hunger
Falckenberg, Otto 152
farce 15, 38
Faulkner, William 23, 55, 189

Fausses confidences, Les (False Confidings) (Marivaux) 35, 37, 46, 190
Faust I and *II* (Goethe) 16, 18, 132, 154, 158–9, 160, 178–9, 186–7, 195
festivals, theatre 47, 51, 140. *See also* Avignon Festival; *Theatertreffen*
Feuillère, Edwige 42
Feydeau, Georges 15, 38, 78, 190
fight choreography 15
film 18, 23–4, 27–9, 90, 91, 92, 95, 104, 111, 112
First World War 26, 112
Fischer, Peter 193, 194
Flaubert, Gustave 60
Fonds Renaud-Barrault 9
Fontenay, Catherine 35
Fotopoulos, Dionissis 195
Fourberies de Scapin, Les (Scapino's Escapades) (Molière) 16, 39, 47
Francis, Eve 32
Franck, Martine 93, 95
François, Guy-Claude 9, 192, 193
Free University of Berloin 140
French Revolution 13, 84, 85, 88, 90, 103–7
Freshwater by Woolf 19
Freud, Sigmund 101
Friedrich, Caspar David 150
Frisch, Max 140

Gance, Abel 104, 140
Ganz, Bruno 10, 134, 136, 138, 150–1, 152, 156, 159, 173
Gare d'Orsay (Paris) 19, 53
Gaskill, William 133
Gautier, Jean-Jacques 75, 77
Gautier, Théophile 96
Genet, Jean 12, 14, 50, 51, 195
Gerettet. See Saved
Ghenghis Khan (Bauchau) 93
Gide, André 8, 28, 32, 35, 38, 47, 55, 189, 190
Giehse, Therese 10, 131–2, 142, 143, 167, 176, 177
Giesing, Dieter 131
Giraudoux, Jean 8, 42, 190

Godard, Colette 29
Goethe, Johann Wolfgang von 16,
    132, 136, 137, 138, 154, 158,
    164, 170–3, 179, 186–7, 193,
    195
Golden Head. See Tête d'or (Claudel)
Gorky, Maxim 14, 15, 95, 132, 143,
    144–7, 158, 174, 175, 191, 194
Gottsched, Johann Christoph 132
government subsidy 7, 10, 19, 35, 44,
    142, 177
Grand Guignol 91
Grands Augustins, 7 rue des 28
Granval, Charles 29, 30, 31
Granval, Jean-Pierre 29, 35, 52
Great and Small (Strauss) 194
Great War. See First World War
Greece 45–6, 65
Greek classics 7, 14, 17, 25, 65, 74, 85,
    95, 109, 137, 152, 155
Griffith, D.W. 104
Gross und klein. See Great and Small
    (Strauss)
Grotowski, Jerzy 84
Groupe Octobre 28
Group Theatre, The (1930s USA) 142
Gruat, Emilie 123
Grüber, Klaus-Michael 14, 152, 153

Hairy Ape, The (O'Neill) 195
Halévy, Ludovic 191
Hamlet (Laforgue) 30–1
Hamlet (Shakespeare) 15, 31–2, 35, 36,
    37, 39, 42, 44, 62, 69, 78, 189
Hammarskjöld, Dag 45
Hamsun, Knut 30, 189
Hannen, Jane (Mnouchkine's mother) 92
Hanover World Expo 158–9, 160, 187,
    195
Hansen, Gregor 154
Hardy, Gérard 95
Harold et Maude 53
Heinrich, Anna Maria 195
Hélène (1936 film) 28–9
Henry IV, Part 1 (Shakespeare) 16, 192
Henry VI (Shakespeare) 15
Herrmann, Karl-Ernst 11, 146, 147,
    160, 193, 194, 195
Herzog, Joachim 194

Hilbert, Ulrich 194
Histoire de Vasco (Story of Vasco)
    (Schéhadé) 47, 190
*Histoire terrible mais inachevée de
    Norodom Sihanoukm roi de
    Cambodge* (The Terrible But
    Unfinished Story of Norodom
    Sihanouk, King of Cambodia)
    (Cixous) 108, 192
Hitler, Adolf 131
Hobson, Harold 55, 77
Hoffman, E.T.A. 165
Honegger, Arthur 8, 34, 35, 189, 190,
    191
House of Atreus. See Atrides, Les
Hübner, Kurt 134, 136, 139, 140
Hugo, Jean 189
Hunger (*La Faim*) (Hamsun) 30, 31,
    65, 66, 68, 69, 77, 189
Hurok, Sol 45
Huster, Francis 54
Huston, John 92

*I Am a Man of the Theatre. See Je suis
    homme de théâtre*
Ibsen, Henrik 132, 147, 178, 179, 194
Iden, Peter 15, 141, 180, 181
*Im Dickicht der Städt. See In the
    Jungle of Cities*
improvisation 96, 101, 105, 114, 115,
    119–20, 123
India 84, 91, 93, 112
Indiade, L' (Indiade, or the India of
    Their Dreams) 84, 86, 89, 108,
    192
Inferno (Dante) 154
Ingrand, Max 190
In the Jungle of Cities (Brecht) 11, 167,
    170, 174, 193
*Intigue and Love. See Kabale und
    Liebe*
Ionesco, Eugène 48, 62, 65, 191
Iphigenia in Aulis (Euripides) 17, 109,
    192
Itkine, Sylvain 28

Jamois, Marguerite 49
Jandeline 30
Japan 14, 45, 47, 66, 93

Jarre, Maurice 35
Jarry sur la butte (Barrault adaptation) 52
Jerusalem Liberated (Tasso) 170
Jessner, Leopold 137, 167
Je suis homme de théâtre (Barrault) 24, 40, 42
Journal of the Plague Year (*L'Etat de siege*) 39
Jouvet, Louis 8, 16, 27, 35, 39, 43, 47, 56, 62
Joxe, Louis 44
Julius Caesar (Shakespeare) 15, 48, 195

Kabale und Liebe (Intrigue and Love) (Schiller) 132, 134, 135–6, 170, 193
kabuki 66, 78, 82
Kafka, Franz 31, 38, 62, 190
Kaiser, Joachim 137
Karasek, Hellmuth 144, 177
Karinska, Irène 30
Karsunke, Yaak 177, 182
kathakali 82
Keep an Eye on Amelia. See Occupe-toi d'Amélie
Keller, Ingeborg 177
Kemp, Robert 55
King Lear (Shakespeare) 195
King's Theatre (Edinburgh) 195
Kitchen, The. See Cuisine, La
Kleist, Heinrich von 132, 150–1, 194
Kleist's Dream of the Homburg Prince (Kleists Traum vom Prinzen Homburg) 150, 194
Knapp, Bettina 9, 11
Kneidl, Karl 194
König, Michael 11, 134, 135, 140, 152
Kortner, Fritz 10, 131–2, 143, 166–7
Kosma, Joseph 8, 28, 38, 190
Kott, Jan 100
Kreuzenberger, Hajo 187

Labiche, Eugène 15, 132, 148–9, 194
Labisse, Félix 8, 17, 28, 38, 190
Laforgue, Jules 30
Lamont, Rosette C. 52
Lampe, Jutta 10, 134, 135, 139, 140, 145, 149, 155, 157, 158

langage du corps, le (the language of the body) 23–4, 27, 60
Langage du corps, Le 53, 191
Laser, Dieter 140
Lasry, Jacques 101, 191
Laurent, Jeanne 94
Lechenperg-Recker, F. 193
Lecoq, Jacques/Lecoq School 93, 97, 99, 100
Lehnstücke 175, 184
Lelouche, Claude 92
Lemarchand, Jacques 77
Lemêtre, Jean-Jacques 9, 17, 90, 108, 192, 193
Lenin, Vladimir Ilich 143, 176, 183
Léotard, Philippe 95, 96
Leroux, Maurice 190
Le Roy, Georges 35
Lessing, Gotthold 132
Lettres françaises, Les (journal) 96
Levasseur, Catherine 14, 26, 29, 48
Lévy, Jean-Benoît 28
Libation Bearers, The (Aeschylus) 154
Liberation of Paris 34
lighting 74–5, 76, 101
Lincoln Center (New York) 195
Living Theatre, The 99
Luther, Martin 132
Lyons, Charles 59

Maclès, Jean-Denis 190, 191
Maisonneuve, Ysabel de 193
Malherbe, François de 12
Malraux, André 48, 50, 51
Mann, Klaus 108
Mao Zedong 142, 176
Marcabru, Pierre 99
Marceau, Marcel 56
Marigny. *See* Théâtre Marigny
Marivaux, Pierre Carlet de Chamblain de 25, 35, 37, 38, 190
Marseillaise, La (film, Renoir) 104
Martin, Didier 193
Marxism 50, 141, 148, 164, 174
Marx, Karl 183
masks 9, 14, 18, 57, 73–4, 75, 78, 94, 100, 108
Masson, André 8, 28, 29, 35, 189, 191
Matias 191

May 1968, events of 12, 16, 50, 51, 95, 100, 101, 104, 107
Meilhac, Henri 191
melodrama 87–91, 104, 110
Melodramatic Imagination, The (Brooks) 90
Memories for Tomorrow. See Souvenirs pour demain
Méphisto 108
Merchant of Venice, The (Shakespeare) 49
Metropolitan Opera (New York City) 195
Meyerhold, Vsevolod 56
Michelet, Jules 12
Middleton, Thomas 140
Midsummer Night's Dream, A (Shakespeare) 16, 100–2, 191
Mignon, Paul-Louis 69
Milan 106, 191, 195
Milhaud, Darius 8, 30, 46, 67–8, 190
mime 23, 24, 59, 61, 63–4
Ministry of Culture/Ministry of Beaux-Arts 50, 54, 94
Minks, Wilfred 136, 138, 139, 160, 173, 193
Misanthrope, Le (Molière) 45
Mise-en-scène de Phèdre (Staging Phaedra) (Barrault) 32
Mitbestimmung (collective agency, political) 141
Mitter, Shomit 10
Mnouchkine, Alexandre (Ariane Mnouchkine's father) 92
Mnouchkine, Ariane 7, 9, 10, 12, 13, 14, 15, 16, 17, 18, 19, 81–125, 191–3
    film 18, 91, 95
    internationalism 82–4, 84, 89, 91, 111
    on directing 12
    social activism 9, 111–12, 115, 119
    workshop 113–14
Mohrt, Michel 77
Moïse et Aaron (Schoenberg) 11, 195
Molière 16, 25, 45, 47, 81, 92, 94, 190, 192
Molière (film, Mnouchkine) 18, 108
Moscoso, Roberto 98, 101, 191
Moscoso, Sophie 9, 10
Moscow Art Theatre 96, 194

Mother Courage (Brecht) 130
Mother, The (*Die Mutter*) (Gorky/Brecht) 10, 142–3, 164, 174–8, 182, 194
Mouloudji 28
Mozart, Wolfgang Amadeus 195
Mrozek, Slawomir 53
Munich Kammerspiele 11, 130, 132, 133, 163, 165, 167, 169, 176, 193
Muret, Marc-Antoine 107
music 34, 35, 38, 67–9, 86, 88, 90, 93, 101, 109, 124–5
Mussorgsky, Modest 195
Mutter, Die (Gorky/Brecht). *See Mother, The*

Nabokov, Vladimir 156, 157
Nagel, Ivan 139, 154, 180, 181
Napoléon (film, Gance) 104
National Theater of Greece 18
National Theatre, London 147
Naufragés du Fol Espoir, Les (Castaways of the Fol Espoir) (Cixous) 108, 111, 193
Nazis 33, 130, 131, 132, 140, 143, 169, 175, 177, 179. *See also* occupation, German, in France
Nederlandse Opera, De 195
neoclassicism 136
Neuber, Karoline 132
Neveux, Georges 190
Nicolai, Serge 123
Nietzsche, Friedrich 13, 191
Nobel Prize for Literature 52
Noël, Jacques 191
Nuits de colère, Les (Nights of Rage) (Salacrou) 35
Numancia (Cervantes) 17, 28, 29–30, 33, 189

Obey, André 8, 17
O'Casey, Sean 140, 194
occupation, German, in France 24, 31, 32, 33, 92
Occupe-toi d'Amélie (Keep an Eye on Amelia, or Look After Lulu) (Feydeau) 15, 38, 78, 190
Odéon. *See* Théâtre de l'Odéon

Oedipe (Oedipus) (Sophocles) 47
Offenbach, Jacques 48, 191
Oiseaux, Les (The Birds) by
  Aristophanes 191
Olivier, Claude 96
O'Mahoney, John 15
O'Neill, Eugene 195
opera directing 11, 18, 130, 186
Ophuls, Max 95
Optimistic Tragedy (Vishnevsky). *See
  Optimistiche Tragödie*
Optimistiche Tragödie (Optimistic
  Tragedy) (Vishnevsky) 143–4,
  145, 148, 194
Oresteia (Aeschylus) 14, 17, 18, 64,
  65, 68, 69, 74, 75, 109, 151–5,
  184, 185, 190, 194
Ostpolitik 141
Otello (Verdi) 11

Pace, Agostino 191
Palais de Chaillot 94
Palalido 106
Paravents, Les (The Screens) (Genet)
  12, 49, 51
Paris Presse (journal) 99
Partage de midi (Break of Noon)
  (Claudel) 31, 34, 38, 49, 190
Patterson, Michael 13, 133, 139, 145,
  165
Peduzzi, Emmanuel 191
Peer Gynt (Ibsen) 147, 148, 151, 164,
  178–82, 184, 194
Peking Opera 93
Pelléas et Mélisande (Debussy) 11, 195
Penchenat, Jean-Claude 95, 103
Personnage combatant, Le (The
  Character Against Himself)
  (Vauthier) 190
Pétain, Philippe 31
Petit Odéon (Paris) 49
Petit-Orsay 53
Petits Bourgeois, Les (Petty Bourgeois/
  Common People) (Gorky) 15,
  95, 191
Petri, Elke 144
Peymann, Claus 160
Phèdre (Phaedra) (Racine) 17, 32, 55,
  62, 66, 70, 74, 76, 189

Philippot, Michel 191
Piccolomini, The (Schiller) 160
Piccolo Theatre of Milan 106, 191
Pierrot 24
*Piggy Bank, The (Das Sparschwein; La
  Cagnotte)* (Labiche) 15, 148–50,
  194
Piscator, Erwin 176
Planchon, Roger 15, 93
Podalydès, Denis 26
Poirot-Delpech, Bertrand 77
Polia, Mildah 55
political engagement 84, 88, 94,
  95, 103, 119, 141–2, 163–4,
  169–70, 174, 178, 181
Polnareff, Michel 191
Pol Pot 89
Poppy, Ricarda 194
populist theatre/popular forms 85, 88,
  91, 94, 97, 102, 103, 104
Portalès, Guy de 31
Porte de Montreuil 191
Poulenc, François 190
Pour Lucrèce (For Lucretia)
  (Giraudoux) 42, 190
Prévert, Jacques 24, 28, 46, 190
Prinz von Homburg, Der (The Prince
  of Homburg) (Kleist) 132, 150–1
Procès, Le (The Trial) (Kafka) 31, 38,
  63–4, 66, 69, 70–2, 75, 77, 190
projections 122
properties (props) 70–3
protests 50, 141, 144. *See also* May
  1968
Prückner, Tilo 140
puppets 81, 84, 104, 105, 110

Quentin, Pol 190

Rabelais (Barrault's adaptation) 12, 52,
  63, 66, 74, 191
Rabelais, François 51, 66, 68, 69, 74,
  191
Racine, Jean 32, 189
Rainer, Wolfgang 177
Ransan, André 77
Raschig, Susanne 136, 194
Redl, Wolf 146, 149
refugees 84, 90, 115–20, 124

Régnier, Marthe 35
rehearsal 10, 11, 27, 30–1, 33–4, 38, 39–43, 51, 61, 82, 90, 96, 97, 98, 100, 105, 115, 119–21, 134, 136, 142, 166, 182
Rehm, Werner 140, 149, 173
Reinhardt, Max 152, 160, 167
Reissner, Larissa 143
religion, religious sensibilities 56–7, 72, 74, 88, 102, 151, 153
Renaud, Madeleine 8, 14, 19, 26, 28–9, 31, 32, 33, 35, 37, 38, 41, 42, 45, 50, 51, 53, 54
Renoir, Jean 92, 95, 104
Renoir, Pierre 35
repertoire 7, 8, 14–15, 17, 25, 36, 39
    rotating repertory (*l'alternance*) 35–8
Répétition, La; ou l'Amour Puni (*The Rehearsal*) (Anouilh) 190
research 12, 13, 51, 104, 147–8, 151, 152–3, 155, 163, 165, 176, 183
Retablo de maravillas (Cervantes) 28
Rheingold, Das (The Rhinegold) 186
Rhinocéros (Ionesco) 48, 65, 70, 71, 191
Richard II 16, 86, 192
Richard III 15
riots. *See* protests
ritual 65, 119, 153, 155
Robespierre 88
Ronsard, Pierre de 12
Rose, Jürgen 168, 193
Rostand, Edmond 31
Rousseau, Jean-Jacques 87, 88
Rowley, William 140
Royal Court Theatre (London) 133
Rules for Actors (Goethe) 137–8
Russian-German Friendship Association 156

Sade, Marquis de 101
Salacrou, Armand 35
Salines d'Arc-et-Sénans 101
Salzburg Festival (Festspiele) 15, 130, 158, 186, 195
Samel, Udo 154
Sander, Otto 140, 149
Sandier, Gilles 96, 101
Sangatte 115–17

Sartre, Jean-Paul 32, 93, 94, 95
Satin Slipper, The. See Soulier de satin, Le
Saved (Bond) 133, 143, 158, 163, 165, 166, 167, 169, 170, 193, 215 n.12
scenery/scene design/scenic space 17, 18, 38, 39–40, 42, 47, 51, 52–3, 69, 70–3, 76, 84, 90, 92, 94, 101, 105, 111, 119–22, 136, 139, 151–2, 160, 168, 169, 172–3, 177, 179
Schaubühne am Halleschen Ufer 7, 8, 10, 11, 14, 18–19, 129, 130, 138, 140, 142, 147–8, 152, 160, 164, 170, 174, 177, 179, 181, 182, 183, 184, 185, 194
Schaubühne am Lehniner Platz (Schaubühne Wilmersdorf) 156, 158, 160, 185, 187, 195
Schéhadé, Georges 8, 47, 190
Schiller, Friedrich von 132, 158, 159, 160, 170, 193, 195
Schitthelm, Jürgen 140
Schlegel, August Wilhelm 132, 214 n.7
Schmidt, Jacques 191
Schoenberg, Arnold 11, 195
Schwiedrzik, Wolfgang 169, 170
Screens, The 133. *See also Paravents, Les*
Seagull, The (Chekhov) 195
Second World War 31, 44, 91, 95, 130, 155, 160–1
1789: la revolution doit s'arreter à la perfection du bonheur 13, 84, 85, 90, 103–7, 191
sexuality 144
Shakespeare, William 11, 14, 15, 16, 25, 35, 38, 48, 81, 85, 86, 94, 100, 108, 132, 151–2, 158, 189, 191, 192, 194, 195
Shakespeare et les français (Shakespeare and the French) (Barrault) 15
Shakespeare Our Contemporary (Kott) 100
Shakespeare's Memory 13, 15, 151–2, 184
Shevtsova, Maria 13
signifying object. *See* properties
silence 57, 62–3, 67

Simon, Alfred 103, 107
Simon Boccanegra (Verdi) 195
Social Democratic Party (SPD), West Germany 141
Société d'Histoire du Théâtre 49
socio-political approaches 9, 19, 85, 88–9, 95, 111, 112, 115, 119, 142, 163, 167–9, 178
Sommergäste (Gorky). *See Summerfolk*
Songe d'une nuit d'été, Le. See Midsummer Night's Dream, A
Sophocles 132
Sorano, Daniel 49
Sorbonne (Université de Paris) 93
Soulier de satin, Le (The Satin Slipper) 8, 24, 31, 32–4, 43, 48, 52, 54, 69, 72, 73
sound effects 38, 67–9, 76
Sous le vent des Iles Baléares (Claudel) 34, 52
Souvenirs pour demain (Memories for Tomorrow) (Barrault) 17, 32, 44
Spanish flu 26
Sperr, Martin 133, 168, 193
Stalin, Josef 143, 144
Stanislavski, Konstantin 56, 95–6, 97, 99, 147, 156
Stein, Herbert (Peter Stein's father) 130
Stein, Peter 7, 9, 10, 11, 12, 13, 14, 15, 16, 17, 18, 19, 130–61, 163–88, 193–5
 directorial approaches 11–12, 141–2, 143, 151, 166, 183–4
 freelance directing 130, 158–60, 164, 165
 mentors 10, 131–2, 143, 167
 space, use of 8, 11, 15, 136, 147, 151–2, 160, 163, 165, 168, 173, 177, 179, 184–5
 text, focus on 132, 135, 136–7, 139, 147–8, 149, 150, 155, 156, 159, 161, 163, 165, 167, 171–2, 176, 179–80, 183, 187
Steins Faust 187. *See also Faust*
Stiefel, Erhard 9, 192
Strauss, Botho 135, 139, 146, 148, 150, 158, 179–80, 194
Strehler, Giorgio 130
Sturm, Dieter 140, 170

Stürmer, Michael 161
Summerfolk (Dachniki) (Gorky) 14, 15, 144–7, 148, 158, 194, 216 n.38
surrealism 28, 29, 58
Syndicat de la Critique 99

Tailhade, Jean-Pierre 95
Tambours sur la digue (Drums on the Dike) (Cixous) 108, 110–11, 193
Tartuffe, Le 16, 192
Teatro alla Scala 195
Teatro Stabile de Torino 195
Tentation de Saint-Antoine, La (The Temptation of Saint Anthony) 60
Tête d'or (Golden Head) (Claudel) 177, 191
Theater Bremen 134
Theater Heute (journal) 133, 134, 135, 165, 170
Theatertreffen (Berlin Theatre Festival) 129, 134, 136, 139, 140, 147, 152, 154, 155, 160, 170
Theatre Aftaab 89
Theatre and Its Double, The (Le Théâtre et son double) (Artaud) 28, 59
Théâtre Antoine (Paris) 30, 189
Théâtre de foire, Le (Fairground Theatre) 54
Théâtre de la Commune d'Aubervilliers 191
Théâtre de l'Atelier (Paris) 27, 31, 56, 62, 94, 189
Théâtre de l'Odéon (Odéon-Théâtre de France) 15, 19, 48–50, 56, 60, 71, 100, 191
Théâtre de l'Oeuvre (Paris) 28
Théâtre des Nations 49, 50, 56
Théâtre d'Orsay 53, 54, 73
Théâtre du Palais Royal (Paris) 48, 191
Théâtre du Rond Point (Paris) 54, 191
Théatre du Soleil (Paris) 7, 9, 10, 14, 16, 19, 81–125, 191–3
Théâtre du Vieux Colombier (Paris) 27, 36, 56, 94
theatre of cruelty 28, 61
Théâtre Marigny (Paris) 35, 36, 44, 45, 46, 47, 48, 54, 189, 190

Théâtre Mouffetard 191
Théâtre National Populaire (TNP) 51, 94
théâtre populaire. See populist theatre
Theatre Populaire (journal) 94–5
Théâtre Sarah Bernhardt (Paris) 48, 190
Théâtre Récamier (Paris) 52, 99
théâtre total. See total theatre
Thomas, Natalie 9, 192, 193
Three Sisters (Chekhov) 15, 156–7, 187, 195
Tieck, Ludwig 132
Titus Andronicus (Shakespeare) 15
TNP. *See* Théâtre National Populaire
Tolstoy, Leo 156
Torquato Tasso (Goethe) 16, 136–40, 145, 164, 170–4, 175, 193
total theatre 33, 39, 58–62, 70
touring 7, 8, 14, 26, 44–7, 53, 111, 125, 140, 155, 174
Tournafond, Françoise 95, 191
translation 15, 16, 18, 32, 35, 38, 132, 133, 155, 167, 168, 179
Tréteaux de France 53
Trial, The. See Procès, Le
Troilus and Cressida (Shakespeare) 15, 195
Trotsky, Leon 143
Twelfth Night (Shakespeare) 16, 87, 192
Tynan, Kenneth 107
Tzara, Tristan 28

United Nations 45
USSR (Union of Soviet Socialist Republics) 14, 47, 144, 156

Valère, Simone 35
Valette, Louis (Barrault's maternal grandfather) 26
Valette, 'Uncle Bob' Robert (Barrault's uncle) 26
van den Berg, Klaus 11, 15
Vaudoyer, Jean-Louis 33, 34
Vauthier, Jean 8, 190
Venice Biennale Teatro 139
Verdi, Giuseppe 11, 195
Verdot, Guy 68
Verne, Jules 112
Vienna Burgtheater 195

Vie parisienne, La (Parisian Life) (Offenbach) 48, 191
Vietnam Discourse. See Viet Nam-Diskurs
Viet Nam-Diskurs (Vietnam Discourse) (Weiss) 169–70, 193
Vieux Colombier. *See* Théâtre du Vieux Colombier
Vilar, Jean 47, 51, 91, 94, 101
Ville perjure ou le reveil des Erinyes, La (The Perjured City, or The Awakening of the Furies) 109, 192
Villeurbanne 16
Vishnevsky, Vsevolod Vitalievich 132, 143–4, 194
Volpone (Jonson) 27
Volterra, Madame 45, 48

Wagner, Richard 136, 186
Wakhévitch, Georges 190
Wallenstein Trilogy (Schiller) 158, 159, 160, 195
Wälterlin, Oskar 140
wardrobe. *See* costumes
Weiffenbach, Klaus 140, 194
Weimar classicism 137
Weiss, Peter 169, 193
Welsh National Opera 195
Wesker, Arnold 97, 98, 107, 191
West Berlin 129–30, 141, 152, 159, 160–1, 164, 169, 174, 194, 195
Wie es euch gefällt. See As You Like It
Wiener Staatsoper 195
Williams, David 9, 145
Wilson, Robert 91
Wirth, Andrzej 185
Wörgerbauer, Ferdinand 160, 195
Woolf, Virginia 19
World War I. *See* First World War
World War II. *See* Second World War

Youngerman, Jack 190

Zadek, Peter 136, 137
Zauberflöte, Die 195
Zetkin, Clara 176
Zipes, Jack 12
Zurich Schauspielhaus 131, 140, 194